Preface

There are two unifying themes to this book. The first relates to the nature of the Supreme Court's role in Canadian politics. As I argue in this book, the constitutional issues that reach the Supreme Court are fundamentally and inescapably political. Constitutional argument asks the Court to help define who we are as individuals and as a people. Such questions cannot be answered through the application of some specialized or technical brand of expertise. What is demanded are political choices and acts of political will.

Many non-lawyers will undoubtedly be amazed that this observation would be regarded as significant or original. Political scientists, for example, have long written about the Court in terms which emphasized the political and discretionary nature of its responsibilities. The fact remains that this perspective has received only partial acceptance in the legal community. Most legal scholarship continues to be organized around a paradigm which regards constitutional analysis as a specialized and technical form of reasoning.

The time has come to abandon this paradigm and create a new way of understanding the constitutional role of the Supreme Court. This new perspective would begin by recognizing the essential continuity between the constitutional analysis of the Supreme Court and more generalized forms of political argument. Under this new conception, constitutional analysis and argument would become a legitimate matter of concern to all Canadians, rather than the preserve of an elite group of specialists or experts.

The second theme of the book builds on the first. I believe that constitutional scholarship must be conceived and practiced within an expanded universe, one which includes and is sensitive to the whole of political and social theory. For lawyers, whose training has been focused almost exclusively on the details and the distinctions contained in particular cases, this is a daunting prospect indeed. What is demanded is nothing less than a fundamental reorientation of one's way of thinking and approaching problems. In concrete terms, it means paying less attention to the details of particular cases and examining the interconnections and themes underlying whole areas of doctrine. It means, further, attempting to identify the assumptions, both explicit and implicit, which underlie and inform the doctrine. It means attempting to understanding the provisional and partial nature of those assumptions and imagining an alternative way of approaching the problems presented.

My analysis of the *Charter* and of federalism builds upon and reflects these two themes. I propose a distinctive and indigenous way of reading the *Charter*, a reading which emphasizes the differences between the *Charter* and the American *Bill of Rights*. The analysis is both descriptive and normative. Criticizing the early judgments of the Supreme Court, I propose an overview of the document which locates it within the communitarian traditions of Canadian politics. This way of understanding the *Charter* is designed to resist the knee-jerk temptation to read the document as though it were an extended footnote to the American Constitution.

My analysis of the federalism decisions of the Court is designed to illuminate the fundamental political choices that are at stake in such litigation. I also attempt to determine the extent to which these court decisions have made a difference in terms of policy outcomes. I argue that the federalism decisions of the Court have often had little or no discernible impact on the choices made by government.

My debts are too numerous to acknowledge adequately. I am particularly grateful for the encouragement and support of Dean John McCamus and the administration of Osgoode Hall Law School of York University. The Law School granted me a six-month research leave in the fall of 1985 which made it possible to complete the bulk of the manuscript. My research assistant, Scott Hutchison, worked tirelessly and also offered numerous perceptive suggestions for

POLITICS
AND THE
CONSTITUTION

The Charter, Federalism and the
Supreme Court of Canada

MONAHAN

M.A., B., LL.M.

Associate Professor of Law
Osgoode Hall Law School
York University

CARSWELL

Toronto • Calgary • Vancouver

1987

Canadian Cataloguing in Publication Data

Monahan, Patrick
    Politics and the constitution

Includes bibliographical references.
ISBN 0-459-30321-X (bound) ISBN 0-458-81600-0 (pbk.)

1. Canada — Constitutional law.   2. Canada.
Supreme Court.   3. Canada. Canadian Charter of
Rights and Freedoms.   4. Federal government —
Canada.   I. Title

K E4216.35.C6M65 1987   342.71′02′02643   C87-094704-4

c c

improvement. The lively debate and argument in the weekly Osgoode constitutional law luncheon group was not only intellectually stimulating but intensely enjoyable. I am particularly indebted to two very good friends, Allan Hutchinson and Andrew Petter. Without their encouragement, insight and moral support, I would never have undertaken such a project, much less completed it.

An earlier version of chapter 3 appeared in *Charter Litigation* (edited by R. Sharpe, 1987) and is reprinted with the permission of Butterworths. Portions of chapters 4, 5 and 6 appeared in "Judicial Review and Democracy: A Theory of Judicial Review" in Volume 21 of the University of British Columbia Law Review (1987). An earlier version of chapter 9 appeared in *The Supreme Court of Canada as an Instrument of Political Change* (Royal Commission on the Economic Union and Development Prospects for Canada, 1985) and is reprinted with the permission of the University of Toronto Press.

Finally, I want to acknowledge the very special debt I owe my wife Monica. Her love, friendship and infectious good humour have sustained me throughout this project, while preventing me from taking myself too seriously. I dedicate the book to her.

Table of Contents

Part 3

The Court and Federalism

Table of Cases

Part 1

Introduction

1

The Politics of Judicial Review

In the mid-1960s, Ronald Cheffins described the Supreme Court of Canada as the "quiet court in an unquiet country".[1] Today, such an observation would be regarded as hopelessly dated. Indeed, a shorthand account of the contemporary Supreme Court's role might well approximate a precise mirror image of Cheffins' original observation: the country having grown "quiet" following the constitutional upheaval of the early 1980s, it is the Supreme Court which now appears "unquiet". Far from being the marginal institution of past decades, today's Supreme Court appears to have assumed an increasingly pivotal role in resolving the constitutional and political conflicts of the nation. This perception flows in large part from the obvious aggrandizement in judicial power associated with the enactment of the *Canadian Charter of Rights and Freedoms*[2] in 1982. But quite apart from the *Charter*, governments in Canada over the past decade have seemed more willing to have major federal-provincial conflicts resolved by the judiciary. With the Court being called upon to adjudicate disputes over energy rents, constitutional reform and incomes policy, political life seems

---

1 R. Cheffins, "The Supreme Court of Canada: The Quiet Court in an Unquiet Country" (1966), 4 Osgoode Hall L.J. 259.
2 Schedule B, Canada Act 1982, (U.K.), c. 11.

to have been judicialized to a degree that would have been unthinkable to the observer of the 1960s. Law has become one of the growth industries of the 1980s.

Yet, despite the growing celebrity of the Supreme Court, we continue to have a relatively primitive understanding of its role in Canadian political life. For the most part, discussions of the Court remain *ad hoc*, episodic and impressionistic.[3] Both criticism and praise of the Court tend to be particularized, framed in terms of the outcomes of individual cases or the evolution of particular areas of doctrine. Canadian legal scholars have rarely attempted to evaluate the Supreme Court in general, or to assess its performance *as a political institution*. Canadian jurists have ignored for the most part what is euphemistically referred to as "grand theory", the larger jurisprudential considerations which have so preoccupied American courtwatchers.

In this book I part company with this established Canadian tradition; I attempt to offer a generalized critical analysis of the Court's performance over the past decade. Of course, much of my analysis will be structured around the details of particular cases. But my ambition is to step back from the trees and to sketch the shape and the structure of the forest. The point of the exercise is to present an overview of the Court's role in the political life of the nation in the mid-1980s.

In embarking on such an enterprise, it will obviously be useful and necessary to draw on insights which have been developed in the American literature on the role of their highest Court. But it bears emphasizing that any analysis of the Supreme Court of Canada must be distinctively indigenous if it is to be successful. One must never lose sight of the important differences in the Canadian and American legal traditions in assessing the role and function of our highest Court. Indeed, my analysis is premised on the assumption that we can best understand our own Court and its tradition by paying particular attention to those features of the tradition which are distinctively or uniquely Canadian.[4]

My focus is the constitutional work of the Court over the past

---

3 See generally *Law and Learning* (Report of the Consultative Group on Canadian Legal Education, Social Sciences and Humanities Research Council of Canada, 1984). For an exception to the generalizations made in *Law and Learning*, see P. Weiler, *In the Last Resort: A Critical Study of the Supreme Court of Canada* (1974).

4 Thus, I will argue that it is possible to develop a generalized understanding of the *Charter* only by focusing on those elements of the document which differ from the American constitutional experience.

decade — I examine the Court's performance as the umpire of Canadian federalism and as the expositor of the *Charter*. There are two reasons for this focus. First, the Court's docket has increasingly become dominated by issues of public law and constitutional law over the past decade. Indeed, the Court's growing emphasis on public and constitutional law has recently become the object of considerable public attention and some criticism amongst the legal community. Some critics of the Court have charged that judicial preoccupation with the *Charter* and with public law generally has reached the point where important private law cases are no longer receiving a fair and appropriate hearing before the country's highest tribunal.[5] For the moment, I want to put the details of this particular debate to one side.[6] The reason for drawing attention to the issue is simply to illustrate the degree to which constitutional law and public law have assumed centre stage in the highest courtroom of the nation.

There is a second reason for focusing my attention on the constitutional jurisprudence of the Supreme Court. Not only have the numbers of constitutional cases increased dramatically over the past decade, but these cases appear to be far more politically significant than any of the other aspects of the Court's work. When the Court decides a constitutional case, it is not simply resolving a private dispute between two parties. At the same time, the Court is also making a determination about the permissible scope of state power. A constitutional decision has the potential to amend or even to rewrite the ground rules for the public policy process in Canada. This is particularly the case since the enactment of the *Charter* in 1982, with the Court now pronouncing on issues as diverse and important as abortion, Sunday closing, and the right to strike. The Court's rulings on these politically sensitive issues could force legislators and the public to rethink fundamentally their assumptions and their approaches to these questions.

In short, I have focused on the constitutional work of the Supreme Court because I believe that this is clearly the most central component on its current responsibilities, both in terms of sheer numbers of cases, as well as the political significance of these cases. By coming to terms

---

5 See *The National*, March 3, 1986, pp. 18-19, in which the President of the Canadian Bar Association calls for the establishment of a committee to investigate the alleged "imbalance" in the docket of the Supreme Court.

6 In Chapter 2, the evolution of the Court's workload is examined in some detail in an attempt to determine whether there is any substance to the claim that the Court is unfairly ignoring private law cases.

with the Supreme Court's role as the constitutional arbiter of the nation, I hope to gain important insights into the Court's role and responsibilities in general.

The issues I deal with are extremely diverse, ranging from the federal-provincial squabbles over resource revenues in the late 1970s, through the constitutional patriation crisis of the early 1980s, as well as the early *Charter* jurisprudence of the Court. There is, however, a central organizing theme to my analysis of these various matters. The starting point of my analysis is the Court's own self-image; I attempt to identify the Court's conception of its role in the political life of the nation. In particular, I examine the extent to which the Court regards itself as a "political" actor, charged with responsibility for making political choices for the nation as a whole. I argue that any meaningful assessment of the Court's contemporary role must begin by first understanding how the Court views itself and the political significance of its own work.

Why should this be so? In essence, the answer is that the Court's conception of its role and mission structures and shapes its work across the whole spectrum of constitutional law. At the risk of oversimplification, this judicial self-portrait can be summarized in the following terms. The organizing feature of the Court's conception of its role is a traditional, if somewhat ill-defined, distinction between legal and political reasoning. The Supreme Court has always maintained that there is a fundamental distinction to be drawn between "legal" reasoning, which is to some degree neutral or objective, and "political" reasoning, which is more open-ended, subjective and value-laden. The law-politics distinction is the cornerstone of the Court's justification for the institution of judicial review. When the Court rules legislation to be unconstitutional, its judgment is supposedly *not* based on any disagreement with the underlying policy of the law; it simply reflects an assessment of the law in light of the objective and manageable standards contained in the constitution itself.

These assumptions about the nature of judicial review often remain implicit in the jurisprudence of the Court, largely because the Court has rarely seen the necessity to justify its constitutional role and responsibilities. But the enactment of the *Charter* in 1982 has given rise to some novel concerns about the "legitimacy" of judicial review in this country. Federalism review is based on a theory of the exhaustion of powers, in which the issue for the Court is simply whether the "proper" level of government has enacted the particular law in question. Since the judicial inquiry is restricted to the question of the proper allocation of power, federalism review is ultimately compatible with the doctrine of parliamentary sovereignty. Not so with *Charter* review. Here, the issue is not whether power has been exercised by the proper organ of the state, but whether certain collective exercises of power are beyond the reach of the state *per se*. The *Charter* is based on a counter-majoritarian principle. The assumption is that certain forms of individual liberty cannot be overridden by any majority, whether federal or provincial.

Because federalism review is essentially compatible with parliamentary sovereignty, Canadian constitutional scholars and jurists have traditionally regarded the issue of the legitimacy of judicial review as a foreign or "American" concern. The enactment of the *Charter* challenges this traditional view, making it necessary to offer some explanation and defence of the counter-majoritarian character of this new form of judicial decision-making. The Supreme Court has offered a number of such justifications in its early *Charter* decisions but the most important and recurring argument relates to the "law-politics" distinction. In the first wave of *Charter* cases, the Court has emphasized the distinctively "legal" as opposed to "political" character of its decisions.[7] According to the Court, its role is simply to interpret and apply the objective and neutral standards contained in the constitution of Canada. The Court does not inquire into the "wisdom" of legislation in deciding constitutional disputes. Nor do judges substitute their values for those of elected officials. Rather, what the Court does is to measure legislation against the values set out in the constitution itself. Ultimately, the point of this line of argument is to downplay the novelty of judicial review under the *Charter* and to emphasize the similarity between *Charter* analysis and federalism review. The Court's claim is that "it is the scope of constitutional adjudication which has been altered rather than its nature, at least as regards the right to consider the content of legislation".[8]

Throughout the course of this book, I offer two central observations about this conception of legal reasoning and this defence of the legitimacy of judicial review. First, I argue that the Court's attempt to divorce "legal" and "political" analysis in constitutional cases is profoundly mistaken. In my view, the Supreme Court is inevitably called upon to make some assessment of the wisdom of legislation

---

7 See, e.g., the judgment of Lamer J. in *Ref. re s. 94(2) of the Motor Vehicle Act (B.C.)*, [1985] 2 S.C.R. 486 (S.C.C.).

8 *Ibid.* at 496.

in order to resolve the constitutional disputes which come before it. The values embodied in the constitutional text are simply too general and indeterminate to dictate uniquely correct answers in the constitutional cases which reach our highest Court. Thus, the act of interpreting constitutional values inevitably requires the Court to redefine and to create the very values which are the subject of the interpretation.

My second observation relates to the consequences of the Court's misconceived defence of the barrier between legal and political reasoning in constitutional cases. The primary consequence is that the Court is required to assess the validity of legislation in an empirical and normative vacuum. Because the Court is unable to acknowledge its inquiry into the wisdom of enactments, it cannot be seen to be openly asking whether the legislature was justified in the choices it has made; thus, for example, the Court is precluded from consciously attempting to measure the costs and benefits of the legislature's choice against the costs and benefits of the available alternatives. Such an analysis would be too overtly "political" and is necessarily off limits. Instead, the Court is limited to asking whether the terms of a law violate the "text" of the constitution, without any meaningful sense of the costs and the benefits of the law or of its alternatives. The truncated character of this type of analysis does not mean that the Court can somehow manage to avoid making political choices. It simply means that the political choices that are made by the Court are made blindfolded, without any clear sense of the costs or the consequences of those choices.

1. THE IMPACT OF CONSTITUTIONAL ADJUDICATION: THE INTERNAL AND EXTERNAL PERSPECTIVES

The larger question which arises from this critique is deceptively simple, yet elusive: "does any of this matter?" Predictably, it is impossible to offer a categorical answer to the question. As is typically the case, the appropriate response in this instance depends in large part on the perspective one adopts in order to frame an answer. Viewed from what might be termed an "internal" perspective — the perspective of the participants in the process itself — claims about the consistency or rationality of constitutional decision-making are necessarily and inherently important. But if one approaches the issue from an "external" perspective — a perspective which attempts to stand outside the judicial enterprise — then the significance of constitutional adjudication becomes much more difficult to assess. From an external perspective, the logical consistency or rationality of legal decisions is of somewhat secondary importance. What matters is not so much whether the decisions are "logical", but rather whether they have significant impacts on other political institutions or on citizens generally. It might be, for instance, that a series of "illogical" court decisions is simply ignored by governments when they come to formulate public policy in the area. In short, from an external perspective, the question "does constitutional adjudication matter?" is essentially a question about the practical instrumental impact of court decisions on policy outcomes.[9]

I will spend a good deal of time in this book examining the internal consistency and logic of the Supreme Court's constitutional analysis. But I hope also to analyze and to criticize the jurisprudence from the broader external perspective which I have identified. In particular, I will attempt to measure the extent to which federal and provincial governments in Canada appear to be constrained in their policy choices by the constitutional decisions of the Supreme Court. In general terms, I will argue that one can understand the nature and extent of these constitutional constraints only by distinguishing between federalism review on the one hand and *Charter* review on the other.

In terms of federalism review, I will suggest that constitutional adjudication operates as a relatively weak constraint on governments. I offer a variety of justifications for this claim. The first and most obvious is the theory of exhaustion of powers, upon which federalism review is based. Because a federalism case merely determines the proper allocation of power, rulings of *ultra vires* do not necessarily mean that "the state" is precluded from enacting a particular law. One possibility is that the results of litigation might be reversed by intergovernmental agreement; the "winning" level of government may simply delegate to the "loser" the disputed jurisdiction. Thus, following the Supreme Court's ruling that the federal government "owned" the resources off the shore of Newfoundland, Ottawa entered into an agreement whereby it granted significant rights of control to the province. In effect, the federal government chose not to take full advantage of the legal rights recognized by the Court. A second

---

9 There is, of course, a rich and growing literature on the issue of the instrumental impact of legal decisions. Much of this literature has found that the impact of court decisions has been vastly overestimated. See, e.g., R. Epstein, "The Social Consequences of Common Law Rules" (1982), 95 Harv. L. Rev. 1717: J. Griffiths, "Is Law Important?" (1979), N.Y.U. L. Rev. 339.

possibility is that, once the Court has ruled that a particular legislative instrument is *ultra vires* a particular level of government, the other level of government might elect to regulate the activity in an essentially identical manner. For instance, after the Supreme Court ruled that certain aspects of an egg marketing scheme were beyond provincial powers, the federal and provincial governments enacted dovetailing legislation which achieved the same practical effect as the original scheme which had been struck down.

Substituting one level of government for the other in this way may or may not be significant. Some commentators claim that provincial governments are more susceptible to "capture" by producer interests, particularly when such interests are heavily concentrated in a particular jurisdiction.[10] If such were the case, it would obviously be highly significant that regulatory authority had been transferred from one level of government to the other. But it is possible that the substitution of one level of government for the other may have little impact on the degree to which individuals are subject to state control.

There is a second reason why governments might be able to overcome the constraining force of federalism review by courts. Governments can achieve a given policy goal through a variety of legislative instruments. In addition to employing "command and control" regulation, the state might impose a tax, grant a subsidy, or deploy a crown corporation. For instance, instead of creating agricultural marketing boards to enhance farmers' incomes, the state might provide special tax concessions, impose import quotas or send them cheques.[11] In many cases, these instruments appear highly substitutable for each other.

It is well-known that certain regulatory instruments are virtually immune from judicial supervision. For instance, of the 177 federalism cases decided by the Supreme Court from 1949 to 1984, there were no cases involving the spending power, one case dealing with state enterprise and four cases challenging a government's proprietary interest. The vast bulk of the cases, approximately 70 per cent of those decided, involved direct regulation or taxation.[12] The result is that certain regulatory instruments — particularly the power to spend

---

10 For arguments along these lines see A.P. Pross, *Pressure Group Behaviour in Canadian Politics* (Economic Council of Canada, 1975).

11 See M.J. Trebilcock *et al.*, *The Choice of Governing Instrument* (1982) at 95-97.

12 See *infra*, Chapter 7.

public money — are largely free from judicial scrutiny on federalism grounds.

This is particularly pertinent because federalism since 1945 has evolved, not through formal constitutional amendment, but largely through creative use of the spending power. Anyone attempting to trace the evolution in power between Ottawa and the provinces over the past 40 years would begin by examining the complex set of intergovernmental agreements dealing with fiscal arrangements and programme funding. There would be little point in consulting the pages of the Supreme Court Reports; constitutional adjudication has been oblivious to the ongoing process of federal-provincial negotiations on taxes and transfers.

In short, I will claim that federalism review by the Supreme Court has operated as a relatively weak constraint on governments in the recent past. The reason is that whenever governments have been confronted by an unfavourable court ruling, they have usually had a range of regulatory substitutes available to them. Thus, my analysis of the instrumental impact of federalism adjudication will focus on the availability and the cost of regulatory substitutes by government. By understanding the extent to which governments are able to substitute around unfavourable court rulings, we will gain insight into the relatively weak constraints imposed on governments by federalism review by the Supreme Court.

The instrumental impact of the *Charter* is another and rather different matter. Although our experience with the *Charter* is much too limited to come to any firm conclusions, there are good reasons to believe that the *Charter* will constitute a far more significant constraint on the activities of government.

First, unlike federalism review, *Charter* analysis is not premised on the theory of exhaustion of powers. This eliminates the possibility of intergovernmental agreement as a means of substituting around *Charter* rulings. Second, *Charter* review appears to be much broader and more universal than federalism review. For instance, federalism review has had virtually no impact on government decisions to spend money. But the spending power will almost certainly come under judicial scrutiny under the *Charter*. The equality provision in s. 15 of the *Charter* means that when the state elects to spend money for purpose "A" but not purpose "B", it may have to justify that decision in Court. The recent litigation involving full funding for separate schools in Ontario is an illustration of the type of challenge that has been made possible by the *Charter*.

My claim is that the *Charter* is likely to have a fairly significant instrumental impact on public policy outcomes. This, in turn, means that the "internal" logic or rationality of this form of constitutional decision-making takes on added importance. If court decisions are found to have relatively minor impacts on governmental choices, then the reasoning employed by the Court is of rather secondary importance. But if, as seems likely in the case of the *Charter*, court decisions are likely to have an important impact on public policy, then the reasoning of the Court in these cases begins to matter a great deal. It makes a difference whether the Court is aware of the various competing interests at stake in constitutional litigation and whether it is capable of balancing those interests in a sensitive and coherent fashion.

2. A THEORY OF JUDICIAL REVIEW UNDER THE CHARTER

This returns me to my original observations about the importance of the Court's own conception of its role under the *Charter*. I will argue that as long as the Court clings to the mistaken idea that its role is simply to interpret the "text" of the constitution, its jurisprudence under the *Charter* will remain barren and haphazard. The Court must reconceive its self-image and its mission. What the *Charter* demands of the Court is nothing less than an exercise in political theory. The Court must attempt to identify the background political ideals which give shape and substance to the *Charter* as a whole. Constructing such a background political theory is a normative exercise, as well as a descriptive one. It requires the Court to develop a concept of the *Charter* and of judicial review which best fits the distinctive traditions of Canadian politics and society. This background political theory can then serve as a basis for making the excruciatingly difficult moral and political choices demanded by the *Charter*.

I attempt to construct such a background political theory in this book. I begin with the observation that there are a number of central differences between the Canadian and the American political traditions. In particular, I argue that Canadian politics has always placed particular emphasis on the value of community, in contrast to the overriding individualism of the American experience. This communitarian element has manifested itself in a more activist role for the state in Canada, as well as the emergence of socialist third parties at both the provincial and federal level.

It seems to have been commonly assumed that the *Charter* represents a radical break with this communitarian political tradition;

according to this scenario, the *Charter* has administered a potent dose of liberal individualism to the Canadian body politic. The prognosis for the patient seems hopeful. In my view, this account of the significance of the *Charter* is vastly oversimplified. There can be little doubt that the *Charter* signals a somewhat greater emphasis on individualistic values in Canadian political life. But to regard the *Charter* as the straightforward embodiment of liberal individualism would be an error of the highest proportions. I argue that the *Charter* is located firmly within the traditions of Canadian politics. Although framed in the rhetoric of liberal individualism, the *Charter* simultaneously emphasizes communitarian values. Nor does the document assume that there is any necessary contradiction between state regulation and individual freedom. The *Charter* seeks to give expression to the notion that state intervention in the market can often serve as the means to enhance individual freedom, rather than to subvert it. In short, my argument is that there are important differences between the *Charter* and the American Bill of Rights. These differences are only to be expected, given the varied traditions of the two countries. In interpreting the *Charter*, it is crucial that our courts and the wider community pay attention to these differences and attempt to give expression to them. This book represents a tentative initial contribution to that interpretive enterprise.

3. PLAN OF THE WORK

The book is divided into two parts, the first dealing with the *Charter*, the second with federalism review. The section on the *Charter* begins with an overview of the practical implications of the document for the political and legal process. The initial chapter is an analysis of the 800 *Charter* decisions handed down by the Ontario and Federal Courts by the spring of 1986. I point out the extent to which various sections of the *Charter* have been used by litigants and the types of governmental action which have been subject to challenge. I also emphasize the wide variation in the "success rate" for different categories of *Charter* arguments. I argue that all levels of court have assumed a relatively "activist" approach to *Charter* interpretation, but that this activism has been particularly pronounced in the Supreme Court of Canada.

The remaining chapters in Part 1 of the book focus on the work of the Supreme Court in the *Charter* era. In the early Supreme Court jurisprudence, there has been considerable attention paid to the "legitimacy" of judicial review. The Court has defended the legitimacy of its role by claiming that its role is peculiarly "legal" as opposed to "political". In Chapter 4, I argue that this defence of judicial review cannot be sustained. Focusing on the Supreme Court's decisions in *Operation Dismantle* and *Oakes*, I attempt to demonstrate that courts under the *Charter* are required to engage in a process of "interest balancing"; there is nothing peculiarly "legal" about this task. Thus, the legitimacy of judicial review cannot be defended successfully in the fashion suggested by the Court.

In Chapter 5, I examine the massive American literature on the legitimacy of judicial review. There are two leading contemporary American approaches to the question, known in the literature as "interpretivism" and "noninterpretivism". After critically analyzing these two approaches, I conclude that they are products of the American constitutional experience and are of rather limited utility in the Canadian context. I claim that any understanding of the *Charter* must highlight, rather than subliminate, the important differences between our document and the American Bill of Rights. In Chapter 6, I turn to the task of developing such an understanding of the meaning of the *Charter*. The argument I present seeks to locate the *Charter* within the communitarian and organic traditions of Canadian politics. I argue for a limited conception of the function of judicial review in the Canadian context and, in this way, to resolve the question of legitimacy.

In Part 2 of the book I turn to the Court's federalism jurisprudence. Chapter 7 is an overview of the Court's work in this area in the past decade. I note the increasing numbers of federalism cases reaching the Court since the mid-1970s, as well as the more activist approach of the Court in these cases. In the past few years, the Supreme Court has shown a greater tendency to declare legislation *ultra vires* on federalism grounds than at any other time in the past 40 years. In short, the Court's approach in federalism cases has paralleled its aggressive attitude in terms of the *Charter*. The Court obviously conceives itself as an important constitutional player in the affairs of the nation, in contrast to its relatively deferential attitude of previous eras.

Chapter 8 is an analysis of what was clearly the most celebrated federalism dispute of the past decade — the federal-provincial battle over constitutional amendment in the 1980–1982 period. My analysis suggests that the dispute was really about a choice between two competing visions of the nature of the country. The first vision saw

Canada in primarily national terms and regarded the central government as the legitimate representative of that overriding national interest. The second, competing vision rejected the whole notion of any overriding national interest, emphasizing instead the primacy of the various regional and provincial communities. I argue that the Court refused to embrace fully either of these opposed visions of Canada's political community. Instead, the Court's reasoning and its rhetoric oscillated between these two ideals; at certain times, the Court's reasoning reflected a pan-Canadian view of the country, while at others, it adopted a provincialist analysis of the issues. I conclude that there is no single, coherent conception of federalism reflected in the Court's jurisprudence.

Chapter 9 attempts to generalize this analysis to other aspects of the Court's federalism jurisprudence. This chapter examines the evolution of the trade and commerce power over the past decade, focusing in particular on the federal-provincial disputes over resource rents in the late 1970s. I argue that it is impossible to identify any overriding principle which explains or justifies the trade and commerce decisions of this period. Arguments and distinctions are deployed in a patchwork and often contradictory fashion. The explanation is not judicial incompetence or perversity, but a decline in the background understandings surrounding Canadian federalism. Without any generalized political consensus regarding the appropriate scope of federal or provincial activity, it is hardly realistic to suppose that the judiciary could devise such a schema on its own.

Chapter 10 is an attempt to place the Court's federalism jurisprudence in a larger political perspective. The issue addressed here is the extent to which the Court's decisions have constrained the policy choices of government. I trace the political response to the high-profile federalism cases of this period and discover that the decisions often had little or no impact on eventual policy outcomes. I attempt to offer a generalized account of the impact of federalism review, emphasizing the fact that the crucial policy issue is the availability of close regulatory substitutes.

I conclude by offering a prognosis of the Court's prospects into the 1990s. The past decade has been a time of great and unprecedented turbulence and transformation for the Supreme Court. For most of its history, the Court laboured in almost total obscurity, its members and its work unknown to the general public. All that has changed radically in the past decade. The Court has been thrust directly into the glare of the political spotlight, first because of its high-profile role in resolving the federal–provincial disputes in the late 1970s and early 1980s and, more recently, because of the *Charter*. I argue that this trend will continue and, indeed, intensify into the 1990s. Canadians have yet to realize the full extent of the new responsibilities which have been thrust upon the Court under the *Charter*. As the Court begins handing down decisions on issues as politically divisive as abortion or the right to strike, we can expect to see greater public awareness and scrutiny of the politics of constitutional decision-making of the Supreme Court.

2

Changing the Court's Business:
The Evolution of the Court's Docket,
1961–1985

The 1960s and early 1970s was a period of remarkable stability and continuity for the Supreme Court of Canada. This stability was reflected first and foremost in the workload of the Court. Each year, the Court heard and decided about 120 cases, divided almost equally between public and private law litigation. There were less than 100 motions for leave to appeal to the Court; the majority of the litigants travelling to Ottawa did so as of right. The Court kept a low profile in constitutional matters, deciding only about two or three constitutional cases per year. Details of the Court's work were virtually unknown beyond members of the legal community.

It is widely recognized that the Court and its workload have been radically transformed in the past decade. The Court is now assumed to be essentially a public law court, increasingly preoccupied with complex constitutional issues. This involvement in high profile constitutional issues has thrust the Court into the public eye; whereas a decade ago the Court's decisions were rarely even reported, today its judgments are regularly regarded as front page news.[1] Moreover, there has been some criticism of the Court's apparent preoccupation with public law and constitutional issues, especially amongst the legal community. These critics have charged that judicial preoccupation with the *Charter* has reached the point where important private law cases are no longer receiving a fair and appropriate hearing before the country's highest tribunal.

Are these widespread assumptions about the evolution of the Court's workload accurate? I attempted to answer this question by analyzing the docket of the Court over the past 25 years. Figure 1 provides an overview of the Court's caseload from 1961 to 1985.

The date in figure 1 confirms the widespread perception that the Court has become increasingly preoccupied with public law issues at the expense of private law litigation. Since 1975, when the Supreme Court was given far greater control over its own docket, there has been a steady increase in the percentage of the Court's time devoted to public law issues. For instance, in the 1961–74 period, approximately one-half of the cases decided by the Court raised issues of public law. In contrast, in the last three years shown in figure 1 (1983–85 inclusive) over three-quarters of the cases decided by the Court were public law cases. Further, the reduced importance of private law cases at the Supreme Court level is reflected in the declining absolute numbers of such cases decided by the Court. In the 1960s, the Court decided nearly 60 private law cases annually. The Court has decided less than 15 private law cases in each of the past two years.

Not only has the public law portion of the Court's docket been expanding, the Court is now deciding far more constitutional cases today than at any time since 1961. In the 1961–74 period, constitutional

---

1 Consider, as an illustration of this phenomenon, the increase in coverage of the Supreme Court by the Toronto *Globe and Mail* since 1979. The following table indicates the number of stories mentioning the Supreme Court of Canada, by year.

Year	No. of Stories Mentioning S.C.C.
1979	330
1980	379
1981	726
1982	468
1983	485
1984	532
1985	512

Source: "Infoglobe"

FIGURE 1
Public and Private Law Cases in the Supreme Court of Canada 1961–1985
Number of Cases

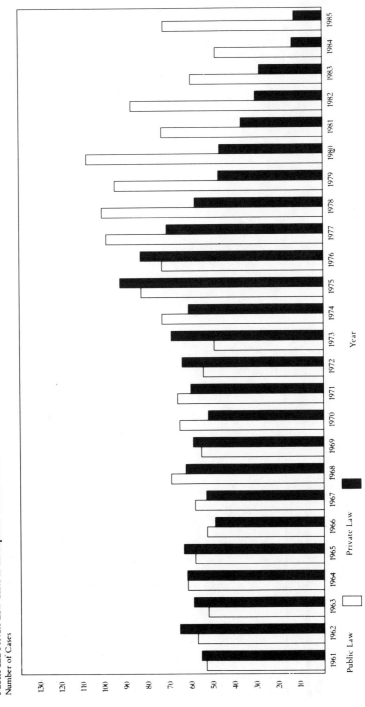

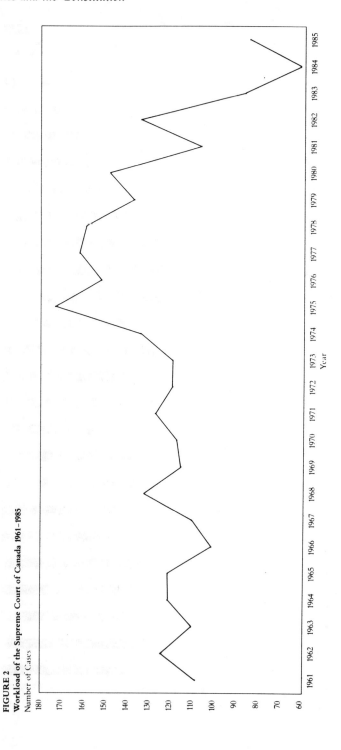

FIGURE 2
Workload of the Supreme Court of Canada 1961–1985
Number of Cases

cases represented a marginal element of the Court's workload; the highwater mark for constitutional adjudication during this period was 1964, when the Court decided a total of five constitutional cases. As table 1 indicates, this situation began to change in the late 1970s and early 1980s, in both relative and absolute terms. In the early 1980s, the Supreme Court was deciding between ten and fifteen constitutional cases per year. By 1985, the first year in which the full impact of the *Charter* was reflected in the Court's workload, there were more than 20 constitutional decisions handed down by the Court. This represented about a quarter of the Court's entire output for the year.

TABLE 1
Constitutional Litigation in the Supreme Court of Canada 1961–1985

Year	No. of Constitutional Decisions	Total Cases
1985	21	85
1984	10	62
1983	11	87
1982	12	132
1981	11	107
1980	14	149
1979	10	138
1978	14	160
1977	7	163
1976	5	153
1975	6	174
1974	3	135
1973	3	120
1972	5	120
1971	5	129
1970	3	118
1969	2	116
1968	0	133
1967	3	111
1966	4	102
1965	4	122
1964	5	122
1963	1	111
1962	1	125
1961	2	109

Thus, there does appear to be solid empirical support for public perceptions about the predominance of public law and constitutional issues before the Supreme Court. Yet, while these perceptions appear generally accurate, they are also radically incomplete and somewhat misleading. There are other aspects of the evolution of the Court's docket which have been ignored in the current debate over the Court's role. Moreover, these other elements of the story are equally significant in understanding the transformation that has taken place on the Court in recent years.

Consider first the data in figure 2 regarding the annual workload of the Court over the past 25 years. Beginning in 1961, and continuing up until 1973, the Court decided an average of 118 cases per year. Moreover, there was relatively little variation from one year to another, with the Court never deciding less than 102 cases and never more than 133 cases during this 13-year period. Then, in 1974, coincident upon the appointment of Bora Laskin as Chief Justice, the annual output of the Court rose dramatically. In 1975, for example, the Court decided an unprecedented total of 174 cases. Over the 7-year period beginning in 1974 and ending in 1980, the Court decided an average of 153 cases per year, with the annual output never falling below 135 decisions. Then, in 1981, the number of cases decided by the Court began to decline sharply. Initially, the Court's annual output simply fell back to the lower levels associated with the 1961–73 period. But this was followed in 1983 by a second sharp decline in the workload of the Court. Over the past three years, the Court has handed down a mere 80 cases a year, far fewer than at any other time in the past quarter century.

Although the annual workload of the Court has fluctuated quite radically over the past 25 years, this fact has rarely been mentioned in contemporary discussions of the Court's role. There is a second, overlooked observation about the Court's workload that emerges from a closer examination of the data in figure 1. This observation relates to a widely-held assumption about the relationship between the decline in private law cases and the increase in public and constitutional law cases. It is commonly said that the "cause" of the decline in private law cases has been a corresponding increase in the number of constitutional and public law cases. Yet, the data in figure 1 fails to confirm the existence of any such causal relationship. The data indicates that there have been far more complex factors at work than a simple trade-off between constitutional and private law cases. Both constitutional cases in particular and public law cases in general began rising dramatically in the late 1970s. This increase in public law litigation was not accomplished at the expense of private law litigants. During the 1975–80 period, there was only a marginal decline in the numbers of private law cases being decided by the Court. It was not until the early 1980s that the numbers of private law cases began to decline significantly. But this decline in private law cases does not appear to be related to an increase in either constitutional or public law litigation. With the exception of 1985, the number of constitutional cases decided by the Court has been virtually constant over this period. Moreover, the number of public law cases has actually *declined* rather sharply since 1980. Thus, to blame the decline of private law litigation in the 1980s on an increase in public law cases is surely misleading. The plain fact is that there has been a decline in *both* public and private law cases decided by the Court in the past five years.

Taken together, these observations suggest an alternative explanation of the evolution of the Court's docket over the past 25 years. This alternative explanation rejects the notion that there has been a steady, orderly progression in the Court's business. This alternative explanation suggests that the Court's work since the early 1960s falls into three distinct periods, each quite different from the others. The first period began in 1961 and continued until 1973. The chief characteristics of this first period have already been outlined; a constant number of cases decided each year, an equal division between public and private law, and little or no emphasis on constitutional issues. The second distinct period, which might be termed the "Laskin era", spans the years 1974 to 1980. During these years, the Court began to devote increasing amounts of its time to constitutional and public law issues. But this new public law emphasis did not significantly limit the right of private law litigants to gain a hearing before the Supreme Court. The explanation for the increase in public law litigation combined with a constant number of private lawsuits is really quite straightforward; the Court simply increased the number of cases it decided each year. This meant that the expanded public law role of the Court could be accommodated without any noticeable cutback in private law litigation. The most recent five years, bridging the final years of Laskin's tenure as Chief Justice and the early years of the Dickson Court, constitute the third distinct period. The dominant characteristic of this most recent period has been a steep decline in the number of cases being decided annually by the Supreme Court. While the decline in the private law area has tended to attract the greatest public attention, both public and private law cases have declined, and in roughly equal proportions.

The question is whether it is possible to explain why the Court's docket has evolved in this particular fashion. Peter Russell, who has observed the decline in the number of cases decided by the Supreme Court, has speculated that the Court may be experiencing a form of "information overload" as a result of the increased demands placed upon it by the *Charter*.[2] Russell argues that the increase in constitutional litigation in the 1980s means that the cases decided by the Court are more complex and important. At the same time, the amount of time the justices can devote to actually hearing cases has been reduced by the increase in leave to appeal applications before the Court. Russell concludes that "[t]he Charter is clearly straining the Supreme Court's workload capacity" and that the Court "is experiencing serious difficulty in getting its work done".[3]

Any attempt to distinguish Supreme Court cases according to their relative "complexity" seems problematic; presumably, all cases that reach the Supreme Court would necessarily be closely bunched at the top end of any such "legal complexity" scale. One potential measure of this variable would be the length of the judgments released by the Court. One might expect that as cases become more complex, they would require longer opinions from the justices. Of course, there is no necessary relationship between the length of opinions and legal complexity; longer opinions may simply reflect the writing styles of the various authors.

TABLE 2
Length of Supreme Court Judgments, 1970–1985

Year	Pages (in bi-reporter)	Average Case Length
1985	1628	19.1
1984	1355	22.8
1983	1429	16.4
1982	2018	15.3
1981	1615	15.1
1980	2304	15.5
1979	2280	16.5
1978	2566	16.0
1977	2007	12.3
1976	1679	15.9
1975	1698	14.2
1974	1392	14.8
1973	915	14.5
1972	956	13.6
1971	1052	13.3
1970	1036	12.5

2 P. Russell, "The First Three Years in Charterland" (1985), 28 Can. Pub. Admin. 367 at 371. Russell also observes that poor health of some justices may also account for the reduced output of the Court.
3 *Ibid.* at 370–371.

The data in table 2 indicates that Supreme Court judgments have been relatively constant in their length over the past fifteen years, averaging between twelve and sixteen pages. However, in the past two years, there has been a significant departure from this established norm, with opinions averaging well over 20 pages. Yet it seems unlikely that this increase can be attributed to the complexity of the legal issues at stake in the cases. In 1984, when the average length of the opinions reached nearly 23 pages, the Court decided only three *Charter* cases. The total of ten constitutional cases reported during the year was actually a slight decrease from 1983. There is no reason to suppose that the other 52 nonconstitutional cases decided in 1984 were any more or less complex, as a class, from those of previous years. The implication is that the increased length of the judgments in 1984 was more a by-product of the writing styles of the justices rather than any characteristics of the cases themselves.

There is a larger point which emerges from this analysis. This point is that it is dangerous to automatically attribute any and all recent changes in the Court's workload to the enactment of the *Charter*. The emerging trends in the Court's docket had already become firmly established *before* the first wave of *Charter* cases reached the Court. For example, by 1983, a year when the Court had only just begun hearing *Charter* cases, there had already been sharp drops in private law litigation as well as the total number of judgments written. Thus, the explanation for these developments must involve something more than a simple judicial preoccupation with the *Charter* or, alternatively, the alleged "complexity" of the opinions being written.

No doubt there has been a variety of factors driving the observable changes in the Court's docket over the past 25 years. The changes in the leave to appeal procedure in the mid-1970s and, more recently, the illness or absence of certain justices have undoubtedly affected the Court's workload.[4] Yet, one additional explanation, which represents more a hypothesis than a conclusion, is that changes in the personnel of the Court are important determinants of its docket. Given the limited membership of nine, a turnover of only two or three of the justices has the potential to effect quite significant transformations in the behaviour of the institution as a whole. It is surely more than coincidence, for example, that the workload of the Court increased dramatically in 1974, precisely the same time that Bora Laskin was appointed Chief Justice. The personnel on the Court today is radically

---

4 For discussion of these points, see P. Russell, *supra*, note 2 at 369-373.

different from what it was in the mid-1970s. Thus, changes which may appear to be the result of dramatic legal events such as the *Charter* may actually be the prosaic product of the preferences and attitudes of those individuals who happen to be sitting on the Court at a given point in time. This explanation of the changing business of the Court may appear overly simplistic, but it seems far more plausible than any alternative explanation that has been offered thus far.

Part 2

———————

The Court and the Charter

———————

3

The Legitimacy of Judicial Review:
How an American Debate Came
to Canada

1. AN OVERVIEW OF THE ISSUE

There are two deep and central puzzles which confront Canadian jurists as they struggle to make sense of the *Charter* and its meaning for Canadian legal and political culture. The puzzles, although not identical, are closely interrelated. The first is the recurring riddle which has haunted American constitutionalists for the past 25 years. It arises from the apparent contradiction between democratic values and the institution of judicial review. Judicial review involves unelected judges overturning the will of a democratically-accountable legislature on the basis of open-ended and abstract constitutional guarantees. The interpretation and application of those guarantees appears to invite the judiciary to "balance" the interests of individuals against those of the collectivity. The problem for American theorists has been how to account for and justify this apparent derogation from democratic principles. After all, courts are far less adept than legislatures in striking the right balance between the interests of individuals and the need for effective governmental programmes. Indeed, it is precisely for this reason that Canadian courts have traditionally resisted various invitations to engage in "interest balancing". The view of Canadian courts has been that interest balancing requires choices "which must, by their very nature, be arbitrary and embody personal economic and social beliefs".[1]

With the enactment of the *Charter*, Canadian lawyers and judges will now have to grapple with this fundamental issue of the legitimacy of judicial review. There is a second, related problem arising from the introduction of the *Charter* in Canada; in a sense, this second problem could be characterized as nothing more than a particularized restatement of the first. As the above passage from *Harrison v. Carswell* suggests, one of the central components of Canada's legal creed has been a belief in the continued viability of the distinction between the realms of law and politics.[2] The cornerstone of this creed has been the legislative supremacy of Parliament, subject only to federalism issues dealing with the proper allocation of power. The role of the courts has been regarded as essentially subordinate; the courts do not make political choices themselves, but merely give effect to the political choices made by others. The *Charter* challenges the dominance of this ruling paradigm. Under the *Charter*, courts are required to balance interests, the very sort of reasoning which *Harrison v. Carswell* declared off limits. Thus, the *Charter* appears to reject all the established axioms about the mature of the judicial role. It casts judges in the role of political actors rather than neutral arbiters. As such, the potential impact of the *Charter* extends far beyond the particular field of constitutional law. The *Charter* has the potential to revise the way we view judges generally, across the whole spectrum of the legal system.

The Supreme Court of Canada has already attempted to resolve these two problems posed by the introduction of the *Charter*. With respect to the first issue — the "legitimacy" of judicial review — the Court has argued that the issue was resolved by the mere enactment of the *Charter* in 1982. As Mr. Justice Lamer argued in the *Motor Vehicle Reference*,[3] the drafters of the *Charter* were well aware of what they were doing when they enacted this document into law in 1982. The very point of enacting the *Charter* was to confer on judges the power to strike down statutes. Thus, it would be illogical and ahistorical to claim that when judges interpret and apply the *Charter*, they are

---

1 Dickson J. [as he then was] in *Harrison v. Carswell* (1975), 62 D.L.R. (3d) 68 at 82 (S.C.C.).
2 See P. Monahan, "At Doctrine's Twilight: The Structure of Canadian Federalism" (1984), 34 U.T.L.J. 47.
3 *Ref. re s. 94(2) of the Motor Vehicle Act (B.C.)*, [1985] 2 S.C.R. 486 (S.C.C.).

acting illegitimately; the judiciary is simply discharging the duty which was inherent in the enactment of the *Constitution Act, 1982*.[4]

As for the claim that *Charter* adjudication requires the courts to make "political" choices, the Court has maintained that its role under the *Charter* is exclusively legal rather than political. The Court has repeatedly emphasized that its task is simply to interpret and apply the objective and neutral standards contained in the constitution. The Court need not inquire into the wisdom of legislation, nor do judges substitute their values for those of the legislature in resolving constitutional claims. The question of the constitutional validity of legislation is totally separate and distinct from the question of the wisdom or merits of that legislation.[5]

This second argument about "wisdom" is simply wrong. In the next chapter, I attempt to explain why judges are inevitably required to assess the policy underlying legislation in order to measure that legislation against the *Charter*. I want to defer discussion of this important question until that chapter. What of the first argument regarding legitimacy — the claim that the whole "legitimacy debate" is essentially an in-house American dispute which has no relevance for the Canadian *Charter*? This argument is based on the fact that, whereas the American Constitution does not explicitly provide for the power of judicial review, in Canada such power was explicitly contemplated by s. 52 of the *Constitution Act, 1982*. Thus, while there may be some residual doubt over the "legitimacy" of judicial review in the American context, such questions simply do not arise in Canada.

This defence of the legitimacy of judicial review is misleading and oversimplified. Of course, it is true that the American Constitution does not explicitly provide for judicial review and that the institution owes its existence to Marshall's opinion in *Marbury*.[6] But the debate over the legitimacy of judicial review in America over the past quarter century has certainly not centered over the merits of *Marbury*. There are no prominent contemporary American theorists calling for the "abolition" of the institution of judicial review. The debate is not over judicial review *per se*, but rather over what type of judicial review can be justified in a democratic polity. In essence, the contemporary debate is between some form of "textualism", which seeks to constrain judges through an objective theory of interpretation, and "noninter-

---

4 *Constitution Act, 1982* [en. by the *Canada Act, 1982* (U.K.), c. 11, s. 1].

5 *Motor Vehicle Reference, supra*, note 3.

6 *Marbury v. Madison*, 5 U.S. (1 Cranch) 137 (1803).

pretivism", which suggests that judges may look to values outside the text in order to give meaning to the constitution.

It is apparent that precisely the same issues inevitably arise in the context of the Canada *Charter*. The issue of legitimacy does not center on whether to have judicial review at all; this "big question" was settled by the enactment of the *Charter* in 1982. What the enactment of the *Charter* did not resolve was the subsidiary and more narrow issue of whether there are inherent limits to judicial review in the Canadian context. Once it is acknowledged that such limits exist, then the issue of legitimacy is joined. The very act of defining the limitations of judicial review requires the identification of those forms of judicial review which fall outside of the limits and are therefore inappropriate or "illegitimate".

As noted above, the Supreme Court itself has repeated on many occasions that its role under the *Charter* is a limited one. The Court believes that its duty is to objectively apply the text of the constitution and not assess the wisdom of legislation. Thus, while the Court has sought to deny the relevance of the legitimacy debate, its own analysis makes such a debate unavoidable. By elaborating a particular conception of its role, the Court has begun the task of defining the forms of judicial review which are legitimate and the forms which are illegitimate. The inevitability of such a debate does not mean that the specific contours of the Canadian debate should simply mimic developments in the United States. Canadians may arrive at quite distinctive and indigenous conclusions over the appropriate function of judicial review. The point is simply that *some* form of legitimacy debate is both necessary and desirable in Canada.

The first section of this book is essentially an attempt to respond to the problem of legitimacy posed by the *Charter*. The ultimate goal is to offer a theory of judicial review which will define the boundaries of the judicial role under the *Charter*. It is apparent, in other words, that this inquiry into the legitimacy of judicial review should not be confused with the separate issue of whether we should have a *Charter* at all. Given that we have a *Charter*, the crucial issue becomes identifying those tasks which are appropriate to judges and those tasks which are inappropriate or illegitimate.

Before I turn to a detailed analysis of this fundamental issue, it is necessary to begin on a more concrete and practical level. Abstract discussions about the legitimacy of judicial review only become meaningful if they are grounded in a pragmatic understanding of how the *Charter* is operating "on the ground". It would be pointless, for example, to attempt to resolve the legitimacy of judicial review without some understanding of how judges have actually been using the *Charter* in the past four and one-half years. One obvious issue that arises is the degree to which courts have demonstrated a willingness to utilize the *Charter* to overturn choices made by the legislature. It is also important to identify whether any particular types of legislation have been more vulnerable to *Charter* attack. The remainder of this chapter attempts to resolve these concrete questions. It represents a snapshot of the first four years of *Charter* litigation.

2. THE EARLY JUDICIAL RESPONSE TO THE CHARTER

While the enactment of the *Charter* was accompanied by high public expectations, many legal scholars doubted whether the courts would utilize their new powers in an aggressive or activist fashion. These scholars pointed to the fact that the courts had virtually ignored the federal *Bill of Rights*,[7] which had been enacted in 1960. The federal Bill had been interpreted in as narrow a fashion as possible, with the judiciary avoiding at all costs the prospect of interfering with the legislative choices made by Parliament.

Less than five years later, it is clear that these predictions about judicial deference in the *Charter* era were completely mistaken. The point is illustrated by the data in table 1, which summarizes the results of the approximately 800 Charter cases decided in Ontario, the Federal Court and the Supreme Court of Canada up to the spring of 1986.[8] Within these jurisdictions, *Charter* claims have been successful in almost one out of every three cases in which they have been raised. This finding is confirmed by studies of *Charter* outcomes in other Canadian jurisdictions.[9] It seems clear that courts at all levels across the country

---

7 *Canadian Bill of Rights*, R.S.C. 1970, App. III.

8 The data was obtained by analyzing all *Charter* decisions summarized for these jurisdictions in either the All Canada Weekly Summaries (A.C.W.S.) or the Weekly Criminal Bulletin (W.C.B.). There were a total of 806 *Charter* decisions for these jurisdictions summarized by June 1986. While this does not necessarily include all *Charter* cases actually decided to that point, the editors of these services claim that they summarize any case in which there are written reasons. These 806 decisions were then coded for pertinent characteristics and the information was analyzed using a SASS statistical program.

Ontario was selected for analysis because it is the jurisdiction which has generated the largest number of *Charter* cases thus far; the Federal Court was also included because of the large number of claims against federal laws which are decided in that jurisdiction.

9 This finding parallels the analysis of W.L. Morton, "Charting the Charter — Year One:

have no intention of continuing the tradition of extreme judicial deference associated with the *Canadian Bill of Rights*. The judiciary regards the *Charter* as an explicit invitation to subject legislative choices to meaningful scrutiny and they are taking that invitation seriously.

TABLE 1
Outcome of Charter Cases in Ontario Courts,
Federal Courts and Supreme Court of Canada, 1982–86

	Number of cases	Percent
Charter claim succeeds	248	31
Charter claim fails	521	65
No clear winner	37	4

Note: All cases summarized in the Weekly Criminal Bulletin and the All Canada Weekly Summaries up to June 1986 are included.

There is even evidence suggesting that the success rate of 31 per cent for *Charter* claims may well rise in the future. If the outcomes in the cases are analyzed over time, the willingness of courts to invoke the *Charter* appears to be increasing. As table 2 indicates, *Charter* arguments were *least* successful in the first two years of the *Charter*'s operation. Conversely, there has been a fairly significant increase in the success rate for *Charter* claims over the 1983–85 period, with approximately 34 per cent of claims in 1985 succeeding.

TABLE 2
Success Rate Over Time for Charter Claims

Year	Success Rate	Number of Cases
1982	29.1%	110
1983	26.5%	230
1984	32.2%	214
1985	34.1%	217
1986	34.3%	35

There is a plausible explanation as to why the success rate for *Charter* claims might well be expected to rise gradually over time. During the early years of the *Charter*, both bench and bar are unfamiliar

A Statistical Analysis" (1984-85), 2 Can. Human Rights Y.B. 239, who found an identical success rate for *Charter* arguments in the first year of its operation. Morton's analysis included cases decided in all ten provinces.

with this form of constitutional adjudication. This means that counsel will be advancing novel or untested arguments which later experience will demonstrate to be untenable. Similarly, one might have predicted an attitude of relative restraint on the part of the judiciary during this early period, given their unfamiliarity with *Charter* analysis and the absence of authoritative higher court rulings. Later, with the establishment of ascertainable margins of argument, the plainly untenable claims would never get to court while the judiciary would be more comfortable with the notion of overturning legislative choices on the basis of vaguely-worded rights guarantees. This suggests that, although a success rate of 30 per cent for *Charter* claims in the first three and one-half years is surprisingly high, the long-term success rate for such claims may well turn out to be somewhat higher.

There is further support for this hypothesis when the outcomes are broken down according to the level of court deciding the case. As table 3 indicates, the general rule has been that the higher the level of the court, the lower the success rate has been for *Charter* claims. In the Ontario provincially-appointed courts, for instance, *Charter* claims have been successful in nearly 43 per cent of the cases in which they have been raised. But the success rate drops to just over 24 per cent by the time litigants reach the Court of Appeal. A similar pattern is evident as one moves from the Federal Court–Trial Division to the Federal Court of Appeal. The exception to the trend is the Supreme Court of Canada. Far from adopting a restrictive attitude towards the *Charter*, our highest Court has pursued an extremely activist line of analysis. Of the first twenty *Charter* cases decided by the Court, the *Charter* claim has been successful on eleven occasions.

Of course, it is necessary to place this success rate of over 50 per cent at the Supreme Court level in its proper context. In seven of the eleven cases in which a *Charter* claim was successful, the Supreme Court was merely affirming a decision of a lower court. Moreover, many of these cases involved claims which were procedural or quasi-procedural in nature. *Singh*,[10] for example, involved the right to a hearing prior to the determination of refugee status; *Therens, Rahn* and *Trask*[11] turned on the right to counsel prior to being required to provide a breath sample; *Oakes*[12] raised the issue of the use of reverse onus

---

10 *Singh v. Min. of Employment & Immigration*, [1985] 1 S.C.R. 177 (S.C.C.).
11 *R. v. Therens*, [1985] 1 S.C.R. 613 (S.C.C.); *Trask v. R.*, [1985] 1 S.C.R. 655 (S.C.C.); *Rahn v. R.*, [1985] 1 S.C.R. 659 (S.C.C.).
12 *R. v. Oakes*, [1986] 1 S.C.R. 103 (S.C.C.).

provisions in criminal statutes; *Dubois*[13] defined the scope of the right against self-incrimination. These decisions certainly do not amount to a legal revolution, either individually or collectively.

TABLE 3
Charter Outcome by Level of Court

Court	No. of Cases	Success Rate
Ontario s. 92 cts.	180	43%
Ontario s. 96 cts.*	386	27%
Ontario Ct. of Appeal	94	24%
Federal Ct. Trial	91	25%
Federal Ct. Appeal	33	15%
Supreme Court Canada	20	55%

*excluding Court of Appeal

At the same time, the clear message from these early cases is that the Court intends to take the *Charter* seriously and that it will interpret it in a vigorous and innovative manner. The strongest statement of this message can be found in the *Motor Vehicle Reference*,[14] in which the Court simply rejected the unmistakable intentions of the drafters and adopted a substantive interpretation of s. 7. In *R. v. Oakes*,[15] the Court set out a test for examining legislation under s. 1 of the *Charter* which is extremely demanding; if this test is to be taken seriously in the future, it will result in a large body of previously uncontroversial legislation being struck down. The underlying assumption in both of these cases is that narrow interpretations of the provisions of the *Charter* are "bad" while broad and liberal interpretations are "good". This assumption has been reinforced on numerous other occasions, as the Court has gone out of its way to emphasize that it does not regard decisions giving narrow scope to *Bill of Rights* provisions as "binding authority" when it comes to interpreting analogous provisions under the *Charter*. The *Charter* is looked upon by the Court as a "constitutional document [that] is fundamentally different from the statutory *Canadian Bill of Rights*, which was interpreted as simply recognizing and declaring existing rights".[16]

If this activist trend on the Supreme Court continues, one would expect to see a gradual increase in the success rates for *Charter* claims

---

13 *Dubois v. R.*, [1985] 2 S.C.R. 350 (S.C.C.).
14 *Supra*, note 3.
15 *Supra*, note 12.
16 *R. v. Oakes, supra*, note 12 at 124, per Dickson C.J.

in lower courts, particularly at the Court of Appeal level. Moreover, this "trickle down" effect will reinforce the aggressive attitude demonstrated by the provincially-appointed courts in the early years of the *Charter*. The suggestion is that the success rate of 31 per cent established for *Charter* claims thus far is likely to go even higher in the future.

3. THE TARGETS OF CHARTER CHALLENGES

Given the rather activist use of the *Charter* over the first four and one-half years of its existence, the obvious issue which arises is: what sorts of governmental activity have been subject to challenge and with what success? The data in tables 4 and 5 attempts to offer a preliminary answer to this question.

There are two points of particular interest which arise from the data in table 4. First, the overwhelming majority of *Charter* claims thus far have arisen in the criminal law context. In the province of Ontario, for example, roughly 85 per cent of all *Charter* cases decided thus far have been criminal cases.[17] Second, courts have been far more activist in criminal as opposed to non-criminal cases. In Ontario and the Federal Courts up until the end of October 1985, success in criminal cases has been much higher than in non-criminal cases.

TABLE 4
Charter Success in Criminal Cases

Type of case	Claim Succeeds	Claim Fails	No Winner	Success Rate
Criminal Cases	202	385	23	33%
Non-Criminal Cases	46	136	14	23%

These results are not terribly surprising. Supervision of the criminal process is a staple item on the judicial menu. Invoking the *Charter* in this context does not appear to require difficult judgments of social policy on the part of the judiciary. Rather, the courts are seen to be using the *Charter* in order to determine the guilt or innocence

---

17 In this category, I include claims arising under the *Criminal Code*, R.S.C. 1970, c. C-34, as well as claims associated with the enforcement of other "criminal" statutes, such as the *Narcotic Control Act*, R.S.C. 1970, c. N-1, and the *Combines Investigation Act*, R.S.C. 1970, c. C-23. I also include claims raised by inmates of the penitentiary system.

of individual accused. On these issues, judicial legitimacy and expertise appears high. Conversely, it is in the non-criminal context that courts are most likely to encounter cases which raise broad issues of economic and social policy. One would expect the judiciary to be more reluctant to cut a wide *Charter* swath through such social and economic programmes, especially in the early days of the *Charter*.

Table 5 examines the extent to which *Charter* claims have been directed at administrative conduct as opposed to statutes. The data indicates that the vast majority of *Charter* litigation to this point has centered on the actions of public officials, primarily police officers and crown attorneys. In Ontario and the Federal Courts, only about one in three *Charter* challenges has involved the validity of a statute or a statutory instrument. Moreover, whenever the validity of a statute has been challenged, the courts have been significantly less likely to uphold the *Charter* claim. Only about one in four challenges to federal and provincial statutes succeed,[18] while slightly over one in three challenges to the conduct of public officials is upheld.

TABLE 5
The Objects of Charter Litigation
Ontario and Federal Courts 1982–86

Object of Challenge	No. of Cases	Charter Claim Succeeds	Charter Claim Fails	Success Rate
Statute	325*	84	224	26%
Conduct of Public Official	475**	163	293	34%
Other	6	2	4	33%

* includes 17 cases in which there was no clear winner
**includes 19 cases in which there was no clear winner

---

18 It has been suggested that courts have been more deferential towards federal than provincial statutes in the early days of the *Charter*. See W.L. Morton, *supra*, note 9 at 254. The cases in Ontario and the Federal Court do not support this claim. In fact, there was greater success in challenging federal statutes than provincial statutes in this sample, as the data outlined below indicates:

Nature of Statute	Challenge Succeeds	Challenge Fails	Success Rate*
Federal	67	160	28%
Provincial	17	58	21%

*includes cases in which there was no clear winner

Once again, these results are not overly surprising. Judicial review would appear most controversial in instances where courts are assessing the validity of a statute or a statutory instrument. Here, the courts are calling into question an explicit policy choice of the legislature or the cabinet. Conversely, where the courts are simply reviewing the conduct of particular public officials, such as police officers and public servants, the question of judicial legitimacy becomes more muted. Such claims are more likely to involve procedural as opposed to substantive challenges to state policies. In fact, it has been argued that this form of judicial review actually enhances democracy rather than subverts it, since it provides a mechanism for individuals to challenge the omnipresent power of bureaucracy over their lives. It has the potential to produce a "participant, rights-conscious citizenry" which is seen as a "necessary, if not sufficient condition for a well-functioning constitutional order".[19] Other defences of this form of judicial review have argued that "bureaucrats are often negligent and even high-handed in their dealings with the public. Rarely in the public eye but exercising significant discretion, civil servants, bureaucrats and policemen are potentially even less accountable than judges".[20]

It should be pointed out that this defence of judicial review slides rather quickly over a number of sticky questions. If the claim is that bureaucrats are acting outside the bounds of the authority established by Parliament, there should be no need to resort to an entrenched constitutional *Charter* at all. Courts can deal with unlawful or unauthorized state action simply by applying general principles associated with the rule of law. If, on the other hand, the bureaucratic conduct has been authorized by Parliament but the complaint is that this otherwise lawful activity violates the *Charter*, then the conflict with democracy is less easy to avoid. Although the litigation may not be challenging the validity of a statute directly, it still calls into question a policy choice that has been made by Parliament. If the courts overturn that policy choice, they are indirectly substituting their views for the views of the elected representatives of the people.

Notwithstanding this caveat, it is clear that the courts have been most aggressive in applying the *Charter* in those areas where its legitimacy is likely to be the highest. Judicial scrutiny has tended to focus on the criminal context and address the behaviour of officials as opposed to the validity of statutes.

---

19 A.C. Cairns, "The Canadian Constitutional Experiment" (1984), 9 Dalhousie L.J. 87 at 113.
20 W.L. Morton, *supra*, note 9 at 241.

4. THE RIGHTS GAP: DIFFERING SUCCESS RATES FOR DIFFERENT CHARTER RIGHTS

In theory, all the rights guaranteed by the *Charter* are supposed to be equally fundamental. They are all subject to the same standard of review set out in s. 1; limitations to any right set out in the *Charter* must be "reasonable" and "demonstrably justified in a free and democratic society". In practice, however, it turns out that courts seem far more receptive to certain rights arguments than they are to others. Table 6 lists the five more frequently litigated *Charter* rights in Ontario and Federal Courts along with the corresponding success rate for each right.[21]

The variation in relative success rates is rather striking, given the large number of occasions on which the various rights have been litigated. Courts have been most receptive to arguments alleging unreasonable search and seizure as well as arguments based on s. 10, primarily the right to counsel in s. 10(*b*). On the other hand, courts have been least receptive to guarantees of "fundamental freedoms" in s. 2, as well as the right to "life, liberty and security of the person" in s. 7. The disparity in relative success rates is such that arguments based on ss. 8 and 10 have been almost twice as successful as arguments based on ss. 2 and 7. Courts have also been relatively unreceptive to *Charter* litigation based on s. 11, which has primarily involved the right to be tried within a reasonable time [s. 11(*b*)] and the presumption of innocence [s. 11(*d*)]. Nor have the courts been particularly enthusiastic about litigation involving s. 15, the guarantee of equality.

TABLE 6
Success Rate for Charter Arguments
Ontario and Federal Courts 1982–86

Charter Right	Cases Raised	Cases Successful	Per cent
s. 11	277	71	26%
s. 7	237	58	24%
s. 8	171	69	40%
s. 10	117	49	42%
s. 2	79	19	24%
s. 15	53	13	25%

Note: Table includes all rights which were litigated a minimum of 50 times.

---

21 Note that in any one case, more than one right might be litigated. Thus, in the sample of 806 cases, there was a total of 1128 separate rights arguments raised. The "success rate" in table 6 refers to the court's acceptance or rejection of a given *Charter* argument, rather than to the final outcome of the case. Of the 1128 arguments, 342 or about 30% were successful, virtually the same as the success rate for *Charter* outcomes noted in table 1.

These results seem consistent with the data on *Charter* outcomes presented earlier. *Charter* claims have been most successful in criminal cases or cases involving challenges to administrative conduct. Thus, it is unsurprising to observe a high success rate for claims under ss. 8 and 10. Claims under these sections have largely arisen in the criminal context and have tended to involve the conduct of public officials rather than the validity of statutes. Conversely, claims under s. 2 of the *Charter* have been more likely to arise in the non-criminal context and to involve the validity of statutes. Thus, one would expect to observe a lower success rate for *Charter* claims under s. 2.

Yet this explanation seems seriously incomplete, since it fails to explain why ss. 8 and 10 alone of the various legal rights have been so successfully utilized by litigants thus far. Most of the legal rights in ss. 7 to 14 tend to arise in the criminal context and to involve challenges to administrative conduct rather than to statutes. But claims arising under ss. 8 to 10 have been far more successful than claims arising under other legal rights provisions.

One plausible explanation for these results is the link between the s. 8 and s. 10 rights and traditional judicial values. The guarantee against unreasonable search and seizure in s. 8 has roots deep within the common law, reflecting traditional judicial concern for the protection of private property. Chief Justice Dickson made this linkage between s. 8 and property rights explicit in his unanimous judgment in *Hunter v. Southam Inc.* The Chief Justice cited the old case of *Entick v. Carrington* for the proposition that "[t]he great end for which men entered into society, was to preserve their property", although this sacred right could be "abridged by some public law for the good of the whole".[22] According to Dickson C.J., although s. 8 of the *Charter* has its roots in common law property rights, it is not limited to the protection of property. Rather, the Chief Justice regards s. 8 as suggestive of some larger right of "privacy", which he defines as "the right to be let alone by other people".[23]

Similarly, it is unsurprising to observe the high success rate for the right to counsel in s. 10 of the *Charter*. The judiciary has always regarded courts and the legal profession as one of the central pillars of Canadian democracy. The Supreme Court's expansive interpretation

---

22 *Entick v. Carrington* (1765), 19 State Tr. 1029 at 1066, per Lord Camden; quoted by Dickson C.J. in *Hunter v. Southam Inc.* (1984), 11 D.L.R. (3d) 641 at 651 (S.C.C.).

23 *Hunter v. Southam Inc., ibid.* at 652.

of s. 96 of the *Constitution Act, 1867* in such cases as *Crevier*[24] and *McEvoy*[25] reflects this preoccupation with the virtues of traditional common law courts and lawyers. In the administrative law field, courts have often been quick to imply rights to counsel and trial-type procedures in hearings before administrative tribunals. In *Jabour,*[26] the Supreme Court affirmed the traditional view that the legal profession could be counted on to act in the public interest even though it was exempt from the discipline of the market.[27]

5. THE IMPACT OF THE CHARTER: A PRELIMINARY ASSESSMENT

The desirability of an entrenched bill of rights has long been a source of controversy in the Canadian legal literature. Given our early experience under the *Charter*, what assessment can be made of this long-standing debate?

The arguments in favour of entrenching a *Charter* are well known. The traditional case for an entrenched bill of rights is essentially that it will make governments more sensitive to individual rights in their formulation of public policy. The traditional arguments against an entrenched *Charter*, on the other hand, are less well known and are often stated in a confused or contradictory manner. Thus, it seems worthwhile to outline in some detail the primary claims of the critics of an entrenched *Charter*.

The traditional argument against an entrenched bill of rights can be stated in the form of two propositions. The first is a proposition about legislatures and the political process, the second, a proposition about courts and the judicial process. The first proposition claims that the political process has always been the most effective mechanism for advancing the cause of social justice in Canada. This is not some

---

24 *Crevier v. A.G. Que.*, [1981] 2 S.C.R. 220 (S.C.C.).

25 *Re Ct. of Unified Criminal Jurisdiction; McEvoy v. A.G. N.B.*, [1983] 1 S.C.R. 704 (S.C.C.).

26 *A.G. Can. v. L.S.U.C.; Jabour v. L.S.U.C.*, [1982] 2 S.C.R. 307 (S.C.C.).

27 How can one account for the higher rate of success associated with the right to counsel in s. 10(*b*) as compared with the various legal rights protected in s. 11? The rights in s. 11 seem to reflect the same sorts of values bound up with the right to counsel in s. 10. But an important difference between the sections is the fact that the rights guaranteed in s. 11 are fairly specific and detailed, dealing with particular aspects of the criminal process. The right to counsel, on the other hand, is a more general and fundamental right, in the sense that it might apply in any of the particular circumstances enumerated in s. 11. In effect, the right to counsel might be seen as a precondition to the enjoyment of any of the specifically enumerated rights in s. 11. Accordingly, it would be quite natural to observe a higher degree of success for claims under s. 10 as compared with claims under s. 11.

naive claim that the outcomes of the political process have always and everywhere been substantively just. The claim is simply that, where the interests of the disadvantaged in Canadian society have been advanced, this has usually been accomplished through political debate and argument. Social programmes and the institutions of the welfare state, whatever their shortcomings, are the progeny of the triumph of politics over economics and the market. In essence, the critics of an entrenched *Charter* reject theories of "limited government". For them, the attempt to construct "checks and balances" around the exercise of state power is an obsession rather than a virtue. Because the critics regard the state as a source of social justice rather than oppression and domination, they want to empower the state so that it might defend and promote the interests of the disadvantaged.

The second proposition in the critique claims that wherever the political process has acted in favour of disadvantaged Canadians, it has done so despite courts and the judicial process, rather than because of them. According to this critique, courts have often resisted state initiatives designed to advance the interests of the disadvantaged in Canada. This judicial resistence is a reflection of undue reverence for economics and the market along with a suspicion of the political process. Rather than recognize the legitimacy of state regulation of market institutions in the name of equality, courts in many instances have stymied such regulation, albeit in the name of what the courts regard as "freedom". The problem is that what courts define as "freedom" is often regarded by the critics as little more than a licence for the powerful to exploit the powerless.

When the two elements of the critique are combined, they suggest that the entrenchment of a *Charter* should be viewed as a setback for rather than a vindication of the cause of human rights in Canada. The first proposition of the critique points out that the primary effect of a *Charter* will be to constrain the ability of the state to pursue its goals. Whenever legislation is ruled invalid, the loser is not "the state" *per se*, but the individual Canadians whose interests the state was defending and who stood to benefit from the law. Thus, the claim that a *Charter* increases "rights" in the abstract is wishful thinking. What a *Charter* actually does is to increase or to protect the rights of certain individuals or groups at the expense of the rights of others. The second proposition of the critique identifies which groups and interests are likely to be winners or losers in this process. Drawing on the attitude of courts in the past, the critics predict that the judiciary will likely be most suspicious of attempts by the state to regulate the market or to undertake redistributive social programmes. This does not mean that entrenching a *Charter* will necessarily dismantle the welfare state. It simply suggests that, on balance, existing social programmes will come under increasing challenge and it will be more difficult to expand such programmes in the future. At the margin, an entrenched *Charter* will protect the interests of those who already possess economic and market power, while discounting the interests of disadvantaged Canadians who depend on the state for support and protection.

What does our early experience under the *Charter* tell us about these various arguments over the merits of an entrenched bill of rights? It is evident, I think, that much of the early experience under the *Charter* cuts against the claims of the critics and in favour of the proponents of an entrenched *Charter*. As we saw in the previous section, the vast majority of *Charter* claims to this point has arisen in the criminal context. Moreover, most *Charter* litigation has centered on the conduct of public officials rather than validity of statutes. These factors suggest that the *Charter* may well have a marginal impact on the regulatory powers of the Canadian state. Parliament's ability to regulate the market and enact redistributive social programmes might escape intact from the process of *Charter* scrutiny.

But there is also evidence in the early *Charter* cases which cuts in the opposite direction. This evidence suggests that *Charter* jurisprudence is being shaped and structured by traditional judicial concerns, such as property rights and the importance of the legal profession. At the same time, other liberty interests, such as rights of free expression, have received much less vigorous protection.

It is also instructive, in terms of this debate, to analyze the performance of the courts in non-criminal *Charter* cases. It is in these cases that courts are most likely to become involved in reviewing social welfare and redistributive programmes associated with the welfare state. It is in these instances that critics' fears about the wisdom of a *Charter* are most intense.

In light of this concern, the data in table 4, above, is reassuring. Courts appear to be adopting a deferential attitude towards legislative choices in the non-criminal context; less than one in four such challenges succeeds. Further, those claims which have succeeded have not impeded in any significant way the regulatory powers of the state. There are two explanations for this. First, many of the successful claims have been procedural in nature. Second, even when a court has overturned a substantive state policy, it has often indicated how the

norms. For example, in *Ontario Film and Video Appreciation Society v. Ontario Board of Censors*,[28] the Ontario Divisional Court struck down a censorship scheme which essentially granted unlimited power to a censor board to edit films. But the court held that some form of censorship could be demonstrably justified in a free and democratic society; the problem in this case was the complete absence of legally enforceable standards to guide the censor board's discretion. This judgment was upheld by the Ontario Court of Appeal and is presently under appeal to the Supreme Court of Canada. In the meantime, however, the provincial government took account of the court's ruling and amended the statute so as to require the censor board to employ criteria set out in regulations. The irony is that the standards in the regulations are just as amorphous as the informal guidelines which the censor board had followed in the past; the only difference is that the standards are now legally binding on the board. Although the new regulations may themselves be challenged in future litigation, for now, the *Charter* has not made a great deal of difference to state censorship in Ontario.

While the relatively marginal impact of these early cases is reassuring, there are certain signals in the cases that are somewhat troubling. First, unlike the non-criminal area, these cases are much more likely to involve challenges to statutes rather than the conduct of public officials. In the non-criminal context, over 57 per cent of the cases involved challenges to statutes, as compared to only 33 per cent in the criminal cases.[29] Second, the interests that are reflected in the non-criminal cases tend to be purely economic or property interests. One indication of this is the important role which corporations have played in such litigation. Approximately 27 per cent of the *Charter* claims in the non-criminal context — more than one of every four such claims — was raised by a corporation. These corporate claims are often framed in terms which tend to disguise their character as property claims. *Hunter v. Southam*,[30] although a criminal case,

---

28 *Ont. Film & Video Appreciation Soc. v. Ont. Bd. of Censors* (1983), 147 D.L.R. (3d) 58 (Ont. Div. Ct.).

29 The figures are as follows:

	Challenges to Statutes	Challenges to Administrative Action
Criminal Cases	186 [34%]	365 [66%]
Non-criminal Cases	80 [57%]	57 [41%]

30 *Supra*, note 22.

illustrates the point. Here, the corporate defendant was claiming a right of "privacy" pursuant to s. 8 of the *Charter*. But "privacy" is an interest commonly associated with human, rather than artificial, persons. What the corporation was describing as a "privacy" interest was actually little more than a property interest in its documents and files.

Corporate claims under the *Charter* have been no more successful than claims by individuals. Yet this is really beside the point. The enactment of the *Charter* has armed corporations with an important new instrument to advance their interests and resist regulation by government. At the margin, it has made state regulation of the corporate sector more difficult. This fact has been largely obscured by the popular rhetoric surrounding the *Charter*, which has repeatedly emphasized its character as a "people's package".

There is a final feature of the non-criminal cases which bears emphasis. These cases offer practical illustrations of the way in which the *Charter* protects the rights of certain individuals, but only at the expense of the rights or interests of other Canadians. In effect, the cases expose the fallacy in the view that the *Charter* merely protects the rights of individuals against "the state" in the abstract. One illustration is provided by the recent case of *Re College of Physicians and Surgeons of Ontario and K*.[31] In this case, "K" was a physician who had been charged with professional misconduct for allegedly engaging in sexual impropriety with two of his patients. The discipline committee of the college had heard the evidence of the two women in a common hearing and found Dr. "K" guilty of professional misconduct. The Divisional Court overturned the finding of the committee on a number of grounds, one of them being that the proceedings had violated the "principles of fundamental justice" protected by s. 7 of the *Charter*.[32]

The defect in the proceedings was procedural and there was nothing to prevent the committee from bringing new charges against Dr. "K". But the effect of the court ruling was to make it marginally more difficult for patients to establish claims of sexual impropriety against their doctors. It is the interests of these patients, rather than simply those of "the state", which were at stake in the litigation.

As a second illustration of this point, consider the recent case

---

31 *Re College of Physicians & Surgeons of Ont. and K.* (1985), 50 O.R. (2d) 14 (Ont. Div. Ct.).

32 The Divisional Court held that the fact that the charge against the doctor had contained particulars of the two complainants violated s. 7 of the *Charter*.

of *Re Beaton and Gatecliffe*.[33] Here, a woman was seeking to enforce an order of child support against a putative father residing in Ontario. The order of support had been issued by a Nova Scotian court, which had found that the putative father was a "possible father", pursuant to Nova Scotian law. Under Ontario law, there would have had to have been a finding that the putative father was the biological father. However, s. 6(1) of the *Reciprocal Enforcement of Maintenance Orders Act, 1982*[34] directed the Ontario court in this instance to take account of Nova Scotia law and apply it. The provincial court found that s. 6(1) violated "principles of fundamental justice" since it imposed an obligation on this putative father which would not be imposed on other putative fathers in Ontario. The provision was therefore unconstitutional and of no force and effect with respect to this particular putative father.

The policy of Ontario's reciprocal enforcement legislation is to facilitate local enforcement of maintenance orders validly made elsewhere. If the foreign court which issued the order exercised its jurisdiction properly, then the order should be enforceable in Ontario without the necessity for a complicated and costly hearing before the the Ontario courts. The underlying philosophy is to prevent individuals from escaping their maintenance obligations by taking advantage of jurisdictional obstacles associated with federalism. The use of the *Charter* in this particular context cuts against the legislative policy. It makes it more difficult and costly to overcome problems of divided jurisdiction. Once again, the loser is not "the state", but those individual Canadians who are entitled to support and depend upon the state to enforce their rights.

These cases are not the stuff of which headlines are made or newspapers are sold. In these garden-variety cases, the court is intervening in a marginal way, utilizing the *Charter* in a largely procedural fashion. What the cases illustrate, however, is the way in which courts can utilize such procedural devices to subtly undermine the policy goals of the legislature. Where the court finds the legislative policy distasteful, it need not necessarily rule the statute as a whole to be unconstitutional. It can simply read a whole series of "procedural" guarantees into the legislation, thereby making the pursuit of legislative policy significantly more costly. Those costs fall on indi-

---

33 *Re Beaton and Gatecliffe*, Ont. Fam. Ct., October 9, 1985, summarized (1985), 33 A.C.W.S. (2d) 194.

34 *Reciprocal Enforcement of Maintenance Orders Act, 1982*, S.O. 1982, c. 9, s. 6(1).

viduals such as the aggrieved patients of Dr. "K" or the child suing for maintenance in *Re Beaton*. For these Canadians, the suggestion that the *Charter* has somehow secured their "rights" would seem puzzling and even bizarre. From their point of view, the *Charter*'s effect had been rather different, taking rights from some and giving them to others.

6. CONCLUSION

Although the *Charter* is only a little more than four years old, it is already possible to offer some generalizations about the nature of *Charter* litigation. So far, *Charter* litigation has been overwhelmingly concerned with the criminal process. Most *Charter* challenges have been to the conduct of public officials rather than to statutes or statutory instruments. Courts have tended to be most activist in those areas where their experience and legitimacy is high, and more deferential in instances where their authority is controversial.

In terms of assessing the impact of the *Charter*, there are many factors in the early cases which suggest that the *Charter* may not pose any significant threat to legislative power. The impact of the *Charter* to this point appears to have been fairly marginal. But it is also evident from the early cases that the judiciary will utilize the *Charter* to advance the same sorts of values which courts have traditionally favoured. The *Charter* makes it somewhat more difficult for the state to regulate those favoured interests or values in the name of the community as a whole. This may not make a great deal of difference as long as courts continue to restrict their activism to the criminal process and/or procedural claims. But in the hands of a more aggressive judiciary, the *Charter* could well develop into a serious constitutional roadblock impeding state efforts to assist disadvantaged Canadians.

The enactment of the *Charter* in 1982 was a historic choice for Canadians. In a few short years, the *Charter* has become one of the sacred cows of Canadian political life; critics of an entrenched bill of rights are few and far between.[35] The data presented in this chapter is not designed either to revive or to finally resolve that long-standing debate. Indeed, the early evidence is far too sketchy and speculative to point clearly in either direction. My point is simply that, as with

---

35 But for a cogent argument that the enactment of the *Charter* was a serious mistake, see A. Petter, "The Politics of the Charter" (1986), 8 Sup. Ct. L. Rev. 473.

everything else in political life, the enactment of the *Charter* will likely turn out to be something of a mixed blessing. In assessing its impact, Canadians would be well advised to keep track of the costs at the same time as they give thanks for the blessings.

4

Law, Politics and the Early Charter Cases in the Supreme Court of Canada

1. THE CONFLICTING TENDENCIES

With only a handful of *Charter* cases decided by the Supreme Court by early 1986, it is obviously difficult to hazard any generalizations regarding the Court's performance or attitude towards the *Charter*, let alone to speculate about future developments. Yet, even at this early stage, it is possible to identify at least two important and somewhat conflicting trends in the cases. These tendencies suggest that the Court has a deep ambivalence towards its new responsibilities under the *Charter* and that there are strong impulses pulling the Court in opposite directions.

One tendency in these early cases, which is the most obvious and therefore uncontroversial, is that the Court seems intent on adopting a fundamentally different attitude towards *Charter* litigation than it did to cases arising under the *Canadian Bill of Rights*. The judicial legacy under the *Bill* was one of endless logical and legal posturing, apparently designed to ensure that the statute's only application would be to laws dealing with drunkenness of Indians off their reserves, in the North West Territories.[1] Such transparent contortions have apparently become passé for purposes of *Charter* litigation. Not only has the Court granted relief in over half of the *Charter* cases decided thus far,[2] its judgments have been robed in the rhetoric of activist judicial review. We have been told that the *Charter* is a "living tree" that must not be contaminated by narrow or technical judicial interpretation. The Court in *Charter* cases should not merely engage in ordinary statutory construction, but must perform a "constitutional role".[3] The Court has seen the banner of Chief Justice Marshall being run up the Canadian legal flagpole and it has saluted: "we must never forget, that it is a *constitution* that we are interpreting."[4]

The second tendency in these early *Charter* cases flows from and, to some extent, qualifies the first. Despite the incessant invocation of activist rhetoric, the Court has stoutly maintained that its role under the *Charter* is "legal" and not "political". The Court's concern is not with the "wisdom" of legislation, but only with the separate question of whether a right guaranteed by the *Charter* has been violated. Madam Justice Wilson forcefully emphasized this point in her concurring opinion in the *Operation Dismantle* case: "The question before us is not whether the government's defence policy is sound but whether or not it violates the appellants' rights under s. 7 of the *Charter of Rights and Freedoms. This is a totally different question.* I do not think there can be any doubt that this is a question for the courts."[5]

Of course, this statement is only meaningful if the issue of legality can be determined without recourse to questions of "wisdom". Madam Justice Wilson's confident assertion that the issues are "totally

---

1 See *R. v. Drybones*, [1970] S.C.R. 282 (S.C.C.); *A.G. Can. v. Lavell; Isaac v. Bedard*, [1974] S.C.R. 1349 (S.C.C.); *Bliss v. A.G. Can.*, [1979] 1 S.C.R. 183 (S.C.C.).

2 The cases in which the *Charter* challenge was successful are: *R. v. Trask*, [1985] 1 S.C.R. 655; *R. v. Rahn*, [1985] 1 S.C.R. 659; *R. v. Therens*, [1985] 1 S.C.R. 613; *Singh v. Min. of Employment & Immigration, Can.*, [1985] 1 S.C.R. 177; *Hunter v. Southam Inc.*, [1984] 2 S.C.R. 145; *R. v. Big M Drug Mart Ltd.*, [1985] 1 S.C.R. 295; *Que. Assn. of Protestant School Bds. v. A.G. Que.*, [1984] 2 S.C.R. 66; *Ref. re s. 94(2) of the Motor Vehicle Act (B.C.)*, [1985] 2 S.C.R. 486; *R. v. Oakes*, [1986] 1 S.C.R. 103; *Dubois v. R.*, [1985] 2 S.C.R. 350; *R. v. Clarkson*, [1986] 1 S.C.R. 383. The cases in which the claim failed are: *Operation Dismantle Inc. v. R.*, [1985] 1 S.C.R. 441; *L.S.U.C. v. Skapinker*, [1984] 1 S.C.R. 357; *R. v. Spencer*, [1985] 2 S.C.R. 278; *R. v. Valente (No. 2)* (1985), 52 O.R. (2d) 779; *Société des Acadiens du Nouveau-Brunswick Inc. v. Assn. of Parents for Fairness in Education* (1986), 66 N.R. 173; *Krug v. R.*, [1985] 2 S.C.R. 255. This includes all Supreme Court cases decided as of June 1986. For further discussion, see Chapter 3.

3 *L.S.U.C. v. Skapinker* (1984), 9 D.L.R. (4th) 161 at 168, per Estey J. (S.C.C.).

4 *M'Culloch v. State of Maryland*, 17 U.S. (4 Wheaton) 316 (1819), quoted by Estey J. in *Skapinker, supra*, note 3 at 170.

5 See *Operation Dismantle Inc. v. R.*, [1985] 1 S.C.R. 441 at 472 [emphasis added].

different" seems based on the fact that the Court is being called on to interpret and to apply a specific "legal" standard, in this case s. 7 of the *Charter*. But the mere fact that statutory language is involved does not, in itself, provide a distinction between legal and political questions. The issue is whether it is possible to apply the statutory language without an inquiry into the "wisdom" of the legislation under review.

Even a cursory analysis of the language and structure of the *Charter* indicates that most *Charter* litigation may well turn on the issue of the "wisdom" of legislative choices. In party, this is a product of the abstract and generalized nature of the rights protected by the *Charter*. The very process of defining the content of the rights protected by the *Charter* seems inherently political. Many of these rights — most notably the right to "equality" and "liberty" — contain little or no substantive criteria; they resemble blank slates on which the judiciary can scrawl the imagery of their choice. But there is a second problem. Having given content to these open-ended rights, the judiciary must then "balance" these rights against considerations of general welfare under s. 1. This process of "interest balancing" seems just another way of asking the fundamental legislative question: "is this worth what it costs?" The process of balancing individual interests against collective interests is a calculation which would have already been made by the legislature when it passed the statute under review. Since the legislature passed the statute, it must have calculated that the interests to be served outweighed those to be sacrificed. Section 1 of the *Charter* appears to invite the Court to assess and to second-guess the "wisdom" of the balance struck by the legislature.

There is no reason to suppose that the Court is better situated than the legislature to make such judgments. "Balancing" of interests is a quintessentially legislative task.[6] We normally look to the political rather than the legal branches of government for calculations of general welfare. Only the legislature is equipped to deal with the vast array of data that is relevant to such an inquiry. Not only does the Court lack the expertise and the resources to consider these legislative facts, the litigants in a private lawsuit are unlikely to place them on the

---

6 There was an ongoing American debate in the 1960s over whether "interest balancing" was appropriate for the judiciary. The weight of opinion tended to the view that it was inappropriate, since it required the court to perform legislative tasks. For a sampling of the various viewpoints, see L. Frantz, "The First Amendment in the Balance", 71 Yale L.J. 1424 (1962); W. Mendelson, "On the Meaning of the First Amendment: Absolutes in the Balance", 50 Cal. L. Rev. 821 (1962).

record. This is why even the most ardent defenders of judicial review concede that interpersonal comparisons of utility are best carried out by the legislature: "[t]he political system of representative democracy may work only indifferently . . ., but it works better than a system that allows nonelected judges, who have no mail bag or lobbyists or pressure groups, to compromise competing interests in their chambers."[7]

The highly politicized nature of the s. 1 inquiry is merely exacerbated by the reference to "reasonable limits" that can be "demonstrably justified in a free and democratic society". In order to give content to this terminology, the courts will have to devise some normative theory about the nature of freedom and of democracy. The trouble with this is twofold. First, there is no fixed or uncontroversial "core meaning" to these concepts; they are "contested concepts", with a rich and sophisticated debate continuing within political theory over their content and application.[8] Second, the judiciary is largely unaware of the nature and subtlety of these theoretical debates; legal training in Canada has always relegated such "political" questions to the domain of the academy or the legislature rather than the courtroom. The enactment of the *Charter* is like an unscheduled "night drop", in which Canada's judges and lawyers have been parachuted unawares into the battlefields of political theory, without weapons, and with no knowledge of the deployment of the contending armies.

In an attempt to avoid this unpleasant scenario, some of the early *Charter* cases have suggested that the reference to "free and democratic societies" in s. 1 directs judges to engage in a comparative inquiry. According to this view, the Court must look to practices in other "free and democratic" societies and determine the limits on rights which are acceptable there. Limitations which are generally accepted in such free and democratic societies are justifiable according to the terms of s. 1.[9] If this analysis were correct, the Court would be relieved of the responsibility of determining for itself the nature of freedom or of democracy. The Court would be mere cataloguer rather than

---

7 R. Dworkin, *Taking Rights Seriously* (1977) at 85.

8 For a survey of some of the recent debates over the meaning of democracy, see C. Pateman, *Participation and Democratic Theory* (1970).

9 For instances of this line of argument, see: *Ont. Film & Video Appreciation Soc. v. Ont. Bd. of Censors* (1983), 147 D.L.R. (3d) 58 (Ont. Div. Ct.); *Germany v. Rauca* (1982), 141 D.L.R. (3d) 412 (Ont. H.C.); D. Macdonald, *Legal Rights in the Canadian Charter of Rights and Freedoms: A Manual of Issues and Sources* (1982) at 18.

lofty theorist, taking judicial notice of the balance that others have struck between individual rights and collective welfare. The s. 1 analysis would be largely descriptive rather than overtly normative.

The mistake in this analysis is as common as it is fundamental. The reasoning attempts to leap from the fact that a state of affairs exists to the inference that this state of affairs is justified. But a moment's reflection will indicate why this leap from the descriptive to the normative cannot succeed. To take a well-known example, blacks in the United States have been subjected to various forms of institutionalized and informal discrimination over the past 200 years. In particular, the education system prior to the 1950s was segregated along racial lines, in keeping with the "separate, but equal" doctrine sanctioned in *Plessy*.[10] When the Supreme Court of the United States came to reconsider the constitutionality of such separate schooling in the famous case of *Brown v. Board of Education of Topeka*,[11] the mere fact that such segregation existed could not count as a constitutional justification in its favour. Constitutional argument is normative; it is about what ought to be, not about what is. The opponents of segregation did not question the fact that such segregation had existed; their point was precisely that the very existence of separate facilities perpetuated racial stereotypes and ensured the continued subjugation of American blacks. Historical or comparative arguments pointing to widespread acceptance of such racial segregation were simply irrelevant in this normative equation. If the state was to justify separate facilities, it had to rely on the inherent desirability of the system, not its pervasiveness.

A similar sort of argument applies in the context of s. 1. If, for example, the Court is hearing a s. 15 challenge to restrictions on combat roles for women in the military, the fact that other nations have seen fit to impose similar restrictions cannot count as a significant reason in their favour. This comparative evidence may be relevant as an indication of the extent to which sexual stereotypes are deeply embedded in the consciousness of liberal democracies. But it tells us nothing about whether or not these restrictions on women satisfy some independent norm of equality. To answer that question, the Court will have to devise its own conception of equality and "balance" it against the interests of the community as a whole.

So we begin with this general premise: the process whereby the

---

10 *Plessy v. Ferguson*, 163 U.S. 537 (U.S. La., 1896).
11 *Brown v. Bd. of Education of Topeka*, 349 U.S. 294 (1955).

Court defines rights and then "balances" them against considerations of general welfare bears a striking resemblance to legislative judgments about general utility. The question under s. 1 of the *Charter* — whether gains in general welfare justify limits on individual rights — appears no different in principle from the question the legislature asks itself when it enacts legislation. Moreover, the concepts of "freedom" and "democracy" referred to in s. 1 are themselves indeterminate and fundamentally contested. Rather than offer any meaningful weights and measures for use in the balancing process, they merely invite the court to devise its own theory of freedom and of democracy.

This returns me to my original observation regarding the frequent invocation of activist rhetoric by the Supreme Court in its early *Charter* judgments. My claim is that, beneath this bravado, the *Charter* has thrown the Court into a crisis over the legitimacy of the judicial role and the relationship between law and politics. While maintaining that the *Charter* must receive a "large and liberal" interpretation, the Court has insisted that its function under the *Charter* is a peculiarly legal and not a political one. But the story hasn't convinced anyone. Instead of arguments aimed at differentiating its function from that of the legislature, the Court has offered only bare and hollow assertion.

2. THE OPERATION DISMANTLE CASE

The most obvious illustration of the Court's continuing but frustrated attempt to maintain the law-politics distinction is the opinion of Chief Justice Dickson in the *Operation Dismantle* case. Faced with the challenge by Operation Dismantle to the testing of the cruise missile in Canada, it was all well and good for the Court to maintain that its responsibility was to determine a "legal" question and not to pass judgment on the "wisdom" of cruise testing.[12] But here was the rub. The essence of the "legal" challenge was that the decision to test the cruise missile would lead to an increase in the arms race and thereby increase the chances of nuclear war. In other words, the plaintiffs were questioning the "wisdom" of the government's decision to test the cruise. They were asking a court to hear evidence on the probable effects of the testing programme and overturn the judgment of the government of Canada on the question. The so-called "legal" and "political" questions were simply different versions of the same

---

12 See the judgment of Madam Justice Wilson, quoted *supra*, note 5.

question: was it in the Canadian interest to allow the testing of the cruise missile in Canadian airspace?

The majority judgment of Chief Justice Dickson refused to dismiss the plaintiffs' claim on the broad basis that their challenge was "political" rather than "legal". To have relied on such a broad proposition would have undermined the Court's bold rhetoric about the fundamental character of the constitutional document and its status as a "living tree". Indeed, the Chief Justice was particularly careful to reassure his readers on that score: "I have no doubt that disputes of a political or foreign policy nature may be properly cognizable by the courts."[13] Instead, the Chief Justice invoked an argument that has a familiar "legal" ring to it in order to dismiss this plaintiffs' statement of claim. The claim must be struck out, according to Dickson C.J., on the narrow factual ground of "causation". The "causal link" between the actions of the government and the violation of the plaintiffs' rights was "simply too uncertain, speculative and hypothetical to sustain a cause of action."[14] It would be impossible to offer sufficient legal proof, as a "factual matter", of the connection between the government's decision and the increased threat of nuclear war.

Given the highly controversial nature of the contemporary claims and counterclaims regarding the nuclear arms race, there is some initial plausibility to this disposition of the case. But if we dissect the steps in the argument more closely, it becomes apparent that "causation" is a rather improbable basis for striking out Operation Dismantle's statement of claim. The central thrust of Chief Justice Dickson's argument is that the plaintiffs' claim is premised on assumptions and hypotheses about how independent and sovereign nations will react to the testing of the cruise. According to the Chief Justice, such reactions are purely a matter of speculation and cannot be "proven" one way or the other. For instance, one of the plaintiffs' allegations was that the testing of the cruise would result in an increased military presence in Canada, which would make Canada a more likely target of nuclear attack. But, as Chief Justice Dickson points out, this argument assumes certain reactions of hostile foreign powers to an increased military presence and also makes an assumption about the degree to which Canada is already a possible target of nuclear attack. "Given the impossibility of determining how an independent sovereign nation might react, it can only be a matter of hypothesis whether

---

13 *Operation Dismantle, supra,* note 5 at 459.
14 *Ibid.* at 447.

an increased American presence would make Canada more vulnerable to nuclear attack. It would not be possible to prove it one way or the other."[15]

Underlying the argument is an assumption about the nature of the distinction between facts and values, and the relationship between this distinction and legal argument. The distinction between facts and values is portrayed in terms that are fixed and absolute. Facts exist "out there", independent of human intervention or desire. They can be ascertained and proven through an objectively correct and neutral methodology. Conversely, anything which is not a "fact" is a mere opinion or conjecture. The world can be categorized and comprehended on the basis of a dichotomy between reason and desire: either something is objectively "true" and discernible by reason or else it is hopelessly subjective and governed by speculation and appetite. It is pointless to seek to demonstrate the truth or falsity of subjective opinions. Thus, the opponents of the cruise testing are "entitled to their opinion and belief", but such opinions lie "in the realm of conjecture, rather than fact".[16]

This fact/value dichotomy serves as a toehold securing the legitimacy of judicial review under the *Charter*. On this view, judicial review under the *Charter* can be distinguished from political argument through an appeal to the objective quality of the proof demanded in legal argument. Judicial review is concerned with objective facts rather than subjective opinions. Courts adjudicate claims which are capable of proof in an objective manner, whereas the political branches of government make mere subjective value choices.

An obvious, if disquieting, example of this is the very action under review, the government's decision to permit the testing of the cruise missile. Since it is impossible to prove whether the cruise programme will lead to an increased risk of nuclear war, it is appropriate that such a decision be taken by the political and not the legal authorities. In effect, the dichotomy between facts and values itself fortifies the barrier between law and politics. Law is both constituted and legitimated by the objectivity of the factual. Politics is passion and subjectivity, the irrational working out of conflicting desire and opinion.

These premises seem wrong on both counts; the distinction between facts and values is not absolute, while legal proof and argument

---

15 *Ibid.* at 453.
16 *Ibid.* at 454.

extend beyond the realm of the factual. As to the first issue, it is a gross oversimplification to suppose that human knowledge comes in only two packages, the one labelled "objective", the other, "subjective". To put this another way, the mere fact that an issue cannot be resolved in some neutral or mechanical fashion does not mean that it must be relegated to the category of mere whim or caprice. It is possible to acknowledge the contingent and value-laden character of an enterprise and yet make rational and meaningful arguments about that enterprise. In fact, an important tradition in contemporary philosophy is premised on the belief that *all* branches of knowledge, including the so-called neutral disciplines of the natural sciences, are shot through with subjective and contingent elements.[17] This contingency does not entail the conclusion that there is nothing meaningful to be said about these subjects, or that one opinion is necessarily as persuasive as any other.

Just as it is misleading to posit an absolute dichotomy between facts and values, so too it is false to claim that legal proof is concerned exclusively with facts. In a sense, this is the point made by Madam Justice Wilson in her rebuttal to the argument of the Chief Justice on the causation issue. Madam Justice Wilson claims that legal argument may properly be heard on issues of "intangible fact". Intangible facts are "inferences from real facts" and may also be the subject of opinion. Wilson J. illustrates her argument through references to the case of *McGhee v. National Coal Board*.[18] The issue in this case, whether the lack of shower facilities caused the plaintiff's skin disease, was a matter of medical opinion, but it was also "in law a determination which the courts can properly infer from the surrounding facts and expert opinion evidence."[19] According to Madam Justice Wilson, the claim of the plaintiffs, Operation Dismantle, was also premised on such intangible facts. Although she entertained doubts whether the plaintiffs could prove their case at trial, she argued that it was not the function of the Court on a preliminary motion to prejudge the issue.

Of course, there is a possible point of distinction between the *McGhee* case and *Operation Dismantle*. Although *McGhee* involved the court drawing inferences based on mere medical opinion, these

---

17 See R. Rorty, *Philosophy and the Mirror of Nature* (1979); T. Kuhn, *The Structure of Scientific Revolutions* (1970).

18 [1972] 3 All E.R. 1008 (H.L.).

19 *Operation Dismantle, supra,* note 5 at 478.

inferences related to events which had already taken place. The plaintiffs had already suffered harm and the only question was whether this harm had been legally "caused" by the defendants. In *Operation Dismantle*, on the other hand, the Court is faced with a situation where the harm has not yet occurred and is by no means certain to occur. In fact, in order to sustain the plaintiffs' claim, the Court would have had to have made a prediction about the reactions of independent and sovereign nations to the foreign policy decisions of the Canadian government.

It is not clear why this point of distinction between the cases should be taken to be conclusive. The issue at this stage of the litigation was simply whether the plaintiffs' claim should be permitted to proceed to trial. Accordingly, the question to be decided was whether courts should be barred from hearing evidence and drawing inferences regarding the reactions of "independent and sovereign nations". Moreover, it should not be sufficient to establish that, in this particular case, the plaintiffs were going to have an extremely difficult time proving their factual allegations. This was simply a corollary of the general rule that, on a motion to strike, the facts pleaded in the statement of claim must be deemed to have been proven.[20]

It need hardly be emphasized that there is no *general* bar to courts hearing evidence and making assumptions about the future reactions of independent and sovereign actors, whether they be individuals or groups. Consider our most basic assumptions about the behaviour of markets. Whenever we predict how a market will respond to fluctuations in price, supply or other variables, we are making a prediction about the reactions of "sovereign and independent actors" — in this case, the consumers in a market. Bearing this in mind, recall the judgment of the Supreme Court of Canada in the *Reference Re Anti-Inflation Act*.[21] In this case, the Supreme Court admitted and relied upon a large body of "extrinsic evidence" in order to determine the constitutional validity of the federal government's anti-inflation programme.[22] This material dealt with the state of the Canadian economy in 1975 and the likely success of the anti-inflation programme in

---

20 See *A.G. Can. v. Inuit Tapirisat of Can.*, [1980] 2 S.C.R. 735 at 740, per Estey J. (S.C.C.).

21 *Ref. re Anti-Inflation Act*, [1976] 2 S.C.R. 373 (S.C.C.).

22 These extrinsic materials included a study by economist Richard Lipsey dealing with the state of the Canadian economy in 1975 and the various policy options in dealing with inflation; a transcript of a speech by the Governor of the Bank of Canada, Gerald Bouey, rebutting the Lipsey study; and a "Comment" by the Ontario Office of Economic Policy on the 1975 economic environment designed to show the need for national action.

bringing inflation under control. In short, the evidence tried to establish how millions of individuals, corporations and other economic actors would react to the government's restraint programme. The Court examined the material, at least for the limited purpose of determining whether there was a "rational basis" for the government's decision to enact the legislation.[23]

It is difficult to understand how an *a priori* distinction can be drawn between the extrinsic material considered in the *Anti-Inflation Reference* and the evidence which Operation Dismantle wished to place before the Court. For example, one of the claims of Operation Dismantle was that the testing would lead to an increased American military presence in Canada, which would make Canada a more likely target of nuclear attack. The objection of the Chief Justice was that this argument made assumptions about the degree to which Canada is already a possible target of nuclear attack, and assumed certain reactions of hostile foreign powers to an increased military presence. According to Chief Justice Dickson, these difficulties meant that it "would not be possible to prove . . . one way or the other" whether an increased American presence would make Canada more vulnerable to nuclear attack.[24]

The obvious response to the argument is that these difficulties might well be overcome through the hearing of evidence and expert testimony. The Court could have heard evidence on the extent to which Canada is already a target of nuclear attack as well as the probable effect of an increased American presence. As in the *Anti-Inflation Reference*, the evidence might be admitted merely to establish whether there was a "rational basis" for the government's decision in this particular case. Thus, the "causation" argument provides an inadequate justification for the Court's holding in the case. This is not to suggest that the Court's holding could not be justified; the point is simply that the justification would have to be framed in terms of some larger considerations of public policy rather than the narrow grounds of causation.

The majority opinion in the *Operation Dismantle* case illustrates the conflicting tendencies at work in the Court's early *Charter* cases. On the one hand, the Court is clearly motivated by a desire to escape the infamy associated with its *Bill of Rights* jurisprudence and to give a "large and liberal" interpretation to the various *Charter* guarantees.

---

23 *Anti-Inflation Reference, supra,* note 21 at 391.
24 *Operation Dismantle, supra,* note 5 at 453.

But the overwhelming concern of the Court is to ensure that this "civil libertarian" stance does not result in the collapse of the distinction between law and politics.

The opinion of the Chief Justice in *Operation Dismantle* highlights the tension between these conflicting tendencies and the failure of the Court in reconciling them. The *Operation Dismantle* litigation was particularly exemplary since it placed the political character of *Charter* litigation in stark relief. The litigation was "political" not simply in the sense that the testing of the cruise missile was a highly controversial issue in the political arena. More important was the nature of the claim raised by the plaintiffs. The essence of their claim was that the government had been wrong to allow cruise testing in Canadian airspace. The plaintiffs wanted the Court to declare that the foreign policy of the government, far from advancing Canadian welfare, was actually increasing the risk of nuclear war. Confronted with the prospect of having to substitute its own opinion about the "wisdom" of cruise testing for that of the government, the Court took refuge in an unconvincing argument about causation. It also took the opportunity to reassert and defend the central distinction between the objectivity of legal reasoning and the subjectivity of political argument.

3. POLITICAL JUDGES AND S. 1: THE OAKES CASE

If this fundamental issue of legitimacy is kept in mind, certain distinctive tendencies and patterns begin to emerge in the other *Charter* cases decided by the Supreme Court. The most striking is the Court's treatment of s. 1. I argued earlier that s. 1 "balancing" of interests appeared to be just another way of asking the basic legislative question: is this worth what it costs? Given the overtly political character of such an analysis, we would expect to observe the Court experiencing particular difficulty in interpreting and applying this section.

The striking feature of the early Supreme Court *Charter* cases was the absence of any meaningful discussion of the principles to govern the application of s. 1. Until the judgment of the Court in *R. v. Oakes*, released in February of 1986, the Court had managed to sidestep the difficult question of how to balance interests under s. 1 without also questioning the wisdom of legislative enactments.

In a number of the early cases, the avoidance of s. 1 analysis appeared somewhat strained and contrived. In the *Quebec Schools* case,[25]

---

25 *Que. Assn. of Protestant School Bds. v. A.G. Que.; Wong-Woo v. A.G. Que.; Orman v. A.G. Que.; Mak v. A.G. Que.; Toma v. A.G. Que.* (1984), 10 D.L.R. (4th) 321 (S.C.C.).

for example, the Quebec government had argued that its restrictions on access to English schooling were reasonable within the meaning of s. 1, in view of factors such as demographic patterns, the physical and linguistic mobility of individuals and the regional distribution of interprovincial migrants. In essence, the government of Quebec was asking the Court to pass judgment on the "wisdom" of its policy with respect to English schooling. The Court refused to enter into such an inquiry, but on the basis of a rather curious argument. The Court held that s. 1 did not have to be considered since "[t]he provisions of s. 73 of Bill 101 collide directly with those of s. 23 of the Charter, and are not limits which can be legitimized by s. 1 of the Charter."[26] The Court's argument appeared to rely on the alleged distinction between "limiting" and "denying" a right: where there is "direct conflict" between a *Charter* right and government legislation, the legislation can be ruled invalid on a categorical basis, without even considering s. 1.

The argument is only convincing if the distinction between "limiting" and "denying" a right is meaningful. The difficulty with the distinction is that it does not appear to offer a determinate basis for deciding cases. A particular state restriction on rights can be made to appear as either a "limit" or a "denial", depending on the level of generality at which the right in question is defined. Suppose a municipality passed a by-law prohibiting all demonstrations or marches in the city for a period of 30 days.[27] There are equally plausible arguments suggesting that this could be either a "limit" or a "denial" of the right to freedom of association. If the 30-day period of the by-law is taken as the operative time frame, then the residents of the city could be said to have suffered a complete denial of their right to associate during that period. On the other hand, if the right of association is defined in more general and abstract terms, it could plausibly be argued that this "general right" had not been completely denied, but only limited for the modest period of 30 days. There is nothing in the concepts of "limit" or "denial" which instructs the jurist as to which of these two alternative arguments is to be preferred. In effect, the terms "limit" and "denial" are not themselves grounds for decision, but mere conclusory labels attached *post hoc* to an analysis determined on other, independent grounds.

Such techniques of confession and avoidance were abandoned in the Court's recent judgment in *R. v. Oakes*. In *Oakes*, Chief Justice

---

26 *Ibid.* at 338.
27 See *A.G. Can. v. Montreal*, [1978] 2 S.C.R. 770 (S.C.C.).

Dickson suggested a general approach for the application of s. 1, as well as a particular framework of analysis to structure its application to particular cases. The opinion of the Chief Justice enjoyed the support of four other members of the Court and thus, for the time being at least, represents the considered opinion of the majority of our highest Court on these issues.

The analysis of the Chief Justice appears to constitute a compelling rebuttal to claims that courts are inevitably inquiring into the "wisdom" of legislation in applying s. 1. Dickson C.J. devises a framework which is designed to put constitutional and "legal" flesh on the political skeleton of s. 1. Armed with the "objective and manageable" standards enunciated by the Chief Justice, lower courts may now robustly measure legislation against the dictates of those neutral standards.

This attempt by the Supreme Court to come to terms with the open-ended quality of s. 1 is a welcome development. But, although the analysis purports to offer neutral and objective standards to guide the application of s. 1, this alleged objectivity is illusory. The framework of the Chief Justice necessarily requires the judiciary to question the "wisdom" of legislation, albeit in a disguised fashion. Thus, far from resolving the "lingering doubts" about the legitimacy of the judicial role under the *Charter*, the opinion unintentionally lends credence to such claims.

David Edwin Oakes was charged with unlawful possession of a narcotic for the purpose of trafficking, contrary to s. 4(2) of the *Narcotic Control Act*.[28] At his trial, the crown established that Mr. Oakes had been in possession of eight 1-gm. vials of *cannabis* resin in the form of hashish oil. The crown then sought to rely on the "reverse onus" provision in s. 8 of the Act, in order to establish the offence of trafficking.[29] The trial judge found that there was no rational or necessary connection between the fact proved — possession of the drug — and the inference asked to be drawn — possession for the

---

28 *Narcotic Control Act*, R.S.C. 1970, c. N-1, s. 4(2). This section draws heavily from: P. Monahan and A. Petter, "Developments in Constitutional Law: The 1985-1986 Term" (1987), 9 Sup. Ct. L. Rev. (forthcoming 1987).

29 Section 8 provides that:

In any prosecution for a violation of subsection 4(2), if the accused does not plead guilty, the trial shall proceed as if it were a prosecution for an offence under section 3, and after the close of the case for the prosecution and after the accused has had an opportunity to make full answer and defence, the court shall make a finding as to whether or not the accused was in possession of the narcotic contrary to section 3; if the court finds that the accused was not in possession of the narcotic contrary to section 3,

purpose of trafficking. He found that s. 8 of the Act violated the right of the accused to be presumed innocent, guaranteed by s. 11(*d*) of the *Canadian Charter of Rights and Freedoms*. Section 8 was accordingly rendered inoperative and, in the absence of any further crown evidence tending to establish an intention to traffick, the accused was acquitted.[30]

This disposition of the case was unanimously upheld by the Ontario Court of Appeal. Mr. Justice Martin, speaking for the Court, concluded that s. 8 of the *Narcotic Control Act* was unconstitutional "because of the lack of a rational connection between the proved fact (possession) and the presumed fact (an intention to traffic)."[31]

The further appeal by the crown to the Supreme Court of Canada was dismissed unanimously, although two separate opinions were issued. Chief Justice Dickson, writing for himself and four others, began by finding that s. 8 of the Act imposed a legal burden on an accused to prove on a balance of probabilities that he or she was not in possession of a narcotic for the purpose of trafficking. The Chief Justice concluded that he "had no doubt whatsoever" that s. 8 violated the presumption of innocence in s. 11(*d*) of the *Charter*. This conclusion followed from the fact that the accused was required to establish his innocence on a balance of probabilities; accordingly, it would be possible to convict an accused who had succeeded in raising a reasonable doubt as to his innocence but had failed to satisfy the balance of probabilities standard. Turning to s. 1, the Chief Justice observed that any s. 1 inquiry "must be premised on an understanding that the impugned limit violates constitutional rights and freedoms — rights and freedoms which are part of the supreme law of Canada".[32] Further, Dickson C.J. held that it is clear "from the text of s. 1" that limits on rights are "exceptions to their general guarantee".[33] The purpose of s. 1 is to allow limits on rights when "their exercise would be inimical to the realization

---

he shall be acquitted but if the court finds that the accused was in possession of the narcotic contrary to section 3, he shall be given an opportunity of establishing that he was not in possession of the narcotic for the purpose of trafficking, and thereafter the prosecutor shall be given the opportunity of adducing evidence to establish that the accused was in possession of the narcotic for the purpose of trafficking; if the accused establishes that he was not in possession of the narcotic for the purpose of trafficking, he shall be acquitted of the offence as charged but he shall be convicted of an offence under section 3 and sentenced accordingly; and if the accused fails to establish that he was not in possession of the narcotic for the purpose of trafficking, he shall be convicted of the offence as charged and sentenced accordingly.

30 See *R. v. Oakes* (1982), 38 O.R. (2d) 598 (Ont. Prov. Ct.).

31 *R. v. Oakes* (1983), 145 D.L.R. (3d) 123 at 147 (Ont. C.A.).

32 *R. v. Oakes*, [1986] 1 S.C.R. 103 at 135 (S.C.C.).

33 *Ibid.* at 137.

of collective goals of fundamental importance".[34] Accordingly, although the standard of proof under s. 1 is the civil standard of proof by a preponderance of probability, this standard must be applied "rigorously" and "a very high degree of probability will be . . . 'commensurate with the occasion'".[35]

The Chief Justice set out two central criteria which must be satisfied by the state before a legal limit on rights can be justified. First, the objective or goal of the law must "at a minimum, . . . relate to concerns which are pressing and substantial in a free and democratic society . . .".[36] Second, the means chosen must be proportionate to the goal. There are three components of a test of proportionality. The means must be "rationally connected to the objective"; the means must impair individual rights as little as possible; and there must be a proportionality between the "effects" of the means and the objective which has been identified as of "sufficient importance".[37]

Applying this framework to s. 8 of the *Narcotic Control Act*, the Chief Justice was of the view that Parliament's concern with decreasing drug trafficking could be characterized as "substantial and pressing". Thus, the reverse onus provision satisfied the first branch of the s. 1 inquiry. But the provision failed the proportionality test, on the grounds that there was no "rational connection" between the basic fact of possession and the presumed fact of possession for the purpose of trafficking. This meant that the presumption required under s. 8 was "overinclusive" and could produce results "in certain cases which would defy both rationality and fairness".[38] The provision could not be justified under s. 1 and was of no force and effect.

The opinion of the Chief Justice suggests that the s. 1 analysis is determinate and objective. The Court need not be concerned with the wisdom of legislative policy, but only with the separate question of whether it satisfies the two-pronged "test" under s. 1. There are a number of features of the analysis which contribute to this sense of objectivity and neutrality. First, the inquiry is framed in terms of the traditional and familiar standard of proof in civil cases, proof on a preponderance of probability. This characterization evokes the imagery of a court deciding a garden-variety dispute between private parties. The court will hear evidence on the s. 1 issue and then

---

34 *Ibid.* at 136.
35 *Ibid.* at 137-138.
36 *Ibid.* at 138-139.
37 *Ibid.* at 139.
38 *Ibid.* at 142.

determine, as it would in any private litigation, whether the civil standard of proof has been satisfied. Of course, the evidence and arguments in a *Charter* case will often be complex and require the court to exercise considerable discretion. But this is not significantly different from the task of a court in complex civil litigation. Since the court's competence in these complex civil cases is generally accepted, there should be no serious qualms about the judiciary embarking on the task of *Charter* adjudication.

There is a second feature of the judgment which is even more crucial in terms of bolstering the legitimacy of the court's role. This is the manner in which the Chief Justice actually applies the s. 1 analysis. The Chief Justice accepts the validity of the state's goal in enacting s. 8 of the *Narcotic Control Act*. He strikes down the provision on the basis that Parliament has pursued its policy in an "irrational" way. The constitutional objection is not to the state's policy as such but to the manner in which it has attempted to carry out that policy. The Court's ruling appears wholly instrumentalist, designed to measure the "fit" between the state goal and the means chosen to achieve that goal. Assuming a decidedly deferential posture, the Court is saying to Parliament: *given* that you have decided to pursue this goal, you have done so in a way that is arbitrary or irrational.

This type of analysis appears to resolve any possible tension between judicial review and democratic values. Under a rationality standard, judges are not purporting to substitute their values for those of legislators. The Court is simply ensuring that legislation accurately reflects the chosen values of the legislators themselves. This could be regarded as the perfection of democracy rather than its negation. Judicial review is promoting precision and care in the drafting of legislation and eliminating needless and arbitrary restrictions of individual liberty. There is nothing "undemocratic" about requiring the legislature to pursue its goals in a precise and careful fashion.

A similar set of assumptions underlies the "least restrictive means" analysis, the second branch of the proportionality test outlined by the Chief Justice. As with the "rationality" standard, "the least restrictive means" test does not purport to dictate to the state which value choices it must pursue or avoid. Rather, it is a limited attempt to identify inefficient legislation. The "least restrictive means" analysis says to the legislature: *given* that you have decided to pursue this goal, you have done so inefficiently. There are other legislative devices available which would allow you to pursue the same goal, but in a manner which would be less restrictive of individual liberty. It seems self-evident that the state should never restrict individual liberty needlessly. Given a choice, the state must select the device that is least intrusive in terms of the fundamental values guaranteed by the *Charter*.

It is hardly a coincidence that the trial court and both appellate courts in *Oakes* resolved the constitutional issue on the basis of the "rationality" standard. Indeed, it is rather safe to predict that whenever courts in the future decide to invalidate legislation, they will focus on the "irrationality" of the law or stress the availability of "less restrictive means". This is because these techniques allow the court to overturn legislation without appearing to be a "super-legislature". The crucial question is whether these techniques actually enable the court to avoid having to assess the wisdom of legislative policy, or whether they simply invite the court to make such a "political" judgment in a more covert fashion.

In my view, courts under the *Charter* can never escape the task of evaluating the policies chosen by the legislature. The "rationality standard", although apparently neutral, requires just such a "political" evaluation on the part of judges. The only real function of the rational basis test is to make the judicial balancing of interests less apparent and therefore more legitimate.

The political character of the rationality standard becomes apparent from a consideration of those instances in which it has been applied in the American context. Consider the following example, developed by Professor Ely from the facts of *Smith v. Cahoon*.[39] Professor Ely asks his readers to suppose that a new and unusually effective truck brake were developed.[40] The legislature would undoubtedly be given a wide degree of latitude in deciding whether to require installation of the new brake. Given the cost of the new brake, it might be open to the legislature to require some, but not all, truck owners to install it. For example, a law which required installation of the brake on all trucks whose weight exceeded five tons might well be valid. The burden on the legislature would be to demonstrate that the distinction drawn by the law was rationally relatable to the goal of promoting traffic safety. It could discharge this burden in a variety of ways; for instance, if it could be shown that the heavier a truck is, the harder it is to stop, then requiring the brakes on heavy

---

39 283 U.S. 553 (1931). In this case, the court struck down an exemption for carriers of farm products and certain seafoods from a Florida law requiring commercial carriers to post security against liability for injuries caused by their negligence.

40 J.H. Ely, "Legislative and Administrative Motivation in Constitutional Law", 79 Yale L.J. 1205, 1237-39 (1979).

trucks promotes safety to a greater extent than requiring them on light trucks.

But not all distinctions could be shown to be rationally relatable to the goal of traffic safety. Professor Ely offers the example of a law which requires the brake to be installed on all trucks, except those carrying seafood.[41] According to Ely, this is an "irrational" law. From the point of view of safety, the distinction between trucks carrying seafood and those carrying other goods is irrelevant; trucks carrying seafood are just as likely to benefit from the installation of the new brake as are any others. Similarly, there is no indication that the installation of the brake on trucks carrying seafood is exceptionally expensive or difficult. Thus, the distinction is not rationally relatable to the goals of either traffic safety or driver economy.

Yet the characterization of the law as "irrational" is surely misplaced. It is true that a distinction based on whether a truck happens to be carrying seafood does not further the goals of traffic safety or driver economy. But there is nothing mysterious about the inclusion of such a distinction in a statute. The purpose of the distinction is obviously to give a preference to the owners of trucks in the seafood business. The exemption will save these truckers the costs of installing the new brake and, presumably, grant them an advantage over their competitors. It is apparent that the law had two purposes, rather than one. The first purpose was to increase traffic safety by requiring most trucks to install new brakes. The second purpose was to ensure that these gains in traffic safety did not come at the expense of increasing the costs of truckers transporting seafood.

Perhaps it might be argued that there is something inherently "irrational" about conferring special benefits or exemptions on one industry as opposed to another. But this argument would be mistaken. It is an uncontroversial feature of our tax laws, for example, that certain industries or individuals may be granted more favourable tax treatment than others. The state might decide to grant special tax exemptions to the oil industry, but not to artists. Thus, in the context of our trucking example, there is very little doubt that the legislature could have granted a special tax concession to truckers transporting seafood but have denied the concession to others. It would be absurd to claim that such a law was "irrational", in the sense that it failed to further its goal. A tax exemption for trucks carrying seafood fits

---

41 This was the distinction employed in *Smith v. Cahoon, supra,* note 39.

perfectly its goal, which is to confer a competitive advantage on such truckers.

Thus, the hypothetical law exempting trucks carrying seafood from installing new brakes is not irrational. The law advances the goal of promoting safety, but not at the expense of truckers carrying seafood. The claim of irrationality is really little more than a judgment that one of these purposes — the goal of preferring seafood truckers — is unacceptable. The court simply ignores the impugned purpose, and then concludes that the legislation does not further the goals which remain.[42]

This analysis is not exceptional or aberrant. Laws are never passed without reasons. Those reasons may be complex and involve a trade-off between a number of competing goals, but reasons always exist. The issue is never whether a law is "rational" or not but, rather, whether it has been passed for good reasons or for bad reasons. Accordingly, the conclusion that the law is "irrational" is not achieved by measuring the fit between a law and its real purposes; it is a product of evaluating the fit between the law and some contrived and restrictive set of judicial purposes.[43]

The generality of this critique can be illustrated through a consideration of recent American Supreme Court cases purporting to apply the rational connection test. Many of the recent cases involve gender classifications in legislation. A typical example is *Weinberger v. Wiesenfeld*,[44] in which the court struck down a provision of the *Social Security Act* which authorized payments to the wife, but not to the husband, of a deceased wage earner with minor children. The payment of benefits was contingent upon responsibility for minor children; according to the court, it was designed to allow the surviving spouse to elect not to work and devote themselves full time to the care of the children. But, according to the court, the classification in the law could not be justified on the basis of such a goal. If the point was to ensure full-time parental care for minor children, distinctions between men and women are irrelevant. The only effect of the classification was to denigrate the efforts of women who work outside the home and to produce less protection for their families than is

---

42 This was essentially the technique employed in *Smith v. Cahoon*, in which the court considered only the goal of traffic safety, and ignored other possible purposes of the law. See *supra*, note 39.

43 For the elaboration and application of this critique to a wide number of contexts, see Note, "Legislative Purpose, Rationality, and Equal Protection", 82 Yale L.J. 123 (1972).

44 *Weinberger v. Weisenfeld*, 420 U.S. 636 (1975).

produced by the efforts of men. As such, the distinction between widows and widowers was "entirely irrational."[45]

Yet the trouble with this law is not so much that it is irrational as that it is premised on a traditional conception of the nature of the family, one which the court happens to dislike. This traditional conception places particular value on women remaining at home on a full-time basis and caring for minor children. Thus, the classification in the law, which paid benefits to widows with minor children but not to other widows or to any widowers, was perfectly tailored to fit this goal. The court's decision to strike down the law was essentially a rejection of such traditional, conservative values regarding family life. The other recent cases dealing with gender classifications can be analyzed in essentially identical terms.[46]

So the "rationality" standard is not simply a neutral process of measuring the fit between the goals of legislation and the means chosen to achieve those goals. Instead, it requires judges to make an evaluation of the adequacy of the goals themselves. In short, the judgment of Chief Justice Dickson in the *Oakes* case, while purporting to downplay the political character of the s. 1 inquiry, merely confirms the necessity of political judgments in *Charter* adjudication.[47]

4. CONCLUSION

So the main story that can be told about the early *Charter* cases in the Supreme Court is rather simple and straightforward. It has been particularly important to the Court to give at least the appearance of breaking with the discredited tradition of the *Bill of Rights* cases. But the Court wants to accomplish this first objective without calling into question the basic legitimacy of the judicial role, in particular, the distinction between legal and political reasoning. The sticking point is that the Court has not yet hit on a method for accomplishing both of these goals simultaneously. Indeed, a careful analysis of the early *Charter* opinions of the Court illustrates the inherently "political" character of the Court's reasoning. I chose to make this point by

---

45 *Ibid.* at 651.

46 See, e.g., *Orr v. Orr*, 440 U.S. 268 (1979). For an insightful analysis of the rationality standard as applied in these cases, see Baker, "Neutrality, Process, and Rationality: Flawed Interpretations of Equal Protection", 58 Tex. L. Rev. 1029 at 1084–1094 (1980).

47 Due to space limitations, I have not considered Dickson C.J.'s particular analysis of s. 8 of the *Narcotic Control Act*. For a discussion of this part of the Chief Justice's opinion, see Monahan and Petter, "Developments in Constitutional Law: The 1985–86 Term" (1987), 9 Sup. Ct. L. Rev. (forthcoming 1987).

focusing on the Court's opinions in *Operation Dismantle* and *Oakes*, but a similar critique could have been offered of any of the other *Charter* judgments of the Court. The value-laden character of the Court's analysis illustrates the hollowness of the claim that the legitimacy of judicial review is a non-issue in the Canadian context. If judicial review under the *Charter* is to be justified, it cannot be on the spurious basis that the adjudicative process is neutral or objective. Any convincing justification must take into account the value-laden nature of judicial review and attempt to reconcile this political role for judges with traditional democratic values.

5

The Use and Abuse of American Constitutional Theory in Charter Analysis

It seems appropriate to review the argument developed in Chapter 4. The starting point was the assumption that reasoning and argument under the *Charter* do not appear to have a peculiarly "legal" quality. The open-ended language of the *Charter*, along with the requirement that judges "balance" individual rights against the interests of the community, seem to invite judgments that are essentially legislative. This raises a fundamental question of legitimacy. By what warrant do unelected judges substitute their views on the wisdom of public policy for that of the legislature? Moreover, how can this law-making activity by judges be reconciled with the traditional claim that law involves a distinctive and technical mode of argument not encountered in the political arena? The early Supreme Court cases under the *Charter* have only dimly perceived the nature of the problem, much less resolved it in any satisfactory manner.

Of course, these issues are not unique to judicial review under the *Charter*. The same fundamental problem of legitimacy has long been a central preoccupation of American legal theory. Given the many similarities between American and Canadian legal culture, it is tempting to assume that this American literature will provide answers to the difficult issues under the *Charter*. In this chapter, I want to explore this possibility by considering the two primary justifications that American theorists have devised to legitimize judicial review. I will suggest that Canadian jurists can certainly profit by becoming familiar with these American approaches. But in my view, American writing on judicial review does not really provide adequate answers to the difficult interpretive issues which arise under the *Charter*. The *Charter* is a uniquely Canadian document. The key to unlocking its secrets does not lie in an alien culture, but in the Canadian political tradition itself.

1. ORIGINALISM AND JUDICIAL REVIEW

A theory which has enjoyed substantial popularity and influence amongst American commentators seeks to resolve textual indeterminacy through an appeal to the original intentions of the framers. According to this theory, the courts should give meaning to the open-ended clauses of the constitution by interpreting them in accordance with the views of the individuals who drafted them.[1] By observing this canon of construction, judges can avoid the charge that they are usurping legislative power. Far from imposing their own values, the courts are merely giving effect to the enduring, fundamental values of the polity as embodied in the constitutional text. To the extent that those fundamental values now appear outdated or simply wrong-headed, the appropriate remedy is a formal constitutional amendment rather than creative judicial interpretation.

It is important to appreciate the distinctiveness of the originalist argument. Originalism does not merely claim that the intentions of the framers deserve to be considered or even to be accorded presumptive weight in the interpretive process. The identifying feature of the originalist argument is the claim that the intentions of the framers should be *conclusive* in resolving textual ambiguity. If it is possible to ascertain how the framers would have applied a particular constitutional provision, then that interpretation must govern, regardless of any arguments or considerations to the contrary.

A virtual cottage industry has sprung up in the past decade aimed at discrediting the claims of originalism.[2] The criticisms fall into two

---

1 See R. Berger. *Government by Judiciary.* (1977); R. Bork, "Neutral Principles and Some First Amendment Problems", [1971] Indiana L.J.; Monaghan, "Our Perfect Constitution", 56 N.Y.U.L. Rev. 353.

2 It would be impossible to refer to even a small portion of this literature here. Perhaps

camps. The first group of critics raise essentially pragmatic objections to the originalist argument. These pragmatic objections are designed to demonstrate the inherent impossibility of ascertaining the collective intention of a group of men who have been dead for nearly 200 years. The critics focus on the illusory nature of "group intent", point out that the framers' intention on many questions was indeterminate, and argue that it is impossible for any contemporary observer to truly understand the "intent" of individuals who lived in eighteenth century America. This last argument is premised on the assumption that the world-view of the framers is so fundamentally foreign to our own that it would be mistaken and presumptuous to suppose that we could ever really appreciate their "intent".

What force do these pragmatic objections hold in the context of the Canadian *Charter*? In general, the objections seem much less persuasive. This does not mean that it is ever going to be a straightforward or mechanical matter to determine the views of the drafters with respect to substantive provisions of the *Charter*. The first and most obvious difficulty will be who is to count as "the drafters". According to the Supreme Court's judgment in the *Patriation Appeals*, constitutional convention at the time of the enactment of the *Charter* required that the "substantial consent" of the provinces be obtained before the joint resolution could be forwarded to Great Britain. This suggests that it would be necessary to canvass the views of provincial, as well as federal, officials in determining the drafters' intentions. Yet we have virtually no record of provincial views on the meaning or application of specific substantive provisions of the *Charter*.

A second problem is that very few members of the federal Senate and House of Commons appear to have formed any independent views as to the meaning of the various *Charter* provisions. Instead, they simply relied on officials in the Department of Justice to provide them with "expert opinion" about the meaning of *Charter* phraseology. The deference of elected representatives towards departmental officials was made crystal clear in the committee hearings on the proposed resolution.[3] Thus, the relevant intention appears to be that of officials in the federal Department of Justice, rather than that of elected representatives in either the provinces or Parliament.

---

the most compelling case against originalism is to be found in P. Brest, "The Misconceived Quest for the Original Understanding" (1980), 60 B.U.L.R. 204; see also R. Dworkin, "The Forum of Principle", in *A Matter of Principle* (1985).

3 See Canada, 32 Parl., Sess. 1, Special Joint Committee on the Constitution of Canada, *Proceedings* (1980-81).

The irony is that, in purely pragmatic terms, the domination of the process by unelected federal officials may be more a virtue than a vice. There is no surer way to foreclose problems of indeterminacy in constitutional provisions than through appeal to a bureaucratic hierarchy. The dominant role played by the federal bureaucracy makes the instrumental task of determining "drafters' intent" much easier than if one had to consult the conflicting and often self-serving opinions of a group of elected parliamentarians. Rather than being confronted with a cacophony of conflicting opinion, one is presented with a single, distilled interpretation of the meaning of various *Charter* provisions. To consider but one example, there can be little doubt as to the views of officials in the Department of Justice on the issue of whether s. 7 of the *Charter* was to receive a procedural, as opposed to a substantive, interpretation. In testimony before the Special Joint Committee on the Constitution, the Department made it clear that they regarded s. 7 of the *Charter* as providing purely procedural as opposed to substantive protection for "life, liberty and security of the person".[4] The Department hoped to avoid the line of American cases based on "substantive due process" and chose the words "fundamental justice" rather than "due process" in an attempt to achieve this result. In sum, if the views of the "drafters" are dispositive, there can be little doubt as to how the ambiguity in s. 7 ought to be resolved.

While the existence of this "expert opinion" may be helpful in overcoming purely pragmatic difficulties in determining the drafters' intentions, it resolves none of the principled, normative objections to originalism. The mere fact that we might be capable of ascertaining the intent of the drafters does not mean that their intention should necessarily govern. Constitutional theories based on original intent must be normative as well as descriptive; the theory must provide a reason why the views of the drafters ought to count in the interpretive process.[5]

---

4 See the comments of B.L. Strayer, then Assistant Deputy Minister, Public Law, Department of Justice, speaking before the Special Joint Committee of the Senate and House of Commons on January 27, 1981:

> Mr. Chairman, it was our belief that the words "fundamental justice" would cover the same thing as what is called procedural due process, that is the meaning of due process in relation to requiring fair procedure. However, it in our view does not cover the concept of what is called substantive due process, which would impose substantive requirements as to policy of the law in question.

Canada, 32 Parl., Sess. 1, Special Joint Committee on the Constitution of Canada, *Proceedings*, No. 46 at 32 (1980-81).

5 Dworkin, *supra*, note 2.

In a sense, it is rather easy to defend the claim that some minimal weight ought to attach to the views of the drafters of a constitution. The argument flows from the basic observation that the process of interpretation is necessarily contextual. Words do not speak for themselves. Language has meaning only within a particular context. To attempt to interpret language apart from the context in which it is used is a recipe for unresolvable indeterminacy. A central feature of linguistic context is the purposes and understandings of the individuals using the language. Thus, on this view, it is self-evident that some attention must be paid to the intentions of the drafters of the *Charter* if we are to make any sense at all of the document.

But this argument does not inform us of the extent to which the views of the drafters ought to figure in the interpretive process. The first issue is whether their views should be accorded conclusive weight in the interpretive process. The best way to resolve this issue is to analyze what might be termed the "interpretive intent" of the drafters of the *Charter*. American writers on judicial review have made an important distinction between two very different senses in which we might use the term "drafters' intent".[6] The drafters' "substantive intent" refers to their views as to the actual meaning of the various constitutional provisions they have enacted. The drafters' "interpretive intent" refers to their understanding of how those substantive provisions are to be interpreted and applied by the courts. The distinction is important because there is no necessary connection between substantive and interpretive intent. The drafters may hold very fixed substantive views as to the meaning of certain constitutional provisions, but may also regard their personal beliefs as irrelevant in terms of the legal interpretation of the provisions; their views on interpretation might be based, for example, on a "plain meaning rule", which would make judicial recourse to legislative history inappropriate.[7]

Defenders of originalism suppose that only the drafters' substantive intent is relevant. But this is obviously mistaken. If one were really serious about fidelity to the intention of the drafters, one would have to begin at least with their views as to the nature of the interpretive process. It would be ironic and bizarre to rely on the drafters' substantive views without first determining whether they

---

6 This distinction has been highlighted by American critics of originalism. See, in particular, the helpful article by Brest, *supra*, note 2 at 205-16.

7 See *ibid.* at 215-16. See also H. Powell, "The Original Understanding of Original Intent", 98 Harv. L. Rev. 885 (1985).

themselves regarded those substantive views as conclusive.

These distinctions are particularly relevant in the Canadian context, since we have a full legislative record outlining the "interpretive views" of the Canadian drafters. This legislative record makes it clear that the Canadian drafters did not envisage their substantive views on the meaning of various *Charter* provisions as being conclusive of constitutional meaning. Rather, their view of constitutional interpretation might be described as one of "modified judicial realism". This "modified realism" was a product of our drafters' analysis of the nature and development of constitutional interpretation in the United States. Notwithstanding the recent protests of legal academics, the American constitutional tradition has never been premised on the belief that the original intention of the drafters should be conclusive on issues of textual indeterminacy. The American courts may have considered the intentions of the framers on occasion, but they have certainly not hesitated to ignore those views when they found other values or interpretations more compelling. As Paul Brest has pointed out, a substantial portion of contemporary American constitutional doctrine has evolved in this way:[8]

> . . . [I]f you consider the evolution of doctrines in just about any extensively adjudicated area of constitutional law — whether 'under' the commerce, free speech, due process, or equal protection clauses — explicit reliance on originalist sources has played a very small role compared to the elaboration of the Court's own precedents. It is rather like having a remote ancestor who came over on the Mayflower.

The drafters of the *Charter* expected that the Canadian constitutional tradition would develop in a broadly similar fashion. Canada's judges were not expected to consult the substantive opinions of the drafters each time they were faced with ambiguous *Charter* language. It was thought that the courts would rely on a variety of "non-originalist" sources, including judge-made rules of statutory construction and previous judicial decisions on similar language. Reliance on these sources meant that judicial interpretations of *Charter* provisions might well diverge from the drafters' substantive intentions regarding those provisions. But the drafters regarded this judicial originality as an inherent feature of constitutional interpretation under the *Charter*. They had a relatively sophisticated and realistic view of the nature of the adjudication process. For them, constitutional adjudication was far from mechanical or formalistic. They were aware of the significant

---

8 Brest, *supra*, note 2 at 234.

degree of discretion available to courts interpreting constitutional texts. Because some degree of judicial originality was inevitable, the drafters saw their task as making educated guesses as to how the courts might interpret particular constitutional language, and choosing the language which was most likely to secure for them the results they desired.

The best way to illustrate this "modified judicial realism" is to consider the discussion surrounding a particular substantive *Charter* provision. The debate over the nature of s. 7 is particularly illuminating. In drafting s. 7 of the *Charter*, the Department had hoped to provide procedural but not substantive protection for "life, liberty and security of the person". Yet there was considerable confusion during the parliamentary hearings as to why the Department had inserted the words "principles of fundamental justice" rather than "procedural due process" in s. 7; to the lay members of the parliamentary committee, the words "due process" seemed to capture the Department's "intent" much more accurately than the novel and baffling "principles of fundamental justice".[9] The response of the Department is illuminating. Justice officials did not claim that the phrase "principles of fundamental justice" was a clearer or more accurate way to capture their intent. Indeed, when pressed on the matter, they had to admit that the words "principles of fundamental justice" were almost totally novel in Canadian jurisprudence.[10] Rather, they noted that the American courts had interpreted the phrase "due process" as guaranteeing substantive protection for property or privacy and they wanted to avoid the courts reading this interpretation into s. 7 of the *Charter*. Barry Strayer, then the Assistant Deputy Minister of Justice, explained the matter in these terms:[11]

> . . . these words [principles of fundamental justice] have not appeared in a constitution or in any type of statute before, but I am bound to add, Mr. Chairman, that there is a good deal of jurisprudence on the term "due process",

---

9 See, in particular, the exchange between the Honourable David Crombie and Barry Strayer, Assistant Deputy Minister of Justice, on this issue: *Proceedings, supra*, note 4 at 38-43.

10 The only instance in which the words had been used previously was in s. 2(e) of the *Canadian Bill of Rights*, R.S.C. 1970, App. III, in connection with the right to a fair hearing. This had been interpreted in *Duke v. R.*, [1972] S.C.R. 917 at 923 (S.C.C.) by Fauteux C.J. as follows:

> Without attempting to formulate any final definition of those words, I would take them to mean, generally, that the tribunal which adjudicates upon his rights must act fairly, in good faith, without bias and in a judicial temper, and must give to him an opportunity adequately to state his case.

11 *Proceedings, supra*, note 4 at 33.

both in Canada and the United States, and some of that jurisprudence in the United States gave rise to the problem that we were trying to avoid with the term "fundamental justice".

But the matter did not rest there. When the resolution reached the House of Commons, there was a good deal of concern expressed over the possibility that s. 7 would limit Parliament's ability to legislate with respect to abortion. Since "conflicting legal difficulties throw that matter into doubt",[12] the Honourable David Crombie proposed that the *Charter* be amended to include the words "nothing in this charter affects the authority of Parliament to legislate in respect of abortion."[13] In speaking against the proposed amendment, the Prime Minister noted that the government's view was that the *Charter* was "neutral" on the issue of abortion. He continued:[14]

> However, as I said yesterday to the member for Etobicoke-Lakeshore, should a judge conclude that on the contrary, the charter does, to a certain extent, affect certain provisions of the Criminal Code, under the override clause we reserve the right to say: Notwithstanding this decision, notwithstanding the charter of rights as interpreted by this judge, the House legislates in such and such a manner on the abortion issue.

It is important to retrace the steps in the government's argument closely. The government believed that the *Charter* was neutral on the abortion issue. But there were no guarantees that the courts would necessarily see it that way. After all, the American courts had taken the words "due process" and read into them a whole series of substantive protections for rights of property and privacy. Moreover, the American courts had done so without relying on the intentions of the framers; the "substantive due process" jurisprudence was a product of the court's *own* views as to the meaning of the Fifth and Fourteenth amendments. This is simply a reiteration of Paul Brest's basic point that "the practice of supplementing and derogating from the text and original understanding is itself part of our constitutional tradition."[15]

The drafters of the Canadian *Charter* recognized this reality and sought to take account of it in their choice of constitutional language.

---

12 Canada, House of Commons, *Commons Debates*, the Honourable David Crombie (27 November 1981).

13 *Ibid.*

14 Canada, House of Commons, *Commons Debates*, the Right Honourable Pierre E. Trudeau (Prime Minister) (27 November 1981).

15 Brest, *supra*, note 2 at 225.

Thus, while the words "procedural due process" might have been an accurate reflection of their intentions with respect to s. 7, they rejected them on account of the American substantive due process jurisprudence. There was no magic in the words "fundamental justice", even though there was an earlier court decision under the *Canadian Bill of Rights* which had suggested that they provided procedural protection only.[16] Thus, if the courts interpreted the words "fundamental justice" as importing substantive protection for rights, Parliament could always resort to the override provision in s. 33 of the *Charter*. In fact, the inclusion of the override provision is itself a recognition of the possibility of creative judicial interpretation under the *Charter*. Because the *Charter* would come to be interpreted and applied in ways that were unforeseen by its drafters, it was prudent to provide a mechanism which would enable Parliament to limit its scope.

This conception of constitutional adjudication is a continuation rather than a contrast with our previous constitutional tradition. Prior to 1982, constitutional interpretation had been concerned primarily with the terms of the *Constitution Act, 1867* (B.N.A. Act).[17] This document has been construed with little or no reference to the actual intentions of the "fathers" of confederation. Nor do the bare words of the statute constitute an accurate guide to its "meaning"; the "classes of subjects" in ss. 91 and 92 are so abstract that a whole range of alternative interpretations of their meaning is possible. Instead, constitutional "law" is composed almost exclusively of previous court decisions which have determined the content of various constitutional provisions. These judicial elaborations are the flesh on the constitutional skeleton.

For many years, academic lawyers complained that these judicial interpretations of the B.N.A. Act did not conform to the expectations of the drafters of the document. The drafters had contemplated a highly centralized federalism for Canada. In place of this quasi-unitary state, the Privy Council had substituted its own idiosyncratic and romantic brand of classical, decentralized federalism.[18] But in recent decades, it has come to be recognized that the supposed "mutilation" of the B.N.A. Act by the Privy Council actually was more in keeping with

---

16 See *Duke v. R.*, [1972] S.C.R. 917 (S.C.C.), interpreting the phrase "a fair hearing in accordance with the principles of fundamental justice" in s. 2(*e*) of the *Bill of Rights*.

17 *Constitution Act, 1867* (30 & 31 Vict.), c. 3.

18 See, e.g., V.C. MacDonald, "Judicial Interpretations of the Canadian Constitution" (1935-36), 1 U.T.L.J. 1.

the underlying Canadian political reality.[19] According to the contemporary view, the country has always been too large and diverse to tolerate the degree of centralism envisaged by the fathers of confederation. The "provincialist" bias of the Privy Council is to be commended rather than condemned; it helped to ensure the continued relevance and vibrancy of federal institutions in Canada. The underlying assumption is that constitutional adjudication should be less concerned with ascertaining the views of the drafters than with ensuring that the constitution is applied in conformity with the changing values and needs of the polity.

What this suggests is that the intentions of the drafters should not be conclusive in constitutional interpretation. But this limited conclusion leaves open the broader question of whether any weight at all should be attached to the intentions of the drafters. The views of the drafters may not be conclusive in resolving constitutional ambiguity, but this does not necessarily imply that their intentions should be simply ignored. Indeed, it would seem impossible or absurd to attempt to construe the *Charter* without taking the intentions of the drafters into account in some minimal fashion. The Court has declared its support for a "purposive" interpretation of the *Charter*, which surely makes the purposes of the drafters of the document relevant and significant. Moreover, the Court's recent jurisprudence surrounding the *Constitution Act, 1867* has made increasing reference to legislative history.[20] Thus, the real issue is not whether the intentions of the drafters are relevant at all but rather what weight ought to be attached to this material.

Professor Dworkin has attempted to answer this question through reference to a distinction between "concepts" and "conceptions". A "conception" is a specific account or understanding of what the words one is using mean, whereas a "concept" invites discussion about what words used to convey some general idea mean.[21] Concepts are not tied to the author's situation and intentions in the way conceptions are. Moreover, a concept is sufficiently vague and abstract such that its content is not usually specific enough to decide troubling cases. People may agree on some paradigmatic case which exemplifies the concept, but its boundaries will remain "contested" and perennially

---

19 See A. Cairns, "The Judicial Committee and its Critics" (1971), 4 Can. J. Pol. Sc. 301.
20 For a helpful discussion of this jurisprudence, see P. Hogg, "Legislative History in Constitutional Cases", in B. Sharpe (ed.), *Charter Litigation*, (1987) at 131-158.
21 R. Dworkin, *Taking Rights Seriously* (1977) at 131.

open to dispute. Dworkin's view is that only the concepts used by the drafters of the constitution are binding on later interpreters; although the drafters may well have had conceptions of their own as to the meaning of constitutional language, these conceptions need not be used in deciding cases. Dworkin's conclusions on this point are apparently derived from the views of the drafters themselves who, according to Dworkin, did not intend to give their own conceptions any special weight.[22]

Dworkin's concepts-conceptions distinction, while extremely suggestive, has been subjected to widespread criticism in the American constitutional literature.[23] Despite the difficulties with Dworkin's approach, it does capture one important truth about the significance of authorial intent in constitutional interpretation: judges deciding cases ought to take serious account of generalized purposes or intentions of the drafters, while at the same time according less weight to their views as to the precise meaning of particular words or phrases. This conclusion follows from the very nature of the process of drafting a constitution. A constitution is designed to state the general and enduring principles which are to govern the life of the polity. The role of the drafters is simply to define those general purposes rather than to decide individual cases. The task of applying the language of the document to particular circumstances is the responsibility of judges rather than the authors. It follows that judges should pay particular attention to the general purposes and policies of the drafters, but accord little or no weight to their opinions on the outcome of particular cases.

This analysis does not depend on Dworkin's distinction between concepts and conceptions which, in any case, probably never occurred to the drafters. The analysis is much more straightforward. My primary suggestion is that the use of legislative history can be structured along a continuum ranging from the more abstract and generalized purposes of the drafters, which should be accorded significant weight, to their views on the application of specific provisions, which are entitled to minimal or no weight. The argument can be illustrated by referring once again to the *Charter*. As we have seen, the drafters expressed a number of opinions as to the effect of s. 7 on particular legislative provisions. For instance, it was claimed that s. 7 would not have any impact on the *Criminal Code* provisions regarding abortion and that

---

22 *Ibid.* at 136.
23 See, e.g., M. Perry, *The Constitution, the Courts and Human Rights* (1982).

Parliament's power to regulate this matter would be unimpaired by the *Charter*. According to the framework offered here, these opinions on the particular application of s. 7 should be granted little or no weight by a court called upon to determine the constitutionality of Canada's abortion laws. At the same time, the drafters offered their views on the general purposes underlying s. 7, emphasizing that the provision was intended to protect procedural rather than substantive rights. These more generalized views are entitled to more serious consideration by a court interpreting s. 7. They relate, not to the application of the provision to particular cases, but to the very point of including the provision in the constitution in the first place. A court interested in a "purposive" interpretation of s. 7 would surely have to accord these views very serious consideration.

What this suggests is that the Supreme Court's treatment of legislative history in *Ref. re S. 94(2) of the Motor Vehicle Act (B.C.)*[24] was seriously inadequate. Lamer J. acknowledged that the senior civil servants and politicians who appeared before the Special Joint Committee were united in their view that s. 7 was confined to questions of procedural justice. But Justice Lamer concluded that this evidence, although admissible, was entitled to minimal weight. He justifies his conclusion on two grounds. First, he states that a few federal civil servants should not be regarded as representative of the "multiplicity of individuals who played major roles in the negotiating, drafting and adoption of the *Charter*".[25] Second, he argues that adopting the views of the drafters would mean that *Charter* rights would become "frozen in time . . . with little or no possibility of growth, development and adjustment to changing societal needs".[26]

Neither of Lamer J.'s arguments is particularly persuasive. The first argument fails to take account of the fact that it was not just a few federal civil servants who advanced a procedural interpretation of s. 7. The proceedings of the Special Joint Committee indicate that all the members of the committee were of the view that s. 7 ought not to receive a substantive interpretation. As for the second argument raised by Lamer J., his objection would be convincing if the Court had been considering the drafters' views on the particular application of s. 7. What was at issue, however, was the drafters' views on the very purpose of the provision. For the court to have given greater

---

24 *Ref. re s. 94(2) of the Motor Vehicle Act (B.C.)*, [1985] 2 S.C.R. 486 (S.C.C.).
25 *Ibid.* at 508.
26 *Ibid.* at 509.

weight to this evidence would hardly have "frozen" the meaning of the section, since the evidence merely went to general principles and did not deal with specific applications of those principles. There would have been adequate scope for the courts to have developed a progressive interpretation of s. 7 while remaining faithful to the fundamental purposes and policies it was designed to serve.

In short, I conclude that the intentions of the drafters do have a significant role to play in constitutional interpretation. Their views should never be taken to be conclusive on issues of doctrinal ambiguity. But the drafters' opinions as to the general purposes underlying particular provisions should be given serious consideration by courts. These authorial intentions are unlikely to compel or dictate specific results in concrete cases, given their inherent generality. Thus, use of legislative history will not relieve the judiciary of the difficult, value-laden task of applying general constitutional language to individual cases. But it is only by consulting history in appropriate cases that the judiciary can hope to engage in a "purposive" analysis of the *Charter* that is realistic and defensible.

2. FUNDAMENTAL RIGHTS THEORIES OF JUDICIAL REVIEW

A second American attempt to reconcile the institution of judicial review with democracy has adopted a much more sophisticated strategy. According to this second view, it is futile to suppose that constitutional adjudication is concerned only with the "plain meaning" of the text or with the views of the framers. The strategy of the second view is to concede a wide scope for judicial originality, but to argue that this originality is justified because of a particular expertise claimed by judges. The justification for judicial review is its concern with "rights".[27] Rights should not be taken to be synonymous with "interests" or "preferences". Rather, rights are a certain body of preferences which are singled out and accorded special weight. The extra weight attached to this limited body of preferences means that it is not a sufficient argument for denying a right that the aggregate satisfaction of preferences would be marginally increased by doing so. In this sense, certain rights theorists have described rights as

---

27 See generally Dworkin, *supra*, note 2.

"trumps"; the special weight accorded certain preferences means that they can overcome arguments based solely on considerations of general welfare.

A rights-based approach to judicial review attempts to construct boundaries around democratic politics. The appropriate domain of political debate involves the calculation of community welfare. The political process is the most appropriate institution to make compromises based on straightforward utilitarian principles. But questions of rights are thought to be within the competence of judges rather than politicians. Rights-based claims implicate problems germane to moral philosophy rather than to politics. For instance, a theory of rights can be tested by imagining circumstances in which the theory would produce unacceptable results and revising the theory accordingly.[28] This type of analysis is likely to be performed in a far more accurate manner by judges than by legislators or individual citizens. Judges are free from political pressure, deciding cases on the basis of reason and principle rather than expedient log-rolling.

This argument, based on institutional competence, is not the only justification offered for rights-based judicial review. Other arguments have suggested that judicial review has an important role to play in heightening the awareness of rights issues amongst citizens generally. The claim is that "rights talk" is a means of uplifting and revitalizing political and moral discourse in our society generally. By forcing the political process to confront the question of individual rights, public morality will become more reflective and self-critical.[29] The most commonly cited American example of this phenomenon is the American Supreme Court's decision in *Brown v. Board of Education*[30] in 1954, a decision which made the issue of desegregation in public schools a major focus of public controversy. Cast as the high priests of moral discourse, the judiciary encourages and orchestrates meaningful public debate on moral issues.

These arguments based on "fundamental rights" have been the subject of extensive debate and critique in the American literature. The critiques have focused on the spurious claims of objectivity and elitism which underlie the fundamental rights position. Perhaps the most compelling critique has been that advanced by John Hart Ely.[31]

---

28 See Dworkin, "Political Judges and the Rule of Law", in *supra*, note 2 at 24.
29 For arguments to this effect, see M. Perry, *supra*, note 23.
30 *Brown v. Bd. of Education of Topeka*, 349 U.S. 294 (1955).
31 See J.H. Ely, *Democracy and Distrust* (1980) at 56-60.

Ely points out that there is no such thing as "a" method of moral philosophy. For instance, the two most renowned contemporary theorists of moral and political philosophy, John Rawls and Robert Nozick, reach radically different conclusions on the requirements of the "just" state. Given this indeterminacy in moral theory, the invitation to judges to act as moral philosophers is a covert invitation for them to impose their own values on the democracy. The values that will be deemed to be "fundamental" will be the ones which seem most important to the upper-middle, professional class from which most lawyers and judges are drawn. Ely condemns such a practice as flagrantly elitist and undemocratic:[32]

> Thus the values judges are likely to single out as fundamental, to the extent that the selections do not simply reflect the political and ethical predispositions of the individuals concerned, are likely to have the smell of the lamp about them. They will be — and it would be unreasonable to expect otherwise if the task is so defined — the values of what Henry Hart without irony used to call 'first-rate lawyers' . . . Our society did not make the constitutional decision to move to near-universal suffrage only to turn around and have superimposed on popular decisions the values of first rate lawyers.

Even if the decisions of judges did not systematically reflect this narrow range of values, it would still be difficult to sustain the case for the legitimacy of activist judicial review. The proponents of activist judicial review are motivated by a profound distrust of the political process on rights issues. They regard the messy compromises of politics as simply inappropriate for determining individual rights; rights are matters of individual entitlement, derived from a process of reason and argument, and should not depend for their recognition upon whether "the people" happen to recognize them or not. The fallacy in the argument is the assumption that the justification for democracy is that it is likely to produce objectively "right" answers. Democratic politics is not guaranteed to produce right answers. No matter how much debate and discussion is encouraged, there is still the possibility that the community will make a choice that is mean-spirited or unenlightened. This possibility seems implicit in the democratic bargain. A choice for democracy means that the community has a right to be wrong. As Michael Walzer has observed, "[t]he people's claim to rule does not rest upon their knowledge of truth . . . but in terms of who they are. They are the subjects of the law, and if the law is to bind them as free men and women, they must also be

---

32 *Ibid.* at 59.

its makers."[33] The distinction that Walzer is drawing is between having a right to decide and having the right answer. Democracy assumes that the people have the former but not necessarily the latter.

There is a final, highly ironic objection to the "fundamental rights" approach to judicial review. The irony lies in the fact that, while these theorists claim to be the champions of principle, their own theories are remarkably unprincipled and *ad hoc*. The problem arises in the following way. If judicial review were actually designed to protect "fundamental interests", the range of issues which would have to be subjected to judicial scrutiny would have to be radically expanded. Judicial review would have to assume a leading role in defining individual entitlement to employment, to housing or to education, since all of these matters are arguably "fundamental" to human development or human "personhood". Yet the American judiciary does not now purport to deal with these issues in any serious or systematic fashion. This leaves the American "fundamental rights" theorist with a major problem: how can a fundamental rights analysis of judicial review be justified when the range of interests which are deemed fundamental is so obviously underinclusive?

There are two possible ways to deal with this problem of underinclusiveness, neither of which is particularly satisfactory. On the one hand, the theorist can arbitrarily narrow the class of interests which are deemed to be fundamental, so that the protected class exactly approximates the current, restricted doctrinal categories. Alternatively, the theorist can claim that large portions of current doctrine are "mistaken" and that the range of constitutionally protected interests should be radically expanded. The difficulty with this latter strategy is that the category of "mistakes" must remain limited and exceptional; otherwise, the theory is no longer an account of current doctrine but rather a prescription for a whole new set of doctrinal understandings. A serious attempt to apply a fundamental rights analysis and critique to current American constitutional doctrine, for example, would undoubtedly produce an unworkable and overwhelming category of "mistakes".

These democratic objections to the judiciary enforcing a set of "fundamental values" are as persuasive in the Canadian as in the American context. But there are a series of additional, equally compelling difficulties with any attempt to import this form of judicial review into the Canadian setting. These difficulties arise from a

---

33 M. Walzer, "Philosophy and Democracy" (1981), 9 Political Theory 379, 384.

fundamental tension between the assumptions underlying the "fundamental values" position and the distinctive quality of the Canadian political tradition.

The assumptions underlying a "fundamental values" version of judicial review are profoundly individualistic. The language of "trump rights" encourages the belief that communities are nothing more than aggregations of private interests. The rightholder is defined by his separation from and opposition to the community as opposed to his membership in it. This is exemplified by the assertion that rights are designed to ensure that the state remains neutral on questions of the good life or of what gives value to life.[34] Since the citizens of the society hold radically different conceptions of what gives value to life, the government must never take a stand on the issue. It cannot justify a decision on the basis that some ways of leading one's life are more worthy than others, "that it is more worthwhile to look at Titian on the wall than watch a football game on television. Perhaps it is more worthwhile to look at Titian, but that is not the point".[35]

This rights-based ethic has an impoverished conception of communal politics. Attempts on the part of the community to define its collective identity are automatically suspect. For the rights theorist, wherever collectivities gather together to express their moral beliefs in law, there lurks the stale but unmistakable odour of totalitarianism. Questions of morality and values are inescapably relative. Such matters of taste must be left in the hands of the individual, freed from the tyranny of the opinions of others regarding his lifestyle.

The constitutional analysis of Ronald Dworkin exemplifies this impoverished conception of community with its corresponding emphasis on the privatization of morality. Dworkin's analysis is premised on the notion that everyone has the right to be treated with equal concern and respect. This concern for equality is violated when the community allows a "corrupting" element to contaminate its calculation of general welfare. Dworkin identifies the corrupting element as a reliance on "external preferences", preferences people have about what others shall do or have. External preferences are vulgar and corrupt because they suppose that a particular form of life or community is more valuable than any other. In this sense, counting external preferences fails to respect the right of everyone to be treated with equal concern and respect. Judicial protection for "fundamental

---

34 M. Walzer, "Philosophy and Democracy" (1981), 9 Political Theory 379, 384.
35 Dworkin, "Can a Liberal State Support Art?", in *supra*, note 2, 221 at 222.

rights" is an attempt to antecedently identify those political decisions that are likely to reflect strong external preferences and remove them from majoritarian political institutions.

The implication is that political debate is purified when individuals frame arguments solely in terms of their personal interests. Far from purifying utilitarian discourse, Dworkin's proposal debases it. In the guise of offering a political discourse that is neutral or egalitarian, Dworkin has simply ordained that only certain values or ideals may be tolerated in political debate and argument. The accepted dialect is that employed by individuals bargaining in their own self-interest. Any appeal to the values or interests of the community as a whole is morally malformed. Apparently, to invoke public as opposed to purely private considerations is to violate the norm of equal concern and respect.

The result is an aggregate of individuals secure in their abstract rights and liberties but divorced from each other. This, of course, is entirely predictable given the background theory of personality which underlies contemporary liberal accounts of politics. The common starting point of these accounts is an abstract and fictitious choosing self which is stripped of all particularity.[36] This abstract self belongs to no particular family or community, has no set of allegiances or commitments and possesses no life plans. The quality of this person's liberation is aptly captured by Michael Walzer: "I imagine a human being thoroughly divorced, freed of parents, spouse and children, watching pornographic performances in some dark theater, joining (it may be his only membership) this or that odd cult, which he will probably leave in a month or two for another still odder."[37]

In a recent essay, Dworkin has attempted to qualify the prohibition he would place on the use of "external" preferences in political debate and argument.[38] The revised thesis would prohibit use of external preferences only in the sense that the mere existence or popularity of those preferences cannot be counted as a reason in their favour. On this basis, Dworkin explains that it was proper to count the "disinterested" political preferences of liberals that tipped the balance in favour of repealing laws against homosexual relationships in England in 1967. Although these preferences might have been "external", the

---

36 See M. Sandel, *Liberalism and the Limits of Justice* (1983), discussing J. Rawls, *A Theory of Justice* (1971).

37 M. Walzer, *Radical Principles* (1981) at 6.

38 See Dworkin, "Do We Have a Right to Pornography?", in *supra*, note 2, 335 at 365-72.

liberals "*expressed* their own political preferences in their votes and arguments, but they did not *appeal* to the popularity of these preferences as providing an argument in itself for what they wanted."[39] The point seems to be that the case for reform would have been just as strong had there been very few heterosexuals in favour of reform even though, as a practical matter, reform might have been impossible.

This qualification seems to collapse the argument into a crude assertion along the following lines: one should only count those views which are "liberal", and therefore "correct", while discounting any contrary views. This is because the claim that conservative arguments depend on the "popularity" of the views in question, as opposed to the inherent correctness of those views, is patently unpersuasive. Conservative opponents of reform would have appealed to the same "class" of arguments as did liberals. Their argument would have been one of principle, based on the assertion that homosexual relationships were morally wrong. Like liberals, conservatives would have regarded the case for continued criminalization of homosexuality to be just as compelling, regardless of the relative popularity of their views. Thus, the suggestion that one can distinguish conservative views from liberal ones based on the fact that the former appeals to the popularity of the views while the latter does not is surely wrong.

It would be possible to argue that this individualistic political philosophy is undesirable on it own terms. The basic objection would be that it stunts the possibility of developing a set of shared ends and values, a precondition to the emergence of a genuine populist democratic practice. But the objection which I want to emphasize is a much more limited and modest one. My claim is that there is a tension between this individualist ideology and the Canadian political tradition and, for that reason alone, this ideology ought not to form the basis of judicial review under the *Charter*.

3. THE CANADIAN TORY TOUCH

Despite the ongoing Canadian "identity crisis", social and political theorists claim to have discovered important and enduring differences between Canadian and American political culture. The differences are said to flow from a distinction between "individualist" and "collectivist" visions of the relationship between the individual

---

39 *Ibid.* at 368.

and society.[40] For an individualist, life is the individual pursuit of happiness rather than membership in a body politic. All roads converge on the atomic, prepolitical individual maximizing his or her self-interest. Thus, social contract theorists like Hobbes and Locke justified the creation of the state by analogy to a self-interested bargain between autonomous individuals in a state of nature. There was little emphasis on the possibility of the state helping to forge communal values or common ends. The state was necessary merely as a means of establishing order in a universe in which the interests of rational maximizers inevitably collided with each other.[41] Restraint was contractual rather than natural.

Within collectivism, individuals are constituted by their membership in an organic community. Society is primarily a community of hierarchically organized classes or groups, rather than an association of antecedently free individuals. The good of the individual is not conceivable apart from some regard for the good of the whole. Thus, restraints on individuals are natural rather than contractual, flowing from the very duties and rights which are implicit in membership in a larger community.

In general terms, the dominant ideology in both Canada and the United States can be described as essentially liberal or "individualist". But the broad similarities between the two societies should not lead one to minimize the important differences between them. Although Canada is broadly liberal, there are important features of the Canadian political tradition which cannot be placed within a purely individualist framework. The most prominent of these features is the fact that socialism in Canada is a national political force, whereas in the United States, organized socialism is dead.[42] The significance of socialist ideas is particularly pronounced in provincial politics, where the CCF-NDP parties have formed governments in three provinces; in the national arena, the NDP has never been able to achieve the status of a major urban party, but it has succeeded in becoming a significant minor party. The presence of these socialist ideas is an indication of the ideological diversity of the Canadian political tradition, particularly the legitimacy accorded collectivist or organic conceptions of society. Socialism is an ideology which combines collectivist ideas with rationalist and

---

40 See generally, G. Horowitz, "Conservatism, Liberalism and Socialism in Canada: An Interpretation" (1966), 32 Can. J. Econ. 143.

41 See generally, C.B. Macpherson, *The Life and Times of Liberal Democracy* (1977): Macpherson, *Democratic Theory: Essays in Retrieval* (1973).

42 See generally, Horowitz, *supra*, note 40.

egalitarian ones; "[i]t is *because* socialists have a conception of society as more than an agglomeration of competing individuals — a conception close to the tory view of society as an organic community — that they find the liberal idea of equality (equality of opportunity) inadequate."[43] Socialists see classes and communities in addition to isolated individuals maximizing opportunities for personal growth. They reject the liberal vision of abstract, bloodless individuals, situated in some situation of hypothetical choice, detached from the actual communities in which they live and work.

The presence of socialism is not the only feature of the Canadian political tradition which belies the exclusivity of liberal individualism. "Tory" values of "ascription" and "elitism" played a much more significant role in Canada's development than in America's.[44] Unlike America, Canada never had a lawless and egalitarian frontier. There has been a weaker Canadian emphasis on social equality and a greater acceptance by individuals of the facts of economic inequality and social hierarchy. Thus, in Canada, the Family Compacts were able to maintain their grip on political life long after the easy victory of Jeffersonian and Jacksonian democracy in the United States. Even after the achievement of responsible government, "there was no complete repudiation of the Compacts and what they stood for."[45] There continued to be a greater acceptance of limitations and of hierarchical patterns, as well as a distrust of American republicanism and democracy. Moreover, Canadian political elites have been far more willing than their American counterparts to use the state for controlling and directing economic development. Perhaps the most articulate and passionate celebration of these Canadian conservative values is George Grant's famous essay, *Lament for a Nation*. For Grant, the United States was a society which was devoted to the rights of the individual above the common good and espoused freedom above order and authority. Canada, on the other hand, stood "in firm opposition to the Jeffersonian liberalism so dominant in the United States".[46] Canadians were less enamoured of change, technology and materialism than their American counterparts. In Canada, tradition, order and stability were important virtues of political life. Other commentators do not share Grant's profound commitment to conservative values, but nevertheless con-

---

43 Horowitz, *supra*, note 40 at 144.

44 See S.M. Lipset, *The First New Nation* (1963).

45 K. McRae, "The Structure of Canadian History", in L. Hartz, *The Founding of New Societies*. (1964) at 239.

46 G. Grant, *Lament for a Nation* (1965) at 33.

clude that Canada is a society tinged with a "tory touch";[47] "In English Canada ideological diversity has not been buried beneath an absolutist liberal nationalism. Here Locke is not the one true god; he must tolerate lesser tory and socialist deities at his side."[48]

There is no universal agreement as to what accounts for the "tory" or, more recently, the "socialist" touch in Canadian politics. Perhaps the most influential explanation has been that offered by Gad Horowitz, who has argued that Canadian liberalism and conservatism interacted in a dialectical fashion to produce socialism.[49] This dialectical hypothesis depicts Canada as a "fragment" society with predominantly bourgeois roots,[50] but with non-liberal "imperfections" which eventually produced socialism. Other writers have attempted to offer an economic or "materialist" explanation for the development of Canadian political culture. Thus, Tom Naylor suggests that toryism in Canada is a product of the underdevelopment of Canada as an industrialist capitalist political economy.[51] According to Naylor's thesis, the Canadian bourgeoisie has always been dominated by mercantile and financial elements, which are less entrepreneurial and are more willing to work through the state to enforce their position; "the willingness of Canadian elites to use the state . . . to control and develop the economy is not the consequence of [tory ideology], but its cause."[52] Finally, other observers have advanced the more prosaic explanation that the strength of Canadian socialism is due primarily to our close relationship with Great Britain which made it easy for British ideas to be imported and accepted.[53]

Whatever the explanation, the important point for present

---

47 R. Whitaker, "Images of the State of Canada", in L. Panitch (ed.) *The Canadian State: Political Economy and Political Power* (1977) at 37; G. Horowitz, *Canadian Labour in Politics* (1968).

48 Horowitz, *supra*, note 40 at 155.

49 See *ibid*. See also "Notes on 'Conservatism, Liberalism and Socialism in Canada'" (1978), 11 Can. J. Pol. Sc. 383. For a critique of the Horowitz thesis, see R. Preece, "The Anglo-Saxon Conservative Tradition" (1980), 13 Can. J. Pol. Sc. 3.

50 The notion of a "fragment society" was originally developed by Louis Hartz. See *The Liberal Tradition in America* (1955) and *The Founding of New Societies* (1964). According to this thesis, the new societies founded by Europeans were fragments thrown off from Europe. They were fragment societies because the ideologies borne by the founders of the new society were not representative of the ideological spectrum of the mother country. The United States was a bourgeois fragment, its settlers being dominated by an individualist ethic to the exclusion of other ideas on the ideological spectrum.

51 R.T. Naylor, "The Rise and Fall of the Third Commercial Empire of the St. Lawrence", in G. Teeple (ed.) *Capitalism and the National Question in Canada* (1972).

52 Naylor, *ibid*. at 39.

53 T. Truman, "A Critique of Seymour Martin Lipset's article 'Value Differences, Absolute or Relative: the English Democracies'" (1971), 4 Can. J. Pol. Sc. 518.

purposes is that Canadian political culture cannot be portrayed as uniformly individualist. The Canadian polity has a rich and continuing commitment to collectivist, organic values in addition to individualist ones. This heterogeneity has important implications for the nature of judicial review under the *Charter.* With the enactment of the *Charter,* there is a danger that Canadian jurists and lawyers will uncritically embrace American assumptions about the nature and function of judicial review. But this would be a mistake. American approaches to fundamental rights have been developed in a political culture that is quite different from our own. To rely, in some wholesale and uncritical fashion, on the answers that American courts and commentators have given to problems of individual rights would be to deny the distinctiveness of the Canadian tradition. Importation of the American model of judicial review without significant design modifications would be to marginalize the enterprise. General Motors may be able to ignore the Canadian-American border, but Ronald Dworkin cannot; approaches to judicial review in Canada must necessarily differ from those in the United States.

This result flows from the very nature of constitutions and of constitutional adjudication. The enactment of a constitution is a momentous instant in the life of a polity. It is a constitutional moment in which the community attempts to articulate those values which are most fundamental and which constitute its identity as a community. Judicial review is the process which seeks to mediate and interpret the values identified at that constitutional moment for future generations. Thus, the whole premise and justification of constitutional adjudication under the *Charter* is that it give expression to fundamental Canadian values as opposed to fundamental American, British or European ones. This does not mean that this expression and interpretation of values need be static or backward-looking. As Alasdair MacIntyre has emphasized, a tradition is a "living tradition" to the extent that the heritage of the past is modified and reconstituted in the present:[54]

> [A]ll reasoning takes place within the context of some traditional mode of thought, transcending through criticism and invention the limitations of what had hitherto been reasoned in that tradition; this is as true of modern physics as of medieval logic. Moreover when a tradition is in good order, it is always partially constituted by an argument about the goods the pursuit of which gives to that tradition its particular point and purpose . . . [A]n adequate sense of

---

54 A. MacIntyre. *After Virtue* (1981) at 206-207.

tradition manifests itself in a grasp of those future possibilities which the past has made available to the present. Living traditions, just because they constitute a not-yet-completed narrative, confront a future whose determinate and determinable character, so far as it possesses any, derives from the past.

This suggests that the profoundly individualistic philosophies of Ronald Dworkin and other American "fundamental rights" theorists are an inapt and foreign foundation for judicial review under the Canadian *Charter*. Constitutional adjudication in Canada must accommodate the communitarian and collectivist aspects of our cultural tradition as well as the individualist ones. It must regard attempts by the community to embody its fundamental beliefs in law as something more than the imposition of one person's "external preferences" on another. Judicial review in Canada must be more than another branch-plant operation of an American head office.

6

A Theory of Judicial Review Under the Charter

Given the political character of constitutional adjudication under the *Charter*, what are the values that should guide Canadian judges as they give meaning to its open-ended provisions? This, I have argued, is the fundamental issue facing Canadian jurists as they attempt to make sense of the *Charter*. As I pointed out in Chapter 4, it is a question which has been largely sidestepped by the Supreme Court in its early *Charter* decisions. Moreover, as I suggested in Chapter 5, the answer to the question is not to be found in the two leading contemporary American theories of judicial review.

In this chapter, I want to offer a general theory of judicial review under the *Charter*. The claim which I defend is premised on a distinction between the substantive outcomes of the political process and the fairness of that process itself. In my view, the point of the *Charter* is not to test legislation against some independent theory of "justice" or "fairness". Courts are not to be regarded as some super-legislature, rewriting laws so that they conform with some substantive theory of what is right or good for society. The resolution of *Charter* issues is not to be found in the philosophies of John Rawls, Robert Nozick or Ronald Dworkin. Instead, the focus of *Charter* adjudication should be much more limited and constrained. I regard the *Charter* as directed primarily towards two distinct, but related, values. The first is democracy itself. Democracy implies more than simply popular rule. It means, in addition, a broadening of the opportunities for, and the scope of, collective deliberation and debate in a political community; it means identifying and reducing the barriers to effective and equal participation in the process by all citizens; it means ensuring that there are no arbitrary and permanent boundaries around the scope of political debate. The second fundamental value which I claim underlies the *Charter* is a related one — that of community. The communitarianism implicit in the *Charter* should not be regarded as an attempt to ignore or obliterate individuals. On the contrary, this communitarianism is premised on the belief that it is only through political communities that individuals define and develop their own individuality. As such, it rejects the simplistic assumption that there is an inevitable contradiction between individual and community. By enhancing the opportunities for communities to define their common identity, we can simultaneously enrich the lives of individuals in those communities.

Readers familiar with the American literature will recognize certain broad similarities between this argument and the work of John Hart Ely. In *Democracy and Distrust*, Dean Ely argues that judicial review is designed to ensure that the political process is open to those of all viewpoints on something approaching an equal basis. Ely's work has been the subject of intense and often effective criticism amongst American constitutional theorists.[1] The critics have relentlessly attacked the central distinction between procedure and substance, which forms the underpinnings of Ely's argument. The main point made by the critics is that Ely's so-called "process-oriented" theory itself requires judges to make substantive value choices. The problem is that Ely regards the making of substantive value choices by judges as illegitimate. Thus, his theory seems to require the judiciary to make just the sorts of value choices which he considers off limits; in short, the theory is hopelessly and inevitably self-contradictory.

It may well be that Dean Ely's theory of judicial review under the American constitution is unpersuasive. But the fundamental shortcomings of the theory are not those identified by Ely's critics. In my view, the fundamental problem with Dean Ely's analysis has very little to do with questions of "internal logic" and everything

---

1 See e.g., R. Dworkin, "The Forum of Principle", in *A Matter of Principle*. (1985); L. Tribe, "The Puzzling Persistence of Process-Based Constitutional Theories", 89 Yale L.J. 1063 (1980).

to do with the basic purposes underlying the American constitution. It is simply implausible to regard the provisions of the American constitution as being directed exclusively towards the enhancement of democratic values. This critique of Ely's theory — since it focuses on the "fit" between the theory and the terms of the American constitution — leaves open the possibility that Ely's basic approach may well be relevant and persuasive in another context. Turning to an analysis of the Canadian *Charter*, I attempt to identify both the similarities and the differences between the *Charter* and the U.S. *Bill of Rights*. What is apparent is that the drafters of the *Charter* either rejected or modified many of the elements found in the American *Bill of Rights*. Significantly, the elements of the American experience which were rejected or modified by Canadian drafters were those constitutional provisions which required judges to vindicate particular substantive values. Those features of the American constitution which required judges to police the integrity of the political process were imported, largely unchanged, into the Canadian *Charter*. Moreover, certain distinctively Canadian elements were included in the *Charter*; these elements were directed towards protecting communitarian and democratic values.

This leads me to conclusions which may appear somewhat counter-intuitive or paradoxical. My claim is that a democratic conception of judicial review, although originally formulated in the American context, actually offers a far more convincing account of the purposes underlying the Canadian *Charter*. My claim is that the drafters of the Canadian *Charter* embraced those elements of the American constitution designed to protect the democratic process, while largely excluding provisions aimed at guaranteeing particular substantive goods or values deemed fundamental. The Canadian drafters went on to add a series of provisions which either recognize the positive contribution of the state in securing individual freedom or protect communitarian values. In short, whatever the purposes of the American *Bill of Rights*, judicial review in Canada ought to serve a limited and constrained set of purposes. A shorthand way of describing those purposes would be to say that judicial review should be conducted in the name of democracy, rather than as a means of guaranteeing or requiring "right answers" from the political process.

Before I outline and defend these claims, I think it important to briefly deal with what might be termed the "section 33" question. It is sometimes said that there is no necessity to develop general theories of judicial review under the *Charter* due to the existence of a legislative override in s. 33. According to this view, it is unnecessary to offer a general theory to justify or explain judicial review because the judiciary does not have the last word on rights issues. If the legislature disagrees with the choices made by the judiciary, then it can simply pass legislation which will operate notwithstanding the *Charter*.

This objection is plainly misconceived. Judges are charged with the task of interpreting the *Charter*. The Supreme Court has already emphasized that this task of interpretation is "purposive"; it must be based on some understanding of the purposes which underlie the various provisions of the *Charter*. Clearly, then, the attempt to identify the meaning and purpose of the *Charter* is an absolutely central aspect of adjudication under the *Charter*. It is only by coming to some general understanding of the policies and principles which are embodied in the *Charter* that the process of judicial interpretation can be rendered meaningful. The fact that the *Charter* includes a power of legislative override is certainly not irrelevant to this enterprise. Indeed, any plausible theory of the values underlying the *Charter* should attempt to take into account, in some way, the presence of s. 33. But the existence of s. 33 is not an objection to the task of identifying meaning. It simply makes that task more complex and subtle.

1. PROCESS VERSUS SUBSTANCE?

In the recent American constitutional literature, John Hart Ely's work stands out; he alone has fashioned a defence of judicial review based on democratic values.[2] His theory builds on the distinction between substance and procedure. For Ely, democracy means that the choice of substantive political values must be made by representatives of the people rather than by unelected judges. The role of the judiciary should be to police the process of democracy rather than its substance. The court should intervene, not to vindicate particular substantive values it has determined are important or fundamental, but rather "to ensure that the political process — which is where such values *are* properly identified, weighted, and accommodated — is open to those of all viewpoints on something approaching an equal basis."[3] This means making sure that the avenues of participation remain open and that legislation which discriminates against "discrete and insular minorities" not be permitted.

---

2 J.H. Ely, *Democracy and Distrust.* (1980).
3 *Ibid.* at 74.

This distinction between substance and procedure has proven to be the weak link in Ely's argument and the focus for the attacks of his critics. In one of the most punishing critiques, Laurence Tribe has argued that if "process" values are seen as primary, this can only be because they are themselves substantive.[4] We value process, according to Tribe, for its "intrinsic characteristics"; it gives expression to "a right to individual dignity, or some similarly substantive norm".[5] Moreover, not only are process values substantive, in applying process values courts must necessarily make substantive value choices. For instance, in applying the equal protection clause, "[a]ny constitutional distinction between laws burdening homosexuals and laws burdening exhibitionists . . . must depend on a substantive theory of which [group is] exercising fundamental rights and which [is] not."[6] Finally, Tribe argues that considerations of substance are more fundamental than those of process. A narrow concentration on process may lead us to accept decisions whose effects strike us as substantively obnoxious. Tribe also believes that there are certain constitutional provisions, particularly the equal protection clause, which ought to be "fully explored" rather than artificially made to fit the mould of process values.

This critique of the procedural/substantive distinction has been particularly devastating for Ely's analysis. The critique pulled the carpet out from under Ely's feet. He could no longer claim that his theory reserved questions of substantive values to the democratically-elected legislature, while asking the judiciary to deal only with questions of process. The critics had demonstrated that, on Ely's own premises, courts would still be forced to make substantive determinations on issues of political morality. By Ely's own admission, the courts had no business making such substantive choices. He had been hoist on his own petard.

Yet, it is possible to begin the analysis at a different point. This alternative starting point assumes that judges interpreting a fundamental constitutional document must inevitably make substantive political choices. [This can only be a starting point (as opposed to a conclusion) because the substantive character of constitutional adjudication tells us nothing about the issue that really matters; what substantive values ought to count in the interpretive process?] This

---

4 Tribe, *supra*, note 1 at 1066-1067.

5 *Ibid.* at 1072.

6 *Ibid.* at 1076.

starting point is by no means incompatible with drawing the following fundamental distinction between two very different types of instructions which might be issued to judges interpreting a constitution. The first instruction would direct the court to attend to the outcomes of the political decisions which came before it. The issue in any constitutional case would be whether the court regarded those outcomes as substantively "just" or right. The second instruction would direct the court to focus its attention on the way in which the outcomes had been produced, as opposed to whether the outcomes were substantively just. On this second view, the issue for the court would be whether the process which had produced the decision in question had conformed to democratic values.

In either alternative, the court would be drawn into making determinations of substantive political morality. But this does not necessarily count as an argument in favour of giving the first instruction to judges as opposed to the second. The mere fact that judges must make substantive choices does not tell us whether judges ought to heed political outcomes *per se* as opposed to the way in which those outcomes are produced. In order to choose between these alternative conceptions of judicial review, it is necessary to construct an independent normative argument that does not depend on the mere fact that constitutional adjudication is substantive.

In this chapter I hope to build on what I take to be the fundamental insight of Ely's analysis — that an entrenched bill of rights need not necessarily be incompatible with democratic values. My argument is essentially quite simple. I claim that the best interpretation of the *Charter* — the interpretation which makes sense of the document as a whole — is an interpretation which gives primacy to values of democracy and community.

My analysis and interpretation of the *Charter* is intended to be both normative and political. The analysis is structured along the lines suggested by Ronald Dworkin in his important writing on interpretive theory.[7] The first element of the analysis is what Dworkin has identified as the element of "fit". Any plausible interpretation of the *Charter* must satisfy some threshold test of fit with the provisions of the document. The point is not to identify some uniquely "correct" interpretation of the "real" meaning of the *Charter*, since the dimension of fit can do no more than provide rough boundaries: "[t]here is . . .

---

7 The analysis and distinctions employed in this paragraph are based on the work of Ronald Dworkin. See R. Dworkin, "How Law is Like Literature", *supra*, note 1 at 146-166.

no algorithm for deciding whether a particular interpretation sufficiently fits that history not to be ruled out".[8] Moreover, the process of determining "fit" should not be regarded as a neutral or objective exercise in which the reader discovers something residing "in" the text. The analysis is necessarily political and evaluative, one in which the reader creates meaning in order to find it.[9] The second dimension of the analysis proceeds at the broader level of substantive political theory. The goal is to offer an account of the *Charter* which demonstrates "the best principle or policy it can be taken to serve".[10] The difference between this stage of the analysis and the question of "fit" is not that one is political and the other is not; plainly, I regard interpretation as inherently and thoroughly political. The difference is more a matter of degree rather than of kind, a question of subtle shading, emphasis and focus. In truth, the two stages of the analysis are not really separate at all, but are inextricably bound up with each other and occur simultaneously.[11]

In the remainder of this chapter I describe and defend a "democratic-communitarian" conception of judicial review under the *Charter*. The theory is based, as the name suggests, on the twin values of democracy and community. But a shorthand way of describing the theory and distinguishing it from leading American theories of judicial review is to focus on its attitude towards the political process. Many of the leading American theories of judicial review display a deep ambivalence and suspicion towards the political process.[12] For these theorists, the political process is dangerous because it permits unruly majorities to suffocate individual choice and freedom. Judicial review is said to be necessary in order to rein in the totalitarian impulses of the community. The judiciary is instructed to create and police a zone of individual autonomy which is placed beyond the reach of the unwashed mob. In my view, this attempt to create artificial boundaries around the legitimate scope of democratic debate and

---

8 *Ibid.* at 160.

9 See S. Fish, "Working on the Chain Gang: Interpretation in Law and Literature", 60 Tex. L. Rev. 551 (1982).

10 *Ibid.* at 160.

11 This is the essential point made by Stanley Fish in his critique of Dworkin. Fish claims that Dworkin continues to adopt a mechanical theory of interpretation since Dworkin supposedly regards the issue of "fit" as revolving around meaning found "in" the text. Yet, Fish's analysis of Dworkin is itself mechanical and picayune, seizing on verbal minutiae and refusing to let go like a dog clinging to a bone. See Fish, *supra*, note 9.

12 I am thinking particularly of the work of Ronald Dworkin. See Dworkin, *supra*, note 1 at 32-71.

dialogue is mistaken. I argue for a programme designed to embrace politics rather than to turn away from it. The ambition and point of my theory is to reduce the barriers around political argument rather than to reinforce those barriers. I argue that there should be no set of social or political arrangements arbitrarily or permanently insulated from democratic debate and argument. The point is to increase the possibility of revision in social life, rather than to freeze into place a partial and provisional set of social arrangements. All aspects of social life should be subject to the revisionary potential of politics.[13]

I argue that this conception of politics satisfies a threshold test of "fit" under the *Charter*. In my view, there are two distinctive and foundational concerns reflected in the *Charter*. The first of these concerns is democracy itself. I argue that democratic values are expressly or implicitly referred to throughout the *Charter*. There are a variety of provisions in the *Charter* directed either towards protecting democratic debate and argument, or towards remedying systemic defects in the process. The second foundational concern, intimately related to the first, is the value of community. Throughout the document there is a recognition of the importance of communitarian values. A variety of provisions is directed towards ensuring that individuals living in communities are provided with the opportunity and the means to define and develop their identities. One way of accomplishing this is negatively, by ensuring that communities are not adversely affected by the *Charter*. The other way of achieving this result is positively, by entrenching certain rights of communities or collectivities in the *Charter* itself.

My claim is not that the values of democracy and community are the only ones reflected in the *Charter*. Rather, I argue that these two values run throughout the document and, in particular, help to explain certain of its important structural features. In Dworkinian terms, my claim is that a theory based on these twin values satisfies a threshold test of "fit" with the *Charter*. At the broader level of political theory, I argue that there are three sorts of considerations which suggest that democratic and communitarian values should form the basis of

---

13 This vision of political life is developed most fully in the writings of Roberto Unger. Unger sets out a distinctive view of human freedom and personality. For Unger, true freedom depends upon the extent to which social life contains the instruments of its own revision. Freedom is realized in the activity of a self "that discovers the divergence between its own transcending capabilities and the limitations of the structures in which it lives, and then stuggles by every means at its disposal to narrow this gap." See R. Unger, "The Critical Legal Studies Movement", 96 Harv. L. Rev. 561 at 662. (1983).

Charter interpretation. The first consideration is the Canadian political tradition itself. As I suggested in Chapter 5, Canadian politics has always placed particular emphasis on communitarian values. Moreover, Canadians traditionally have regarded the state as a vehicle for creating individual freedom, rather than as the antithesis of such freedom. Claims for social justice have been advanced and have succeeded in the political, rather than the judicial, arena. The reading of the *Charter* which I suggest attempts to build upon this political tradition.

A second consideration is based on the value of democracy itself. Democracy regards consent as the only legitimate basis for the exercise of state power. Either the people themselves or their democratically-accountable representatives should have responsibility for making political choices. A democratic conception of judicial review attempts to reinforce this ideal. It regards judicial review as a mechanism to protect existing opportunities for democratic debate and dialogue as well as to open new avenues for such debate. The democratic conception stands in contrast to various "justice-based" theories, designed to circumscribe and to by-pass the political process.[14] By inviting judges to test the substantive fairness of political outcomes against some independent normative standard, justice-based theories limit the opportunities for popular participation and control. Rather than encouraging individuals to debate and define the conditions of their communal life, conflict is arbitrated by deferring to an elite judiciary.

A third consideration, which I advance in support of the democratic-communitarian approach, is the intrinsic value of community itself. The conception of community I have in mind is not some romantic ideal of a conflict-free and tightly-knit little world. But neither is the community simply the aggregation of private interests. Instead, it is an ideal which claims that individuals are themselves constituted, in an important if not exclusive sense, by their membership in community. Thus, political debate and argument on the fullest range of issues is valued not because it will necessarily yield right answers to issues of political morality, but because it is a necessary feature of a community defining and revising its own identity. This perspective values the process whereby citizens define their own traditions, conventions and expectations as opposed to seeking to emulate the choices of the inhabitants of some ideal or hypothetical

---

14 See Dworkin, *supra*, note 1.

commonwealth. It is a choice, as Michael Walzer has asserted, for politics and pluralism over universal truth. The particularity of a community's experiences "are valued by the people over the philosopher's gifts because they belong to the people and the gifts do not — much as I might value some familiar and much-used possession and feel uneasy with a new, more perfect model."[15]

2. THE QUESTION OF FIT: WHAT THE CHARTER "HASN'T GOT IN IT"

A recent television advertisement for a well-known brand of cereal attempts to market the product by emphasizing "what it hasn't got in it". The star of the commercial declares that he likes the cereal because it doesn't contain any broccoli and he, of course, "hates broccoli". This commercial has always struck me as rather inane. Nevertheless I want to suggest that the "what it hasn't got in it" approach is surprisingly useful in terms of understanding and interpreting the *Charter*. In particular, I want to suggest that there are a variety of elements of the American Bill of Rights which were deliberately excluded from the *Charter*. I want to focus initially on those excluded elements, and to ask what they tell us about the overall purposes of the *Charter*. In blunt terms, my thesis is that by identifying "what it [the *Charter*] hasn't got in it", it becomes possible to come to some understanding of what it "has" got in it.

What is the relationship between the American constitution and democratic values? Democratic institutions are certainly one important focus of the American constitution, but it is difficult to regard theme as the exclusive or even the overriding theme of the document. There are a variety of clauses which are directed towards the preservation of certain "fundamental values" which have little or nothing to do with furthering democracy. In fact, far from promoting democracy, the document seems preoccupied with drawing boundaries around the political process and preventing unruly majorities from interfering with established rights, particularly property rights. In the 1780s, state legislatures had passed a variety of debtor relief laws which were widely viewed as violations of property rights. A particular concern for federalist thought at the time was to protect property against tyranny by the majority; the ambition was to minimize the threat implicit in popular political power rather than to facilitate political

---

15 M. Walzer, "Philosophy and Democracy", 9 Political Theory 379, 395 (1981).

participation or democratic empowerment.

A central purpose of the U.S. constitution was to confine political life to the "public realm", while ensuring that the state did not interfere with private rights of property or contract. This dichotomy between public and private realms was premised on the belief that individuals possessed a prepolitical zone of "pure" autonomy or freedom. The zone of pure autonomy was prepolitical, in the sense that it did not depend upon the state for its existence or legitimacy. The boundaries of individual autonomy were defined primarily by the institutions of property, contract and the market. Within this eighteenth century world view, market ordering was not a form of coercion or a system of state regulation; markets reflected the absence of regulation, a sphere in which voluntarism and freedom might flourish. State regulation was thus characterized as the coercive control of individuals by the collectivity. Constitutional guarantees such as the "contracts clause" or the "takings clause" were designed to check the potential excesses of popular rule. Armed with such constitutional guarantees, the judiciary would police the boundary between the zone of autonomy and the realm of legitimate democratic debate. Judicial review would be one means of ensuring that the people did not encroach on the private sphere reserved for individuals.

The drafters of the American constitution did not rely exclusively on formal limits in order to protect the propertied minority; they also devised a complex system of checks and balances which would enable minorities to block popular majorities intent on violating rights. The ultimate goal was limited government, not majority rule. Jennifer Nedelsky summarizes the mood and thrust of federalist thought in the following terms:

> The Federalists came to emphasize protection from republican government, rather than exploring or optimizing republican principles. They accepted the widely held view that government by consent was necessary to prevent tyranny, and was required by the imperative of natural rights and the equality of man. Moreover, they recognized that political exigencies required that any viable political proposal appear to comport with the popular attachment to republican principles. They thus took the principle of consent as a given, and turned their attention to the dangers inherent in governments based on such principles. The result was a subtle but important shift in focus from the promise of republican government to the containment of its threats.[16]

---

16 J. Nedelsky, "Private Property and the Formation of the American Constitution", (Public Law Workshop, Osgoode Hall Law School, October 1985) at 15.

John Hart Ely, who claims that the American constitution is primarily directed towards protecting democracy rather than substantive values, has some difficulty in accounting for the emphasis on property and contract in the document. He acknowledges that there are a number of provisions which are "value-oriented", but argues that the provisions which do not fit within his framework are "few and far between". He believes that in order to characterize the "value-oriented" provisions as the dominant theme of the constitutional document, "one would have to concentrate quite single-mindedly on hopping from stone to stone and averting one's eyes from the mainstream".[17] Thus Ely argues that the "contracts clause", although protecting the substantive value of contractual rights, has not played a significant role during most of the twentieth century. As for the Fifth Amendment's requirement that private property not be taken for public use without just compensation, Ely interprets this as promoting democracy rather than the value of property as such: its point is to "spread the cost of operating the governmental apparatus throughout the society rather than imposing it upon some small segment of it".[18]

It is quite unnecessary to determine whether Ely's attempt to marginalize the contracts clause or the takings clause are convincing in historical terms. My point is much simpler. Whatever the precise meaning of the various clauses in the U.S. constitution, it is clear that eighteenth century political assumptions about "limited government" are today totally discredited. It has been axiomatic, at least since the legal realists in the 1920s and 1930s, that the traditional dichotomy between public and private realms is largely illusory. There is no such thing as a zone of pure autonomy, free of state regulation. Property, for example, is itself the creature of the state, rather than its antithesis. The state defines those interests which qualify as property and then intervenes to ensure that they are protected. The same can be said of contractual rights or of markets generally. In effect, it is simply fallacious to attempt to "eliminate" state intervention in markets; the state is already there, defining the entitlements and intervening to protect them. The conceptual underpinnings of the eighteenth century preoccupation with limited government have been demonstrated to be false.

Thus, the Canadian *Charter* was drafted in an era in which the

---

17 Ely, *supra*, note 2 at 101.
18 *Ibid.* at 97, quoting Sax, "Takings and the Police Power", 74 Yale L.J. 36, 75-76.

notion of "private ordering", the very basis of the American consti- tution, had lost much of its meaning. One would expect, accordingly, to observe quite significant differences between the *Charter* and the American Bill of Rights. In fact, this is precisely what one does observe. The agenda of Canadian constitutionalists in 1982 was a far cry from that of American Federalists 200 years earlier. The preoccupation with limited government had largely disappeared, replaced by a concern to ensure that the *Charter* did not frustrate state efforts to expand freedom and pursue the cause of social justice. There was a recognition, in other words, of the fact that there is no necessary tension between the state and freedom; the state can create or enhance freedom as well as limit it. The overriding goal of the *Charter* was to regulate and to structure the way in which state power could be used, rather than to define the boundary between public and private.

This agenda is reflected first of all in what the drafters of the *Charter* sought to exclude from the document. The *Charter* includes no contracts clause and no takings clause. In fact, the drafters took the view that the *Charter* did not provide any protection for "economic" as opposed to "political" rights. Section 7, the Canadian equivalent to the American due process clause, was supposed to protect only the right to a fair procedure as opposed to an entitlement to a substantively just outcome. The drafters were emphatic in their view that s. 7 would not entitle judges to inquire into whether or not the outcomes of the political process were "fair". Thus, the point of s. 7 was to structure and to mediate the exercise of state power, rather than to draw artificial boundaries between "public" and "private" realms. The drafters believed that it was inappropriate for judges to define state policy on issues of public concern; the task of the judges was simply to ensure that the policy chosen by Parliament was applied in a fair and even- handed fashion.

In short, the *Charter* makes no reference to those elements of the American Bill of Rights premised on ideals of "limited government". What, then, were the elements of the American constitution which were imported for use in Canada? There are a number of important parallels between the *Charter* and the U.S. Bill of Rights. First, the "fundamental freedoms" in s. 2 of the *Charter* are analogous to the guarantees of free speech, free press and peaceful assembly in the American constitution. The "democratic rights" in ss. 3 to 5 of the *Charter* parallel similar sorts of rights in the American constitution. A number of the "legal rights" in s. 8 to 14 of the *Charter* draw on similar American provisions. Finally, and most importantly, s. 15 of the *Charter* enshrines the value of "equal protection" which has been so central to American constitutional development.

What is important to note about these various provisions is how they differ from a "contracts clause" or a substantive due process clause. A contracts clause, for example, focuses on a particular substantive value which is deemed fundamental and attempts to insulate that value from the democratic process. The various elements of the *Charter* identified above are motivated by different concerns. The fundamental freedoms in s. 2 are closely linked to democratic values. No genuine democracy could function without basic guarantees regarding free expression, a free press and freedom of association. The same can be said of the democratic rights in ss. 3 to 5. The legal rights protected by ss. 8 to 14 of the *Charter* do not have this obvious and direct link to the democratic process. But, at the same time, these constitutional guarantees do not attempt to dictate or to constrain the outcomes of political debate. Instead, they ensure that, regardless of the particular policy chosen by the state, this policy can only be implemented if a detailed set of norms, most of them procedural, are observed.

What is the ultimate point or purpose of the various rights protected in ss. 8 to 14? It is sometimes suggested that these rights are reflective of the idea of "privacy" or, perhaps, of "individual dignity". But these readings appear singularly unpersuasive. Sections 8 to 14 cannot reflect the idea of "privacy" for the simple reason that many of them create positive entitlements. Section 10, for example, recognizes a positive right to retain and to instruct counsel upon arrest; s. 11 recognizes rights to be tried within a reasonable time, to be presumed innocent until proven guilty and to the benefit of a jury trial for certain types of offences; s. 14 recognizes a right to an interpreter in certain circumstances. Nor is it clear how these particular entitlements necessarily flow from the idea of "individual dignity". The connection between individual dignity and the right to counsel or the right to a jury trial is obscure, at best. A more plausible reading of ss. 8 to 14 is the suggestion that they reflect two sorts of concerns. The first is that of procedural regularity and principles associated with the rule of law. The second is the notion that there should be some attempt to counterbalance the overwhelming advantage enjoyed by the state over the individual in the context of legal proceedings. The state has virtually unlimited resources at its disposal in most legal proceedings. Sections 8 to 14 are an attempt to moderate that "inequality in bargaining power". These provisions envisage a number of specific procedural and substantive protections for the individual while at the same time imposing a number of burdens on the state.

Whatever the purposes of ss. 8 to 14, my limited point at this stage is that these provisions do not seek to draw boundaries around democratic debate and dialogue. They are directed towards the standards governing the administration and the enforcement of laws, and thus, impact only indirectly on their substance. What of the final element of the *Charter* identified above, s. 15? The guarantee of equal protection is one of the most important, but also one of the most ambiguous, provisions in the *Charter*. The "real" meaning of equality is surely one of the most highly-contested issues in modern political theory. The point I want to make here, however, is limited to the following; given the indeterminacy associated with the idea of equality, it is possible and plausible to interpret this provision as designed to remedy the defects of the political process. I want to defer until later in this chapter a detailed account of what such a democratic interpretation of equality would look like.

3. THE CHARTER AND COMMUNITY

Thus far we have identified a number of provisions in the *Charter* which parallel similar provisions in the American Bill of Rights. But this analysis accounts for, at best, only half of the *Charter*. The remaining half of the document contains provisions which are distinctively Canadian and which therefore find no parallel in the American experience. What are the values embodied in these distinctively Canadian provisions?

The first such provisions are the guarantees regarding official languages and minority language education in ss. 16 to 23 of the *Charter*. It is evident that there is no necessary connection between these guarantees and the idea of democracy *per se*. The language guarantees are quite obviously the product of the historic and central role which language and duality have played in the Canadian political tradition.

There are two features of these provisions that require particular emphasis. First, these guarantees reflect a positive, rather than a negative, conception of freedom. The language provisions reject the equation of freedom with the idea of being "let alone". The operative conception of language freedom is one which includes a positive opportunity to use and develop one's language. To take but one example, s. 20 guarantees a positive "right to communicate with, and to receive available services from, any head or central office of an institution of the Parliament or government of Canada in English or French".[19]

There is a second distinctive feature of these provisions, also related to the nature of freedom. Language freedom, as defined by ss. 16 to 23, is neither wholly individualist nor wholly communitarian. Instead, a complex and symbiotic relationship between individual autonomy and community values is posited. Community is both a prerequisite for individual freedom and a corollary of it. The complex and delicate linkage between individual and community is reflected most clearly in those provisions which make the exercise of individual rights expressly contingent on the presence of community. For example, the right to communicate in English or French in s. 20, although guaranteed to "any member of the public", becomes operative where "there is a significant demand for communications with and services from that office in such language. . . ."[20] This "significant demand" proviso makes the exercise of the individual's right wholly contingent on the existence of a language community. Similarly, the right to minority language education, although guaranteed to "citizens of Canada", only applies "wherever in the province the number of children of citizens who have such a right is sufficient to warrant the provision to them out of public funds of minority language instruction."[21] Again, there is a linkage between the language rights of individuals and the existence of language communities. Language rights for individuals cannot exist in isolation; they are wholly dependent on the presence of community.

Even those language provisions which are not expressly contingent on the existence of community implicitly assume it. For instance, s. 19(2) of the *Charter*,[22] although framed in exclusively individualistic terms, in reality reflects broader social and communitarian concerns. This is the point made by Chief Justice Dickson in his eloquent dissent in *La Société des Acadiens du Nouveau-Brunswick Inc. v. Association of Parents for Fairness in Education, Grand Falls District 50 Branch*:

> What good is a right to use one's language if those to whom one speaks cannot

---

19 *Constitution Act*, 1982 [en. by the Canada Act, 1982 (U.K.), c.11, s.1] Pt. I (*Canadian Charter of Rights and Freedoms*) s. 20. The reader will note that the analysis offered here differs significantly from my earlier views, as set out in "Judicial Review and Democracy: A Theory of Judicial Review" (1987), 21 U.B.C.L. Rev. 87 at 158.

20 *Ibid.* at s. 20(1)(*a*).

21 *Ibid.* at s. 23(3)(*a*).

22 Section 19(2) provides that "Either English or French may be used by any person in, or in any pleading in or process issuing from, any court of New Brunswick".

understand? Though couched in individualistic terms, language rights, by their very nature, are intimately and profoundly social. We speak and write to communicate to others. In the courtroom, we speak to communicate to the judge or judges. It is fundamental, therefore, to any effective and coherent guarantee of language rights in the courtroom that the judge or judges understand, either directly or through other means, the language chosen by the individual coming before the court.[23]

In short, what is most distinctive about the language provisions in the *Charter* is their rejection of the supposed "fundamental contradiction" between individual and community.[24] The language guarantees are neither wholly individualistic nor wholly communitarian. They recognize the boundary between self and other, refusing to obliterate the individual in the name of the community. But, at the same time, these constitutional provisions give profound expression to the idea that individuals cannot and do not exist in isolation. They affirm the pervasive contextuality of all human endeavour, of the deep human longing to "open ourselves to personal attachments and communal engagements whose terms we cannot predetermine and whose course we cannot control."[25]

Apart from the language guarantees, the remainder of the *Charter* contains a number of "general" provisions dealing with a series of apparently unrelated issues. Section 25 provides that the *Charter* shall not be construed so as to derogate from aboriginal or treaty rights of the aboriginal peoples of Canada. Section 27 states a general rule of interpretation, to the effect that the *Charter* is to be construed "in a manner consistent with the preservation and enhancement of the multicultural heritage of Canadians". Section 29 states that the *Charter* does not derogate from guaranteed rights regarding denominational schools. These seemingly unconnected provisions share two common features. First, each of these provisions is a distinctive product of the Canadian political tradition, finding no analogue in the American constitution. Second, each is designed to preserve or to enhance communitarian values. Like the language provisions in ss. 16 to 23, they are a recognition and a reaffirmation of the importance of

---

23 Reasons for judgement of Dickson C.J., *Société des Acadiens du Nouveau-Brunswick Inc. v. Assn. of Parents for Fairness in Education, Grand Falls Dist. 50 Branch*, [1986] 1 S.C.R. 549 at 566 (S.C.C.).

24 For a discussion of the centrality of this "fundamental contradiction" to liberal thought see D. Kennedy, "The Structure of Blackstone's Commentaries", 28 Buffalo L. Rev. 205 at 211-212 (1979); G. Frug, "The City as a Legal Concept", 93 Harv. L. Rev. 1057 (1980); P. Brest, "The Fundamental Rights Controversy: The Essential Contradictions of Normative Constitutional Scholarship", 90 Yale L.J. 1063 (1981).

25 R. Unger, Passion: An Essay on Personality. (1984) at 20.

community in the Canadian political tradition. The purpose of s. 25, for example, is to ensure that the distinctive traditions of aboriginal communities are not undermined by the *Charter*.[26] Section 27 requires interpretations which enhance and preserve multiculturalism. The denominational school rights referred to in s. 29 are also motivated by a desire to protect religious and language communities. The inclusion of these references to community reinforces the idea that the *Charter* is not simply a reflection of liberal individualist values.

Interpretations of the *Charter* must seek to make sense of the document as a whole. The fact that the document is replete with references to community ought to make a difference in the interpretation of provisions which are ostensibly wholly individualist. The significance of ss. 16 to 23, for example, is that they present a distinctive vision of the relationship between individual and community. This "post-liberal" conception must be taken into account in the interpretation of the fundamental freedoms found elsewhere in the document. This approach, which seeks to read the *Charter* as a single document, is preferable to the approach endorsed by the Supreme Court of Canada in *La Société des Acadiens du Nouveau-Brunswick Inc. v. Association of Parents For Fairness in Education*.[27] In the *Acadiens* case, Mr. Justice Beetz posited a fundamental dichotomy between the language rights in s. 23 and the other rights guaranteed by the *Charter*. For Beetz J., the language rights were a product of "political compromise". These "political" rights were said to lack the universality and generality of other rights in the *Charter*, which are founded on "principle".

Justice Beetz's analysis overestimates the novelty of the language guarantees; as we have already noted, there are a number of other provisions which are also clearly motivated by communitarian concerns. In the next section of the chapter, we will discover that there are additional provisions which adopt a similar perspective. More importantly, Beetz J.'s analysis is problematic since it seeks to compartmentalize the *Charter*. He even goes so far as to suggest that there are fundamentally different rules of interpretation which should apply to the different provisions in the document. There is certainly no suggestion in the document itself that this compartmentalization was intended. Further, Beetz J.'s analysis makes no attempt to read

---

26 Of course, the protection for aboriginal communities in s. 25 is complemented by s. 35(1), which entrenches the "existing aboriginal and treaty rights of the aboriginal peoples of Canada".

27 *Supra*, note 23.

the *Charter* as a single document. It is ultimately rooted in a narrow textualism, an approach which ignores the fundamental constitutive character of the *Charter*.

4. THE STRUCTURE OF THE CHARTER: SECTIONS 1 AND 33

One of the distinctive structural features of the *Charter* is s.1, the "reasonable limits" clause. This clause articulates a standard for justifying limits on *Charter* rights; constitutional rights are subject to "such reasonable limits prescribed by law as can be demonstrably justified in a free and democratic society."[28] In theory, at least, it was not strictly necessary to draft a separate "limitations clause". Common sense alone indicates that since rights and freedoms inevitably collide, the rights of any one individual or group cannot be absolutely protected. This much is clear from the American constitutional experience. The American constitution does not contain a separate limitations clause and yet, the U.S. Supreme Court has recognized that rights cannot be interpreted in an absolutist fashion. Thus, s. 1 must be taken to mean more than the truism that "rights are not absolute". What additional meaning can be attributed to the provision?

In the first wave of *Charter* cases, courts have tended to characterize s. 1 as imposing a special burden of justification on the state. According to this way of thinking, the presence of s. 1 suggests that *Charter* analysis take place in two distinct steps. First, there is an analysis of the right itself; here, the court determines whether legislation violates a particular provision of the *Charter*. If there is a *Charter* violation, the court moves on to the s. 1 analysis. The court will uphold the violation under s. 1 only if the state can satisfy the most stringent requirements of proof and argument. Section 1 allows limits on rights only "where their exercise would be inimical to the realization of collective goals of fundamental importance."[29] The point of s. 1, according to this methodology, is to ensure that limits on rights are "exceptions to their general guarantee".[30]

The effect of this analysis is to make it extremely difficult for the state to uphold limitations on individual rights. There are two background assumptions underlying the analysis. The first is that values of "freedom" and "democracy" referred to in s. 1 are best vindicated

---

28 *Supra*, note 19 at s. 1.
29 See *R. v. Oakes*, [1986] 1 S.C.R. 103 at 136 (S.C.C.).
30 See generally, the judgment of Dickson, C.J.C. in *Oakes*, *ibid.*

by "liberal" interpretations of rights. This assumption, in turn, depends on the idea that there is a necessary tension or opposition between state "intervention" and individual freedom. If one begins with these background ideas, it makes sense to regard broad interpretations of individual rights as "good" and limits on those rights as "bad".

Yet, there is an alternative view of the purpose of s. 1. This alternative conception sees s. 1 as a reflection of the idea that there is no necessary tension between state power and individual freedom. The reason is deceptively simple. State regulation, while it might limit the opportunities of some citizens, will also expand the opportunities of others. Since state regulation has this "double-barrelled" effect, imposing constitutional limits on what the state can do will not enhance freedom *per se*. The effect of constitutional limits is to expand the freedom of some individuals, while simultaneously restricting the freedom of others.

This basic idea — that constitutional limitations both create and limit freedom — finds more explicit recognition elsewhere in the *Charter*. A good illustration is s. 15(2), which states that equality rights in s. 15(1) do "not preclude any law, program or activity that has as its object the amelioration of conditions of disadvantaged individuals or groups. . . ."[31] This is a saving provision, aimed at protecting legislative jurisdiction. Why was such a saving provision included? The obvious reason is that without such a provision, certain legislative programmes aimed at the "amelioration of conditions of disadvantaged individuals or groups" might be found to be a violation of equality rights in s. 15(1). Such programmes are vulnerable under s. 15(1) for the simple reason that they are discriminatory. The essential purpose of "affirmative action" programmes is the singling out of target groups for special treatment. Section 15(2) is an explicit attempt to preserve the state's power to discriminate in favour of disadvantaged individuals or groups. Suppose it were suggested that s. 15(2) be construed in a narrow or restrictive fashion, for example, by requiring the state to satisfy some stringent standard of justification. Such a restrictive approach to s. 15(2) would obviously not serve the cause of "freedom". Instead, a narrow interpretation of s. 15(2) would simply mean that the opportunities available to disadvantaged individuals or groups would become more limited.

Another provision which reflects similar ideas is s. 6(4) of the *Charter*. Section 6(2) of the *Charter* guarantees a right to move to and

---

31 *Supra*, note 19 at s. 15(2).

to take up residence in a province, as well as a right to pursue the gaining of a livelihood in any province. Section 6(4), like s. 15(2), is a limiting and a saving provision. It provides that mobility rights shall not preclude state regulation aimed at "the amelioration in a province of conditions of individuals in the province who are socially or economically disadvantaged if the rate of employment in that province is below the rate of employment in Canada". Here again is an explicit recognition of the double-barrelled character of constitutional limitations. The guarantee of mobility rights in s. 6(2) does not simply expand freedom in the abstract. It expands the freedom of individuals seeking to move to a particular province, *but only at the expense of individuals already living in the province.* Thus, in reality, the constitutional choice is not between "the individual" and "the state". The choice is between the interests of individuals seeking to move into a province versus the interests of individuals already living in that province. Section 6(4) is an attempt to preserve the ability of the state to discriminate in favour of its own residents. It is a recognition of the idea that a broad interpretation of mobility rights does not simply constrain "the state", but also imposes burdens on individual Canadians.

This analysis of mobility and equality rights can be generalized. Constitutional limitations on state power always have a "double-barrelled" effect, increasing opportunities for some while reducing opportunities for others. Thus, the constitutional choice, although ostensibly between the "state" and the "individual", also implicates the competing interests of individuals. The inclusion of s. 1 can be seen as a recognition of this fundamental feature of *Charter* analysis. It is the generalized analogue of ss. 6(4) and 15(2). It suggests that courts must never entertain the delusion that constitutional limitations are costless. Constitutional limitations always involve direct or indirect costs for certain individuals, groups or communities. Section 1 is a clear signal that courts are always to take these competing demands into account. Rather than facilely assume a contradiction between individual freedom and state regulation, the court must recognize the complex and delicate balance between individual, community and state.

What would be the practical consequences of adopting such a view of s. 1? The main consequence would be a rejection of the presumption that limits on constitutional rights are "exceptions to their general guarantee". Since constitutional rights simply expand the freedom of some at the expense of others, there would be no *a priori* reason why limits on rights should be seen as "exceptional". Courts would have to devise some independent and flexible set of criteria in order to determine when to read constitutional constraints broadly and when to read them narrowly. Section 1 itself contains some suggestions as to the criteria to guide the balancing process. The section refers to limits on rights which can be demonstrably justified in a "free and democratic society". For some, the reference to "democracy" may seem singularly unhelpful. Democracy is far from a precise political concept and there is often room for disagreement whether some procedure is or is not democratic.[32] Yet, despite this indeterminacy, s. 1 is surely an indication of the centrality of democratic ideals under the *Charter*. Section 1 indicates that the ultimate criteria to guide courts in their resolution of constitutional claims is the idea of democracy. This reinforces the basic suggestion I have been making thus far: the best interpretation of the *Charter* is one which sees it as a reflection and a reinforcement of democratic ideas rather than as a negation of those ideas.

The other structural feature of the *Charter* which deserves special mention is s. 33, which permits legislatures to override certain protected rights. There has been some suggestion that s. 33 is a blot on the *Charter*. The Canadian Bar Association, for example, has called for the repeal of s. 33, arguing that it trivializes the fundamental character of constitutional rights. This critique of s. 33 assumes that the provision is a constitutional anomaly. Yet, in my view, precisely the opposite is the case. Section 33 is simply an articulation of a number of fundamental ideas which we have seen throughout the *Charter*. The first idea is that there is no necessary contradiction between individual freedom and the exercise of state power. The state can create freedom as well as limit it. This means that expansive interpretations of constitutional constraints are not necessarily to be preferred to restrictive interpretations. Section 33 is a powerful and blunt expression of this idea. Like ss. 6(4) and 15(2), it is a saving provision, designed to protect legislative jurisdiction. Unlike those other sections, however, s. 33 provides for legislative, rather than judicial, determination of the proper scope of constitutional rights. The purpose is not to legitimate tyranny. The purpose is simply to ensure that the political process will not be subject to unreasonable or perverse judicial interpretations.

---

32 The indeterminacy surrounding the idea of democracy is one of the objections raised by Ronald Dworkin against the "process-based" theory of Professor Ely. See, Dworkin, *supra*, at 59. I will try to deal with this issue of indeterminacy in the next section of this chapter.

The other idea implicit in s. 33 is a basic trust in the political process itself. Section 33 suggests that the rights and freedoms of Canadians can be protected most effectively by the political process, rather than by the judicial process. It is intellectually fashionable, particularly in the United States, to dismiss the political process as unprincipled and arbitrary. Critics of the political process typically rely on a very limited number of historical examples to support their case. Pointing to instances in which majorities have denied the rights of minorities, these critics suggest that the only answer is to hand politics over to the judiciary. Yet the critics' analysis of the historical record is truncated and misleading. What is ignored is the fact that the cause of social and economic justice, in Canada at least, has almost always been advanced through the political, rather than the judicial, process. Andrew Petter has put the matter succinctly:

> The victories that have been won in this century on behalf of workers, the unemployed, women and other socially and economically disadvantaged Canadians are victories that have been achieved, for the most part, in the democratic arena. They are victories that have been won by harnessing the powers of the modern state to redistribute wealth and to place limits on the exercise of "private" economic power. . . . Such progress has been achieved through political action aimed at displacing the common law vision of unbridled individual autonomy with a countervision of collective social responsibility.[33]

Section 33, like ss. 1, 6(4) and 15(2), is a reflection of this basic idea. It is a concrete commitment to the primacy of politics, and a commitment to the idea that liberty is not the enemy but the product of governmental institutions. On this view, the goal is not to construct a set of boundaries around public institutions. The goal is to make public institutions more accountable and responsive. What we need is more politics rather than less.

The idea the the *Charter* should be interpreted as the embodiement of democratic ideals is certainly not new. Indeed, shortly after its enactment, the Chief Justice of Canada suggested that it was possible to reconcile the *Charter* with democratic theory. Here is the Chief Justice's articulation of the fundamental purposes of the *Charter*:

> Democracy is the periodic determination of the common will by the free expression of the genuine and informed will of the individual. There must be freedom of thought, conscience and opinion, or there can be no expression

---

33 A. Petter, "Immaculate Deception: the Charter's Hidden Agenda" (unpublished manuscript, 1986) at 3-4.

of the genuine will of the individual. There must be freedom of information, assembly and association, or there can be no expression of an informed will of the individual. There must be freedom of speech, or there can be no "expression" of the will of the individual. There must be universal suffrage and free elections, representation by population and required sittings and elections of legislative institutions, or there can be no "expression of the common will." The right to privacy is a prerequisite to freedom of speech, expression, thought, conscience, opinion, assembly and association. It is inconsistent to guarantee these rights directly when a person's knowledge that his privacy might be violated will indirectly inhibit the exercise of the guaranteed rights. All of the above rights are prerequisites to the proper exercise of democracy.[34]

Thus I am suggesting that the two central themes running through the *Charter* are the ideas of democracy and community. Yet, even if it were conceded that this was a plausible reading of the *Charter*, a number of important problems would remain. First, the idea of democracy seems so vague and indeterminate that it appears rather unhelpful as a basis for judicial review. How do democratic values make a difference in terms of the interpretation of specific provisions of the *Charter*? Second, even if the idea of democracy were determinate enough to make a difference, what distinguishes this reading of the *Charter* from other possible readings? Why is the reading of the document which I suggest a better reading of the document as a whole? It is to these important questions that I now turn.

5. THE DEMOCRATIC IDEAL

Few concepts in political theory are more contested than that of democracy. Much of the current controversy centers over the extent to which democracy requires that citizens play an active role in making decisions which affect their lives. The current practice of democracy certainly gives rather limited expression to this participatory ideal. Rather than make decisions themselves, citizens in modern democracies simply choose the experts or representatives who will make such decisions on their behalf. The great challenge for modern democratic theory has been to justify the highly elitist character of contemporary democratic practice.

A variety of justifications have been offered, most of them

---

34 The Right Honourable Mr. Justice Brian Dickson, "The Democratic Character of the Charter of Rights", in F.L. Morton, *Law, Politics and the Judicial Process in Canada*. (1984) at 327 (quoting the Committee on the Constitution of the Canadian Bar Association).

centering on the "realism" of representative forms of democracy.[35] The starting point of such arguments is Robert Dahl's observation that "Homo Civicus is not by nature a political animal".[36] The vast majority of citizens are largely apathetic about public affairs.[37] Those individuals who do engage in the minimal political act of voting do not engage in a rational, informed analysis of the issues; rather, voting studies have consistently confirmed that questions of party loyalty, candidate's personalities, prejudice and custom are the chief determinants of voter choice. Moreover, elite theorists regard the low levels of citizen participation and interest as desirable. There is strong evidence to suggest that mass publics are less sympathetic to democratic norms and individual rights than are political elites.[38] If participation were increased, it is argued that the result would be to exacerbate political tensions and jeopardize political stability. Elite theorists claim that it is far better to leave important political decisions to an informed and tolerant elite which is somewhat insulated from the vulgar and authoritarian attitudes of individual citizens. Such analyses have been particularly influential in Canadian political theory; it has been argued that the leaders of Canada's various cultural groups have sought bargains at the elite level in an effort to avoid conflicts among the masses of the various subcultures.[39]

Critics of representative democracy have charged that this limited public participation is neither necessary nor desirable.[40] They have lamented the disappearance of the classical Greek notion of "public freedom" — the belief that individuals should take responsibility for creating and changing the terms on which they lead their lives.[41] The source of the trouble is said to be the proliferation of private and inward-looking conceptions of freedom. Freedom is commonly conceived of as nothing more than the absence of restraint, as "an inner realm into which men might escape at will from the pressures of the

---

35 The classic defence of representative democracy remains the work of Joseph Schumpeter. See, J. Schumpeter, *Capitalism, Socialism and Democracy.* (1943). For other writing in this tradition, see R. Dahl, *Voting.* (1954); R. Dahl, *A Preface to Democratic Theory.* (1956).

36 R. Dahl, *Who Governs?* (1961) at 225.

37 See, e.g., S. Verba and N. Nie, *Participation in America.* (1972); W. Mishler, *Political Participation in Canada* (1979).

38 See H. McClosky, "Consensus and Ideology in American Politics", 64 American Political Science Review 361, 375 (1964).

39 See R. Presthus, *Elite Accommodation in Canadian Politics.* (1973).

40 See, e.g. H. Arendt, *On Revolution.* (1963); C. Pateman, *Participation and Democratic Theory.* (1970).

41 See Frug, *supra*, note 24 at 1068.

world".[42] This purely negative conception of freedom has cheapened and trivialized its meaning. Instead of continuing to view freedom as protection for our private lives, Arendt and others urge us to recapture a forgotten, alternative vision of the idea; freedom as active participation in public decision-making. The truncated character of the contemporary vision of freedom has made the task of creating shared, reflective public values an impossibility. In short, it has undermined values of community in favour of an empty cult of privatism.

Given these radically different visions of democracy, it may be surprising to discover that many of the differences between these competing positions are empirical in nature. A central issue in dispute, for example, is the extent, causes and consequences of citizen participation in contemporary democracy. The basic contention of elite theorists is that apathy and authoritarianism are natural and inevitable; increased participation is both impractical and dangerous. Participatory democrats, in contrast, maintain that apathy is learned rather than natural and that increased citizen participation would contribute to individual empowerment without endangering social stability. Such empirical assertions are testable and, indeed, there is an extensive body of social science evidence relevant to the controversy.

This evidence confirms the observations of elite theorists with respect to the behaviour of an "average citizen". Historically, citizen participation in Canada has been limited primarily to voting, with less than one-quarter of the eligible population participating in more intensive forms of political activity.[43] But concentration on average levels of participation obscures the fact that there are significant differences in the levels of participation of various identifiable groups in Canadian society. Social standing, ethnicity, religion, sex and age are all effective predictors of one's level of political participation.[44] The higher an individual's occupation, income and education, the more likely it is that he or she will participate in politics. Citizens of Anglo-Celtic descent participate more extensively in most areas of political life. Women participate less extensively in virtually every form of political activity than do men. In terms of age, those in middle age, from 35 to 65, participate more extensively than do older citizens or those ages 21 to 35.

---

42 Arendt, *supra*, note 40 at 120.
43 The leading study on the issue of participation in Canada is Mishler, *supra*, note 37.
44 See generally, *ibid.* at 88-113.

What this suggests is that levels of political participation are learned rather than given. There is nothing inherent in "human nature" which tends towards apathy and public disinterest. Levels of political participation are the products of human experience and motivation rather than biological necessity. Moreover, there appears to be a strong relationship between the quantity of citizen participation and its quality. Those citizens who participate the most exhibit the highest levels of political tolerance and tend to be better informed about issues of public policy. Conversely, prejudice and dogmatism have been found to be most prevalent amongst those least active in politics.[45] The relationship between political efficacy and participation has been confirmed by studies of democracy in "non-political" settings, such as the family, the school and the workplace. Citizens who are given the opportunity to participate in decision-making in these settings are likely to carry a generalized sense of personal competence into the political sphere.[46] Thus, participation by untrained and inexpert citizens does not breed mob rule. Rather, it increases the individual's self-esteem while promoting tolerance and respect for the interests of the community as a whole.

This suggests the possibility of pushing beyond the debate between the defenders and the critics of current forms of representative government. The starting point of the analysis would be the current practice and understanding of democracy, rather than some utopian, classical democratic community. Thus, the analysis would accept the proposition that professional politicians and bureaucrats will continue to be responsible for the day-to-day management of public policy. But the widespread citizen apathy and ignorance which characterizes contemporary liberal democracies would be lamented rather than praised. The positive value of citizen participation for political life would be recognized. Citizen participation would be valued for its role in producing better informed and tolerant citizens. It would also be seen as a means of ensuring greater responsiveness on the part of state officials to the needs and desires of the public as a whole. The overriding goal would be to enhance the opportunities for popular debate, argument and accountability. This approach would encourage

---

45 Although there is little Canadian evidence on this issue, numerous American studies have found a correlation between levels of political activity and a greater degree of tolerance as well as a higher sense of political efficacy. See H. McClosky *et al.*, "Issue Conflict and Consensus Among Party Leaders and Followers", 54 American Political Science Review 406 (1960); McClosky, *supra*, note 38.

46 Mishler, *supra*, note 37 at 108-110 (summarizing literature on this issue).

citizen involvement in political activities which were more intensive than voting. It would also support participation in such "non-political" settings as the family, the school and the workplace as a means of encouraging political efficacy and education.

The second stage in the analysis would be to situate democratic values within a larger historical framework. Viewed in terms of political developments over the past 200 years, democracy is a manifestation of what Roberto Unger has termed "modernism". Unger defines modernism in the following terms:

> By modernism I mean the movement in art and theory that from the early decades of the twentieth century, attacked the hierarchies of value and the constraints upon personal and collective experimentation that distinguished Western bourgeois society, sometimes to replace them with other, preferred constraints and hierarchies, but more often with the aim of permanently weakening all those structures of practice or belief that remain impervious to criticism and transformation in the course of normal social activity. According to the modernists, freedom requires, indeed represents, a struggle against arbitrary compulsion.[47]

Democracy is a reflection and response to precisely these sentiments. It is a reaction against the view that there is a natural or inevitable structure to social arrangements. The contexts that define human activity are the products of human reason and desire rather than the sacred embroidery of divine will or impersonal fate. Given the artifactual nature of any set of institutional arrangements, it follows that those arrangements ought to be subject to some form of meaningful debate and criticism. Democracy is the forum and the means for that debate. It seeks to subject formative structures and hierarchies to criticism and revision in the course of routine political activity. It liberates social life from the illusion that current institutional arrangements exhaust the realm of possibility. Democratic politics is built on the revolutionary discovery of plasticity in social life — the idea that there is a difference between the way things are and the way they might be.

This elaboration of democracy translates into two general principles which might provide a framework for judicial review. The first principle is a right of equal access to and participation in the political process. Judicial review would attempt to protect the basic infrastructure of liberal democracy — rights of assembly, debate and free elections. No citizen ought to be excluded from participation in the

---

47 R. Unger, *supra*, note 13 at 660.

process of collective debate and argument except on compelling grounds. But this first principle must not be interpreted in purely formal and negative terms. The emphasis must be on *equal* access and participation as opposed to participation *per se*. The court's analysis must take account of the fact that formal access does not guarantee equal access; moreover, it must appreciate the particular concern of legislatures in the past to bridge the gap between formal and effective rights of access. The state does not act merely to impair freedom, but also to ameliorate it. Freedom is not just the absence of restraint, but the ability to participate effectively in collective decision-making. This suggests that where the state acts in such a way as to improve equal access, there should be a strong presumption in favour of the constitutional validity of such a measure.

The second principle is complementary to the first. I have suggested that democracy implies plasticity and transformation in social arrangements. Thus, judicial review should always attempt to maximize openness and the possibility of revision in social life. It should resist the impulse to freeze into place, through constitutional fiat, a particular set of economic, social or political arrangements. Rather, the goal should be to ensure that all social arrangements are subject to meaningful debate and transformation through the political process. The judiciary should strive to be part of a politics that is "governed by a radical skepticism with regard to every stopping place that is suggested, suspicious of every attempt to limit the enquiry".[48]

These principles may seem overly abstract to be of any value in adjudication. Perhaps the only way to illustrate the practical "bite" of these principles is by drawing out their implications for concrete constitutional issues. A small word of caution is in order in this regard. The theory of judicial review which I am defending is not intended to serve as some comprehensive hornbook which will enable lawyers to "look up" the answers to *Charter* problems. This is not the purpose or function of general theory. The more modest ambition is to provide a larger backdrop which will lend structure and intelligibility to legal analysis under the *Charter*. It is an attempt to identify the point of the enterprise. The theory helps to identify the types of arguments and considerations which ought to count in interpreting the *Charter*, as opposed to those which ought to be deemed irrelevant. It offers a measuring rod for choosing between various competing and plausible definitions of a right protected by the *Charter*. It offers weights and

---

48 M. Oakeshott, "The Concept of a Philosophical Jurisprudence", *Politica*, 348 (1938).

measures to assist the court in "balancing" rights against larger considerations of social utility.

6. THE QUESTION OF WELFARE RIGHTS

It might be thought that one implication of the democratic approach is that the judiciary ought to assume the task of wholly reconstituting the nature and practice of democracy. For instance, given the widespread evidence that levels of political participation decline with social and economic status,[49] it might be thought necessary for the judiciary to provide citizens with the material and intellectual resources to enable them to participate fully in the democratic process. One implication is that the judiciary should read into the constitution a set of "welfare rights" which guarantee minimum levels of income, housing and education. A number of American writers have argued in favour of such welfare rights on the basis that, without a minimum level of material resources, problems of unequal access will never be overcome.[50]

But this welfare rights approach is neither "logical" nor desirable in principle. The difficulty is that constitutionalizing such rights would vastly limit the scope for democratic debate and dialogue rather than expand it. The judiciary, rather than the legislature, would have to assume responsibility for defining the scope and character of the welfare system. It would have to determine how much money to allocate to social programmes and the trade-offs between such programmes and other measures in the government's budget. Once the judiciary embarked on such a project there would be no turning back. Ultimately, budgets and tax measures would have to be drafted by judges and lawyers rather than the legislature. It is precisely this result that the democratic conception of judicial review was designed to avoid in the first place.

Moreover, the "welfare rights" approach ignores the historical fact that it has always been legislatures rather than courts which have taken the initiative in improving equal political access. Elected representatives, acting through the democratic process, have been responsible for putting in place the basic elements of the modern welfare state. The judiciary, far from promoting such redistributive

---

49 See R. Dahl, *Democracy in the United States*, 3rd ed. (1976) at 450.
50 See, e.g. Michelman, "On Protecting the Poor Through the Fourteenth Amendment", 83 Harv. L. Rev. 1383 (1969).

or social welfare measures, has often been keen to block them. Thus, the basic responsibility for improving equal access and participation should remain with the legislature rather than courts, in keeping with the historical record.

7. EQUALITY RIGHTS

In general terms, the approach to equality rights which I prefer is one directed towards the manner in which political outcomes are produced rather than the substantive equality of the outcomes themselves. But in what way could the process of decision-making, as opposed to the outcomes themselves, be said to violate a norm of equality? John Hart Ely, in struggling with this difficult issue, formulated an answer based on the concept of "prejudice" towards discrete and insular minorities. While acknowledging that "prejudice" was a "mushword", he suggested that the core notion of prejudice was a "lens that distorts reality".[51] We act out of prejudice when we inflict inequality for its own sake, "to treat a group worse not in the service of some overriding social goal but largely for the sake of simply disadvantaging its members".[52] Ely argues that we are likely to develop such prejudice against a minority which is "discrete and insular". Where there is little social contact between the minority and society as a whole, it is likely that unjustified stereotypical generalizations about their characteristics will arise.

Yet the concept of "prejudice" seems a rather implausible basis for argument under an equal protection guarantee. It requires a court to inquire into the motives behind legislation and make extremely fine distinctions. How, for example, is the court to distinguish between "prejudice" on the one hand and a simple preference for one's own interests over those of the minority on the other? There seem to be relatively few public policy choices which inflict harm "for its own sake"; most choices prefer the interests of certain groups at the expense of those of others. Nor can it be said that, in instances where the inequality between two groups is very great, the advantaged group is imposing burdens on the basis of "prejudice". In principle, there is no constraint on the social cost which a special interest group will find it expedient to impose on other groups in society in the course

---

51 Ely, *supra*, note 2 at 153.
52 *Ibid.*

of obtaining a larger share of output for itself.[53] A finding of "prejudice" seems little more than a rhetorical, pejorative construct which legitimizes overturning legislative choices with which judges happen to disagree.

The empty character of the "prejudice" criterion is exemplified by the fact that Ely himself appears to abandon it in his discussion of whether particular groups qualify as "discrete and insular minorities". For instance, in the case of women, Ely does not claim that they have been the victims of harm inflicted "for its own sake". Rather, he suggests that the trouble is that women have been operating at an "unfair disadvantage" in the political process. They have been largely excluded from the political process, which has been pervasively dominated by men.[54] He concludes, however, that this exclusion is a historical phenomenon and that any lack of participation by women in the 1980s must be due to their own conscious choice:

> On this score it seems important that today discussion about the appropriate "place" of women is common among both women and men, and between the sexes as well. The very stereotypes that gave rise to laws "protecting" women by barring them from various activities are under daily and publicized attack and are the subject of equally spirited defense. . . . Given such open discussion of the traditional stereotypes, the claim that the numerical majority is being "dominated", that women are in effect "slaves" who have no realistic choice but to assimilate the stereotypes, is one it has become impossible to maintain except at the most inflated rhetorical level.[55]

It is no doubt true that many of the existing "stereotypes" about women are under attack in both popular and elite circles. But it is nevertheless true that social and economic inequality between the sexes remains a pervasive fact of North American society in the 1980s. The underlying social and economic position of women may have improved over the past 25 years, but it remains vastly inferior to that of men according to virtually all measures. The continuing unequal status of women may have relatively little to do with motives such as "prejudice" and much more to do with more observable factors such as access to and participation in the political process.

As was indicated above, women continue to participate less extensively in the political process than do men, although the gap between the sexes is generally narrowing. The gap in participation

---

53 See M. Olson, *The Rise and Decline of Nations*. (1982) at 44.

54 Ely, *supra*, note 2 at 164-166.

55 *Ibid.* at 166.

rates remains particularly stark in terms of the number of women seeking and securing public office. Women remain the most under-represented group in elected assemblies today.[56] Elected women become rarer as one moves from the level of municipal politics to the federal level. On the federal level, although the number of women running for office doubled from 1972 to 1979, less than 14% of the candidates in the 1979 general election were women. Less than one in ten women running for federal office in the 1970s was elected, as opposed to a success rate of one in five for male candidates. This unequal success rate was not a product of "false consciousness" on the part of women who, after all, comprise approximately half the electorate. An analysis of the 1979 election traced the failure of women to get elected to two factors. First, the pattern of recruitment by the major parties was such that women tended to be nominated in so-called "lost cause" ridings, where the party had little prospect for success. Second, there was a substantial increase in the number of women contesting election as independents with little realistic chance of winning.[57]

The situation of women is merely a special case of the more general phenomenon outlined earlier in this section; rates of political participation vary considerably based on factors such as ethnicity, social status, age and gender. This suggests an alternative conception of the equality norm in a process-based theory of judicial review. On this view, the norm of equality is designed to take account of the fact that certain groups and individuals possess unequal access to the political system. Despite guarantees of formal access, certain groups may nevertheless come to enjoy a *de facto* monopoly over state power, leading to the exclusion of certain minorities from effective partic-ipation in the system. The equality norm is an attempt to counter the presence of these systematic, but subtle, defects in the process. It claims that it is appropriate for the judiciary to subject decisions reached through such a tainted process to a heightened standard of review.

For this theory to be plausible, it is necessary to make an important assumption about the relationship between political participation and the outcomes of the policy process. Simply put, the assumption is that participation makes a difference. The argument is that the political

---

56 M. Janine Brodie, "The Recruitment of Canadian Women Provincial Legislators, 1950-75", 2 Atlantis 6 (1977); M. Janine Brodie and Jill Vickers, "The More Things Change . . . Women in the 1979 Federal Campaign", in H. Penniman, ed., *Canada at the Polls 1979 and 1980: a Study of the General Elections.* (1981) at 322.

57 Brodie and Vickers, *supra,* note 56 at 326-327.

process will tend to ignore or to discount the interests of those who are unequally represented. Similarly, the process will tend to favour the interests of those groups who are most vocal and politically active. The argument is captured by John Stuart Mill, who observed that "in the absence of its natural defenders, the interest of the excluded is always in danger of being overlooked; and, when looked at, is seen with very different eyes from those of the person who it directly concerns."[58]

It should be cautioned that there is relatively little empirical evidence regarding the consequences of participation for public policy. But there are strong theoretical reasons for assuming that varying rates of political participation and awareness will have an impact on the policy process. Recent studies of the policy process have advanced a model of "political rationality" to explain public choices.[59] According to this model, impersonal considerations such as technical efficiency offer relatively weak predictors of public policy. The model of "political rationality" predicts that politicians will seek outcomes which will maximize their own interests, namely, the likelihood of their securing re-election. This model would suggest that even relatively modest changes in the composition of the politically active segments in society would stimulate significant changes in government priorities.

The evidence which is available suggests that participation does matter and that government is most responsive to the interests of those who participate the most extensively and in the most demanding political activities.[60] For example, the gradual expansion of opportunities for working-class participation in political life has induced greater attention to the interests of the disadvantaged, particularly in provinces where the CCF-NDP has constituted a major party. My claim is not that the state will always and everywhere favour the interests of the politically powerful while ignoring those of the politically inactive or uninformed. There is no crude, determinist conspiracy at work here. The point is simply that differential rates of participation constitute a systemic bias in the process, making it

---

58 J.S. Mill, "Considerations on Representative Government", bk. III, in *Utilitarianism, Liberty and Representative Government*, quoted in Mishler, *supra*, note 37 at 133.

59 See M.J. Trebilcock *et al*, "The Choice of Governing Instrument" (Economic Council of Canada, 1981).

60 See W. Mishler, "Political Participation and Democracy", in M.S. Whittington and G. Williams, eds., *Canadian Politics in the 1980s* (1981) at 138-139.

politically irrational for elected representatives to weight competing interests in an even-handed manner.

The principle of equality of access offers a far more convincing explanation of American equal protection doctrine than does a theory based on the indeterminate notion of "prejudice". Consider the issue of racial equality, the central and continuing focus of equal protection doctrine. According to Ely's analysis, the court can identify legislation which violates the norm of racial equality by examining the motivation underlying racially discriminatory legislation. Legislation which is enacted in order to inflict harm "for its own sake" violates the norm of equality, while legislation which simply prefers the interests of certain racial groups at the expense of others is the normal and legitimate product of the political system. The first difficulty with this claim has already been pointed out in the discussion of gender; because all legislation prefers the interests of certain groups over those of others, it is impossible to identify legislation which inflicts harm solely for its own sake. Yet, even if the distinction were meaningful, why should the issue of motivation prove conclusive? Surely *all* laws which single out certain racial minorities for discriminatory treatment are suspect, not simply a narrow class of laws which inflicts harm "for its own sake". The reason why all such discriminatory laws are suspect is that certain racial minorities have historically been denied equal access to the political system. The absence of equal access has this important implication: it does not matter whether the discriminatory legislation was enacted out of a simple preference for the interests of the majority over those of the minority, or whether it was motivated by "prejudice". In either event, the legislation is the tainted fruit of a tainted process. The disadvantaged minority did not have an equal voice in the process and for this reason it is illegitimate for the majority to have disregarded the minority's interests.

The notion that equal protection analysis should be triggered by unequal access to the political process is by no means a simple or mechanical concept. It still requires the judiciary to make substantive judgments of political morality. But it avoids a pointless and elusive inquiry into the motivation behind racially discriminatory legislation. Moreover, it illuminates more recent developments in American equal protection analysis. The extension of heightened judicial scrutiny to classifications based on gender seems a response to the fact that women, like blacks and other racial minorities, have lacked an equal voice in the political process. Moreover, the criteria of political access offers a principled basis for holding that affirmative action programmes do not violate the constitutional norm of equality. It is true that such programmes "discriminate" against certain groups or individuals on the basis of racial criteria. But the difference is that the groups or individuals who stand to lose through affirmative action programmes have never been denied access to the political system. Rather, they are individuals like Allan Bakke, a white male whose interests historically have been vastly overrepresented in the political process. If the legislature determines that the interests of someone in Allan Bakke's position must give way in the face of the claims of certain racial minorities, Mr. Bakke has no basis for a constitutional complaint.

Of course, the question of affirmative action was dealt with explicitly in the Canadian *Charter*. Section 15(2) provides that the guarantee of equality rights in s. 15(1) does not preclude programmes designed to ameliorate the conditions of "disadvantaged" individuals or groups. But it is comforting to discover that s. 15(2) can be explained and justified on principled rather than expedient grounds. In addition, the analysis advanced here offers some basis for distinguishing those groups which should be deemed to be "disadvantaged" for the purposes of s. 15(2). In short, the principle of equal access to the political system constitutes the background purpose of both ss. 15(1) and 15(2) of the *Charter*. Reliance on this principle will not eliminate doctrinal ambiguity. But it will enable the courts to sort through the mass of conflicting claims that are certain to arise under the equality clause in an intelligible fashion.

8. FREE EXPRESSION

It is not my intention to deal comprehensively with all the issues which arise in terms of the guarantee of "freedom of expression" under s. 2 of the *Charter*. My focus is the narrow but vexing question of government attempts to regulate the amount of money that can be spent by candidates or individuals in election campaigns. In both Canada and the United States, the state has taken steps to insulate the electoral process from the effects of money. In both jurisdictions, the courts have interpreted constitutional guarantees of free speech so as to prohibit or to limit the regulation of campaign finance. In the United States, the Supreme Court struck down attempts by Congress to limit the amount of money which could be spent by a candidate or by an individual on the candidate's behalf.[61] In Canada,

---

61 See *Buckley v. Valeo*, 424 U.S. 1 (1976).

a provision in the *Canada Elections Act*,[62] which prohibited "third party" advertising during an election campaign was ruled invalid due to the guarantee of freedom of expression in s. 2 of the *Charter*.[63]

The reasoning of the American court was that campaign expenditures constituted speech "at the core of the first Amendment". The only "compelling" reason justifying government restriction of such speech was to prevent corruption or the appearance of corruption in the political process. Since the expenditure of money merely expressed an opinion and did not raise the spectre of corruption, attempts to regulate such expenditures were unconstitutional.

The approach of the Canadian court in the *National Citizens Coalition* case was far less categorical. The government apparently made no attempt to justify the limits on third party spending on the basis of a fear of corruption. The government's primary justification for the legislation was the need to ensure a level of equality amongst all participants in federal elections. It was argued that since parties and candidates are subject to spending limits, the absence of spending limits on third parties would give unfair advantage to wealthy interest groups. Mr. Justice Medhurst did not indicate whether this principle of equality was a legitimate government objective. His Lordship added that the court could not consider whether there may have been other, less restrictive means available to achieve the objective. This would be rewriting the legislation, which was a "political", as opposed to a "legal", task. Medhurst J. based his finding of invalidity on the simple fact that there should be "actual demonstration of harm or a real likelihood of harm to a society value before a limitation can be said to be justified". In this instance, the government had advanced nothing more than "fears or concerns of mischief that may occur", and this evidence was insufficient to justify the limitation on rights of expression.[64] This analysis, although dealing only with the narrow question of third party spending, is an implied attack on the regulation of expenditures by candidates as well. It is hard to see how the government could demonstrate that there was any more "actual harm" from candidates' expenditures as opposed to expenditures by third parties.

How might a democratic theory along the lines I propose deal with the issue of election campaign finance? The first point to note is that the theory does not necessarily "demand" or "require" a

---

62 *Canada Elections Act*, R.S.C. 1970, c. 14 (1st Supp.).
63 See *National Citizens Coalition Inc. v. A.G. Can.*, [1984] 5 W.W.R. 436 (Alta. Q.B.).
64 *Ibid.*

particular result. But in general terms, I would be far more sympathetic to campaign finance regulation than either the Canadian or the American courts have been. If we begin with the proposition that freedom is not simply the absence of restraint, it becomes possible to conceive of the regulation of campaign finance as ameliorating freedom rather than limiting it. The point of the legislation is to restrict the ability of certain wealthy groups or interests to dominate election campaigns through the expenditure of money. The legislation is designed to ensure that no one political perspective is permitted to drown out the competing messages in the electoral marketplace. This justification becomes convincing once you push beyond questions of formal access and negative freedom and focus instead on issues of equality of access and positive freedom.

Basic democratic values suggest that government attempts to improve equal access is an objective that is weighty or "compelling". Far from mandating that certain factions or interests be permitted to dominate the political process, democracy implies that such radical inequality subverts the proper working of the process. If this assumption is accepted, the question then becomes an instrumental one of matching means to ends; has the government pursued its objective in a way that does not unnecessarily compromise other important societal values? One need not use a sledgehammer to kill a fly. This is one way of construing Mr. Justice Medhurst's statement that the government could not justify its legislation on the basis of "concerns of mischief which may occur". The implication seems to be that, given the limited amount of third party spending in the past, there was no need for the government to impose an absolute prohibition on all spending. The government could have achieved its objective through a more finely tuned regulation, such as the previous legislation which had permitted a "good faith" defence.[65]

Mr. Justice Medhurst claims that he is not engaging in any such instrumental analysis of matching means to ends. But once the basic governmental objective of equality in the electoral marketplace is accepted as legitimate, the only remaining issue is whether the

---

65 The specific restriction considered in the case had been an amendment to the Act, enacted in 1983. It had abolished a "good faith" exception which had existed in the legislation. The exception provided that a defence could be claimed by third parties if they could establish that their expenditures were incurred with respect to an issue of public policy, and had not been incurred in collusion with a party or candidate for the purpose of defeating provisions on spending restrictions. For a short history of the legislation, see judgment of Medhurst J., *ibid.* at 442-444.

means. This is indeed a "political" or normative analysis, as Medhurst J. recognizes. But it has long been a commonplace feature of constitutional adjudication in the United States and the same will necessarily be so in Canada.

The analysis advanced here does not yield a "right" answer to the constitutional issue. But it does suggest that the American approach, with its narrow focus on "corruption" as a justification for campaign finance regulation, ought not be followed. The analysis of the American courts is predicated on a wholly negative view of freedom, with no recognition of the fact that the legislation is designed to enhance positive freedom and effective access to the political arena. Constitutional argument in this instance should be limited to the narrow issue of whether the means chosen by the government to achieve this important objective is unduly restrictive of other social values.

9. SECTION 1 ANALYSIS

In earlier portions of this book, I have been highly critical of the s. 1 analysis suggested in the *Oakes* case. I argued that the *Oakes* test was overly restrictive and inflexible. I also pointed out the highly political character of the "proportionality" test put forward by the Court.

Yet the fact that the proportionality test requires political choices by courts does not necessarily mean it ought to be abandoned. The inescapable reality of the *Charter* era is that the judiciary will inevitably be drawn into making fundamental value choices. The issue is not whether or not political choices will be made by courts. The issue is whether those choices will be made well or badly.

Viewed against this backdrop, there are certain compelling attractions to some form of proportionality test as the basis of s. 1 analysis. A proportionality approach does require an assessment of the goals of legislation, but this analysis occurs at the margin. The starting point of the analysis is the particular regulatory framework enacted by the legislature and the goals of that framework. The analysis then attempts to assess the costs and benefits of alternative regulatory instruments which might have been employed to achieve similar goals. The analysis is necessarily empirical and pragmatic, measuring the effects and the costs of the various alternatives against their stated goals. The analysis would also be flexible. There would not be a fixed standard applicable in the same way to all cases.

The obvious objection to this type of empirical, means-ends analysis is that courts are ill-equipped to make such complex factual and normative judgments. But the answer to this objection is quite straightforward. Courts under the *Charter* will be dealing with complex factual and normative issues. The real question is how to ensure that courts are sensitive to those complexities. Notwithstanding the well-known institutional limitations of courts, they are surely better off attempting to assess the relationship between the means and the ends of laws on the basis of evidence and argument as opposed to mere intuition.

The process of forcing legislatures to justify the fit between the means and ends of legislation is not necessarily incompatible with democracy. The virtue of the exercise is that it forces the legislature to be more self-critical, not only in the context of litigation, but also in the drafting of laws. One of the positive effects of the *Charter* is likely to be a generalized sensitivity by legislatures to the values recognized in the document. Far from subverting democracy, this process has the potential to enhance it. By forcing the political branches to re-evaluate the trade offs involved in proposed and existing legislation, laws are likely to be more carefully drafted and more sensitive to the diversity of interests in the political community.

10. WHY DEMOCRACY AND NOT JUSTICE?

A defender of an outcomes-based theory of judicial review might concede that a democratic theory was intelligible and coherent. However, he or she might continue to maintain that the concern of courts ought to be with justice rather than democracy. Professor Tribe, for example, argues that substance is more fundamental than process in constitutional argument; we object to certain laws because they strike us as substantively repugnant, not because they have been enacted in an improper fashion.[66] Tribe and other defenders of an outcomes-based theory claim that their conception of judicial review is not necessarily inimical to democratic values. They regard judicial review as an institution which stimulates moral argument in a polity. The court, by subjecting legislative judgments to the harsh light of principle, will produce a public morality that is more reflective and self-critical. This dialectical relationship between court and polity "enables us to take seriously . . . the possibility that there are right answers to political-moral problems."[67] Judicial review calls some issues from the "battleground of power politics to the forum of principle", where conflicts

---

66 L. Tribe, *American Constitutional Law*. (1978).
67 M. Perry, *The Constitution, the Courts and Human Rights*. (1982) at 102.

between individual and society "will once, someplace, finally, become questions of justice".[68]

Judicial review may well spark a debate over issues of principle. But it is an elite debate in which only elite voices are heard. This is illustrated most clearly by the low public awareness of Supreme Court decisions. Numerous opinion surveys have confirmed that the public has marginal awareness of legal institutions and decisions.[69] Only about half of the American public can recall any Supreme Court decision.[70] Those respondents who are able to cite a specific decision are likely to have an unfavourable opinion of it, by a margin of at least two to one.[71] Measures of public confidence in various governmental institutions typically rank the Supreme Court below both the President and Congress.

Nor has the American Supreme Court assumed the role of moral prophet or teacher. Over time, public opinion on important constitutional issues has either remained unchanged or moved in a direction opposite to that favoured by the Supreme Court. In the 1960s, the school desegregation decisions were favoured by about 60% of respondents, while the school prayer decisions were opposed by a margin of about three to one.[72] By the 1970s, large majorities remained opposed to the school prayer decisions. In contrast, public support for the Court's desegregation decisions had eroded drastically. Although a majority of respondents remained committed to desegregation in schools, the judicial remedy of busing was opposed by 82% of whites and 33% of blacks.

This empirical evidence suggests that the elimination of popular control in favour of an elite institution like the Supreme Court does not actually promote the long-term cause of justice and equality. The faulty assumption is that values like justice and freedom can be defined in some external, elite forum and then simply announced to a grateful, stupefied public. But the reality is precisely the opposite. Public values cannot be abstractly defined in some prepolitical setting and then imported, like bottle mineral water, into the polluted atmosphere of politics. Values such as justice and equality are the products of politics,

---

68 R. Dworkin, *supra*, note 1 at 71.

69 For a summary and analysis of this literature, see Hyde, "The Concept of Legitimation in the Sociology of Law", Wisconsin Law Review 379 at 408-412 (1983).

70 Murphy and Tanenhaus, "Public Opinion and the United States Supreme Court", 2 Law and Society Review 357 at 366 (1968).

71 *Ibid.* at 370. See also, Adamany and Grossman, "Support for the Supreme Court as a National Policymaker", Law and Policy Quarterly 405 (1983).

72 The survey data is collected and analyzed in Adamany and Grossman, *supra*, note 71 at 422-424.

not its antecedents. They take root in a public that engages in debate and argument and is given the opportunity to nurture notions of reasonableness and commonality. Conversely, when citizens are deprived of control over their own lives, public values and civic energy are corroded. Morality becomes a matter for specialists rather than citizens. Because citizens are no longer competent to define their own values and traditions, public morality will atrophy rather than be purged. The appointment of the philosopher king merely exacerbates the very problem it was designed to remedy.

There is no panacea for bigotry or prejudice. Certainly it would be naive and utopian to suppose that narrow-minded attitudes will automatically disappear within a genuine democratic community. Democracy does not guarantee civic enlightenment. But if the collective morality of the community is to become more informed, this will be achieved through more rather than less democracy. By designing institutions which facilitate ongoing civic participation, citizens will be given the opportunity to participate in public talk and public action. It is only through such public talk that small-minded or superficial attitudes might be exposed and attacked.

Judicial fiat is no substitute for such civic deliberation. Rule by judiciary supposes that the only way to deter oppression is to impose external restraints on the political process. But because such external restraints deny the competence of citizens to arrive at informed ethical judgments, they undermine the very process of reflection and self-criticism which might lead to a more mature collective morality. Elitist politics breeds only a mob; to produce citizens, one needs democracy.

Part 3

The Court and Federalism

7

The Law and Politics of Federalism:
An Overview

1. INTRODUCTION

There is little doubt that public awareness and interest in the Supreme Court has been awakened in the past decade primarily because of the enactment of the *Canadian Charter of Rights and Freedoms*. As we saw in the first part of the book, the *Charter* is thought to have heralded the triumph of values of law and legality over those of unbridled political power. But it is not the *Charter* alone that has spawned a perception that Canadian political life is becoming increasingly judicialized. The politics of Canadian federalism appear to be increasingly dominated by the courts in general and the Supreme Court in particular. With the demise of "co-operative federalism" and the heightening of intergovernmental tensions,[1] as well as the loosening

---

1 See D. Smiley, *Canada in Question: Federalism in the Eighties*, 3rd ed. (1980), who details the rise of what he terms "executive federalism" in the 1970s, in which federal-provincial relations became the prerogative of elected, political actors rather than of members of the bureaucracy. Smiley suggests that this development has led to increased tensions between the respective levels of government, since the political actors are less likely to seek compromise and are less likely to view disputes as mere technical issues which can be resolved in a neutral, apolitical manner.

of traditional limits on standing,[2] the courts rather than the political backrooms have apparently become a primary stage for federal politics. In this theatre, lawyers and judges rather than bureaucrats or ministers block and direct the action.

Of course, the most visible and memorable instance of this was the protracted dispute over the patriation of the constitution, in which the Courts became the forum for a bitter struggle by the provinces to resist the unilateralism of the federal government. But numerous other high profile federal-provincial disputes, including those over oil revenues, the ownership of the off-shore, Senate reform and incomes policy all ended up in the Supreme Court, often at the instance of governments themselves. As one provincial government put it: "These are fundamental federal-provincial issues and they are being resolved by an institution not in the mainstream of the political process."[3] By the middle of the 1980s, it seemed obvious, if somewhat troubling, that the Canadian judiciary had assumed center stage in the politics of Canadian federalism.

The second part of this book is an attempt to make some assessment of the Court's involvement in federalism over the past decade. In this chapter, I offer an extremely crude overview of the evolution of federalism in Canada since 1945. I then examine the Court's federalism workload over the past ten years, indicating the extent to which its presence and influence in this area has grown. The Court has been deciding more federalism cases in the past decade than ever before, and it has become increasingly activist in its decisions.

Subsequent chapters offer in-depth analysis of a number of the Court's more controversial federalism decisions in recent years. Chapter 8 looks at a series of decisions handed down by the Court in the late 1970s and early 1980s dealing with powers of constitutional amendment. I will argue that, while the decisions are ostensibly consistent with each other, in reality there are fundamental inconsistencies and tensions between the various majority opinions. These tensions are indicative of the essentially political nature of the Court's decision-making in the federalism area. At bottom, the Court is being called upon to choose between competing visions of the nature of the Canadian political community. The complex and shifting configuration of the opinions in the constitutional amendment cases reflects the

2 *Min. of Justice, Can. v. Borowski,* [1981] 2 S.C.R. 575 (S.C.C.); *Thorson v. A.G. Can.,* [1975] 1 S.C.R. 138 (S.C.C.).

3 "Reform of the Supreme Court of Canada", *British Columbia's Constitutional Proposals* (Paper No. 4, October 1978) at 45.

different visions of the country espoused by the various members of the Court.

In Chapter 9, "Federalism and the Economy", I examine a controversial series of recent cases interpreting the trade and commerce power. Perhaps the most controversial of these cases were the decisions of the court involving provincial schemes to regulate and tax natural resource industries. Provincial governments had been particularly critical of these decisions, suggesting that they reflected a bias on the part of the Court against provincial interests. I examine whether these charges of bias can be substantiated. I also attempt to measure whether the decisions of the Court had any significant impact on the ability of the provinces to regulate the natural resource sector.

In general terms, I argue that the federalism jurisprudence of the Court in the past decade has been just as "political" as any of its decisions under the *Charter*. But I also suggest that there has been a tendency to exaggerate the instrumental impact of the Court's federalism decisions. Although many of the Court's decisions have received considerable public attention and criticism, I argue that much of this attention has probably been unwarranted. If governments are unhappy with particular judicial results, there are often alternative regulatory instruments which can be employed to substitute around that result. This suggests that there would be little point in attempting to revise significantly or limit the federalism jurisdiction of the Supreme Court.

2. THE SETTING:
THE EVOLUTION OF FEDERALISM 1945–1985

The 1940s represented a watershed for Canadian federalism. Prior to 1940, Canada had been premised on an essentially classical model of federalism. Governments possessed authority over "spheres" of jurisdiction. While there was undeniably considerable consultation and coordination, each level of government regarded it as legitimate to act independently of the other within its allotted sphere. Moreover, there was an intelligible and widely-understood line of demarcation between the responsibilities of Ottawa and the provinces. This was the era of "constitutionalism" — the notion that a legally enforceable document should define the society's federal institutions and establish standards for their evaluation.[4]

---

4 See G. Schochet, "Constitutionalism, Liberalism and the Study of Politics", in J. Pennock and J. Chapman, eds., *Constitutionalism* (1979) at 1, 4. Of course, I do not mean to imply

The last four decades have witnessed the demise of constitutionalism. By 1940, it was apparent that the division of responsibilities expressed in the British North America Act had not merely become irrelevant; these "watertight compartments" now constituted a costly obstacle in the public policy process, particularly in terms of the evolution of the welfare state in the post-war era.

Canada was faced with a fundamental political choice. On the one hand, it could recut the federal-provincial deck of cards, redealing the "spheres" of jurisdiction so that they more closely conformed with the functions and demands of government in the mid-twentieth century. This first option represented a continued commitment to the morality of constitutionalism. Alternatively, the players could have ostensibly continued to play their existing hands, while simply dealing themselves more cards from a second deck in order to strengthen their weak suits. This pragmatic, flexible alternative would have appeared to leave the terms of the federal-provincial deal undisturbed. In fact, it would have amounted to a fundamental transformation in the rules of the game. With each player free to add more cards to his hand at will, at some point the hands of the players would become virtually indistinguishable from each other. The terms of the original deal would be little more than a distant and irrelevant trifle. In fact, the central notion which gave the game its integrity in the first place — the idea that each player should be restricted to holding only certain suits or cards — would eventually seem a mindless and absurd limitation.

Canada in the post-war era chose the second alternative over the first, with precisely these predictable consequences. Rather than seek a fundamental redistribution of "spheres" of jurisdiction, the whole notion of discrete and identifiable spheres of legislative authority was itself abandoned. Converts to modernism, Canadian policymakers now espoused the dogma that all things were inextricably related to all other things. The trouble with the "watertight compartments" view was not so much that it was undesirable; more precisely, it was unattainable, the product of a naive and simplistic world view. Rather than "spheres of jurisdiction", the reconstituted federalism was to be organized around the notion of "levels" of government defending "interests". Each level of government was now concerned with

---

that this ethic of constitutionalism dominated all aspects of political discourse at the time. My point is limited to the realm of federal-provincial relations. Nor do I mean to suggest that there were not features and practices of federalism at the time that did not fit within the assumptions of constitutionalism. My point is merely that the federal tradition largely conformed to this ethic in the period prior to 1940.

virtually the whole range of public policy issues. The hands of the players had indeed become indistinguishable from each other. The only way to differentiate the players from each other was to identify the various social, economic and political interests they represented at any given moment. Having banished considerations of principle, federalism was essentially just another form of *Realpolitik*.

One important indication of the new federalism was the growth of federal transfer payments to the provinces.[5] In 1949, federal cash transfers to the provinces (excluding tax-rental payments) amounted to 5.9 per cent of federal spending; by the 1957–62 period, transfers had nearly doubled, to 10.2 per cent of federal spending; by 1971–72, transfers had doubled again, to 23 per cent of federal spending. In effect, nearly one-quarter of all federal spending in 1970 was being directed to objectives nominally within provincial jurisdiction.

At the same time, provincial governments were becoming increasingly dependent on federal transfers for revenue. Whereas federal transfers to provinces had amounted to 13.4 per cent of provincial revenues in 1949–52, the proportion had increased to slightly over 25 per cent by 1971–72. Moreover, these transfers increasingly took the form of conditional grants as opposed to unconditional transfers; at their peak in 1967, conditional grants represented 83 per cent of federal payments to provinces.[6]

It would be mistaken to suppose that these developments necessarily implied greater centralization of power. First, the very fact that the post-war growth of government was taking place in areas of traditional provincial jurisdiction meant that the federal government increasingly required the cooperation of the provinces in order to achieve what were styled "national" policy objectives. Moreover, beginning in the early 1960s and led by the Lesage administration in Quebec, provincial governments became committed to explicit programmes of regional economic development.[7] The Lesage programme included policies with respect to regional economic development, vocational training, the exploitation of natural resources, cultural

---

5 The figures in this paragraph are taken from K. Dowd and A. Sayeed, "Federal-Provincial Fiscal Relations: Some Background" in T. Courchene, D. Conklin and G. Cook, eds., *Ottawa and the Provinces: The Distribution of Money and Power*, vol. 2 (1985) at Table 9, 253, 268.

6 See generally Royal Commission on the Economic Union and Development Prospects for Canada, *Report* vol. III (1985), at 237-247.

7 For a description and analysis of these trends, see D. Smiley, *Constitutional Adaptation and Canadian Federalism Since 1945* (Royal Commission on Bilingualism and Biculturalism, 1970) at 29-32.

affairs, and the channelling of private savings into provincial economic development. In short, Quebec now regarded itself as being responsible for developing an autonomous and distinct provincial community, not only in cultural, but in economic terms. Moreover, the province was no longer willing to play the subordinate role that had been envisaged by the federal drafters of the New National Policy in the 1940s. By the mid-1960s, the other provincial governments began committing themselves to similar programmes of comprehensive economic development. Already, the new phenomenon had a name: "province building".[8]

The terms of the debate had now changed. The discourse was no longer about "rights", but about "interests". Cooperation and consultation was not simply required when one government pursued policies in areas nominally under the jurisdiction of the other, such as shared-cost programmes. Collaboration was seen as essential in any case in which the policies of one government had effects on those of another. Premier Lesage of Quebec defined the new assumptions at the federal-provincial conference of 1965, when he argued that "a government may not do exactly as it pleases simply because it has legal authority in a given field."[9] Even when a government was legislating in fields that fell within its own jurisdiction, "it must see that its actions are compatible with those of the other legislative authorities, and do not infringe on their rights and privileges."[10]

The notion that governments exercised "exclusive jurisdiction" over "classes of subjects" as set out in the B.N.A. Act had become a kind of meaningless sham. Anyone who actually believed or asserted such claims to exclusivity was not merely foolish, but rude. Thus, when Premier Lesage had informed an earlier federal-provincial conference in the 1960s that Quebec intended to pursue its "rights" in the courts, this was widely interpreted as a challenge to the federal system itself.[11] Lesage was attempting to pay heed, rather than mere lip service, to the discredited values of constitutionalism. The power of the new orthodoxy was reflected in the fact that Lesage was roundly criticized, not just by the federal government, but by the other provinces, for his betrayal of the understandings surrounding the new federalism.

---

8 See Smiley, *supra*, note 1.

9 J. Lesage, "Opening Statement" (Federal-Provincial Conference, July 1965), quoted in Smiley, *supra*, note 7, at 83.

10 *Ibid.*

11 *Ibid.* at 40.

Indeed, it was only in Quebec that voices were raised in defence of constitutionalism, most notably by Pierre Elliott Trudeau. In his brilliant essay, "The practice and theory of federalism",[12] Trudeau documented the "sometimes subtle, sometimes brazen, and usually tolerated encroachments by one government upon the jurisdiction of the other."[13] Trudeau was particularly critical of the use of the federal spending power in order to ensure that the provinces were properly exercising the rights they held under the constitution. The provisions of the B.N.A. Act had become an illusory constraint: "it almost seems as though whenever an important segment of the Canadian population needs something badly enough, it is eventually given to them by one level of government or the other, regardless of the constitution."[14] The trouble with this federal practice, according to Trudeau, was that it undermined democratic values. When one government intervened in an area falling under the other's jurisdiction, it blurred accountability to the electorate and retarded democratic debate and argument.[15]

Yet Trudeau's arguments went unheeded, even after he had become leader of the federal Liberals and Prime Minister. By the 1970s, the era of "cooperative federalism" had given way to "executive federalism",[16] but the basic assumptions regarding overlapping of jurisdictions remained the same. It was only in the late 1970s and early 1980s that serious efforts were made to "disentangle" federal and provincial responsibilities. In large part, this effort at disentanglement came at the initiative of the federal government. For a variety of reasons, the federal government had lost faith in the established system

---

12 See M. Oliver, ed., *Social Purpose for Canada* (1961) at 371.

13 *Ibid.* at 382.

14 *Ibid.*

15 "To give but one example: from the Quebec point of view, the most serious objection to federal grants to universities was obviously not that the universities had enough money or that the federal money had a particular odour; it was that once the universities had their bellies filled with federal grants they would see no reason to oppose that provincial government which had persistently failed in its constitutional duties by leaving education in such an impoverished state; and Quebeckers would chalk up another failure in their struggle to master the art of self-government." *Ibid.* at 384.

16 These are the terms used by Smiley, *supra*, note 1. According to Smiley, "cooperative federalism" was characterized by collaboration on specific programmes on an *ad hoc* basis; the governments tended to be represented by technical officials, who shared a common set of values and programme objectives. The move to executive federalism replaced these programme officials with politicians or high-ranking bureaucrats, who were much less likely to share any common set of values or assumptions. Smiley argues that executive federalism is more likely to promote conflict, since the individuals involved come to the bargaining table with fundamentally contradictory goals and visions of the country.

of federal-provincial collaboration.[17] The federal government claimed that executive federalism had given the provinces power to irresponsibly block reforms which were clearly in the interests of all Canadians. The constitutional "straightjacket" was cited as an exemplary instance of this provincial veto power. It was also thought that the federal government had become isolated from individual citizens. The provinces were able to claim exclusive political credit for the delivery of goods and services which had been partly financed by federal money.

The re-election of the Liberal government in 1980 signalled the beginning of an era of unilateralism by the federal government. Unilateralism was pursued simultaneously on a number of fronts, including the constitution, energy policy and the fiscal arrangements. The defining characteristic of the federal strategy was that it embraced policy areas in which federal-provincial cooperation and agreement had become the accepted norm. In the constitutional area, there was a widespread understanding that provincial legislative powers would not be disturbed without prior provincial consent.[18] Energy policy throughout the 1970s had been formulated through bilateral pricing agreements between the federal government and the energy-producing provinces. Fiscal transfers to the provinces had been the subject of extensive federal-provincial bargaining dating back to the tax-rental agreements of 1947. In all of these crucial policy areas, the federal government now asserted the right and responsibility to act unilaterally.[19] Such action was legitimate, according to the federal government, because the national government was the voice of the national interest. Transcending the parochialism of the provincial premiers, Ottawa alone could "speak for Canada."

---

17 The federal critiques of executive federalism are summarized in McRoberts, "Unilateralism, Bilateralism and Multilateralism: Approaches to Canadian federalism" in R. Simeon, ed., *Intergovernmental Relations* (Royal Commission on the Economic Union Research Studies, 1985), vol. 63. The arguments outlined in the following paragraph are drawn from McRoberts' account.

18 The Supreme Court of Canada, in its judgment on the patriation of the constitution in September 1981, concluded that there was a "convention", or political norm, requiring provincial consent in cases where provincial legislative powers were to be altered. See *Ref. re Amendment of the Constitution of Can. (Nos. 1, 2, 3)* (1981), 125 D.L.R. (3d) 1 (S.C.C.).

19 In October 1980, the federal government tabled a joint resolution in the House of Commons which sought an amendment to the British North America Act without the consent of the provinces; in October 1980, the federal government announced the National Energy Policy, which sought to alter the distribution of economic rent from the energy sector; in the spring of 1983, under Bill C-150, the federal government separated the cash contribution for the hospital insurance and medical care programmes, and then imposed "six and five" restraint limits on transfers for post-secondary education.

Yet this era of federal unilateralism did not signal a return to the pre-war classical federalism of watertight compartments. Instead, it merely confirmed the extent to which the classical orthodoxy had become outdated. On all fronts, the provinces moved to block the federal initiatives, often through recourse to the courts. Thus, rather than a return to classical federalism, the developments of the past decade signalled the emergence of what one commentator has termed "double unilateralism".[20] Under this model, both levels of government continue to act in the same general policy areas, but in an antagonistic rather than cooperative fashion. The issue for federalism in the eighties is "not whether the two levels of government will be involved [in the same areas of public policy] but whether they act unilaterally or will collaborate in one fashion or another."[21] The prevailing view is captured by the Royal Commission on the Economic Union and Development Prospects For Canada (the MacDonald Commission), which reports that there is no merit to efforts to restore a classic model of watertight compartments.[22] Overlapping of authority and *de facto* concurrence are "not only inevitable but also desirable".[23] Shared responsibility makes governments compete with one another to respond to citizens' problems, which in turn will temper the self-interest of state officials. To require governments to adhere to an incoherent and outdated set of categories contained in the B.N.A. Act would be to frustrate this competition for public support. The MacDonald Commission's realism both epitomizes and legitimizes the current discourse about federalism.

3. THE EVOLUTION OF JUDICIAL REVIEW

With constitutionalism losing its legitimacy, commentators in the 1960s became convinced that judicial review was becoming an increasingly marginal activity. Governments seemed less willing to have their disputes resolved by the courts, with the most contentious areas of federal and provincial conflict being resolved without resort to the judiciary. Business interests were apparently less inclined than in the past to support judicial challenges to federal power. Judicial review had been supplanted by political processes of adjustment and compromise, as courts were "being retired" from their posts as

---

20 McRoberts, *supra*, note 17 at 93.
21 *Ibid.*
22 See *Final Report*, vol. III, at 254-258.
23 *Ibid.* at 256.

supervisors of the federal balance.[24] The prevailing view in the late 1960s was captured by Donald Smiley: "Judicial review results in a delineation of federal and provincial powers where the perceived needs of the federal system are for a more effective articulation of these powers. In general, the prospects are remote that the courts will reassume a major role as keepers of the federal balance."[25]

A mere fifteen years after Professor Smiley issued this confident prognosis, he appears to have been hopelessly mistaken. All of the indicators which suggested that judicial review was declining in importance have now dramatically reversed themselves. The norms of negotiation and compromise, so widely accepted in the 1960s, had been largely repudiated by the late 1970s and early 1980s. The federal government pursued a policy of unilateralism on the constitution and energy rents, matters which had formerly been the subject of collaboration. The response of the provinces was to attempt to block the federal initiatives through resort to the courts. This thrust the Supreme Court center stage in crucial federal-provincial conflicts over constitutional amendment and energy policy.

Nor did private interests appear reluctant about invoking federalism arguments in order to avoid state regulation. A recent and prominent instance of this is the private challenge to the federal *Canada Health Act*,[26] litigation which has profound implications for the tangled edifice of intergovernmental transfers that has been the bedrock of the new federalism since 1945. Finally, the courts themselves appear to be assuming an increasingly activist stand, more willing to invoke federalism norms to limit state activity. Particularly in the *Patriation Appeals*, the Supreme Court cast itself as the guardian of the federal character of the constitution against encroachments by the central government. All of these developments have induced scholars to revise their assessments about the marginality, if not about the legitimacy, of judicial review. The new conventional wisdom asserts that the courts are assuming an increasingly critical role in the evolution of federalism.

These claims about increasing judicial involvement in federalism matters are confirmed by the figures in Table One. In the 5-year period ending in 1985, the Court decided almost as many federalism cases as in the decade between 1970 and 1980. Perhaps more significant is the increase in the percentage of the Court's time spent on federalism

---

24 J.A. Corry and J.E. Hodgetts, *Democratic Government and Politics* (1959) at 557-579.

25 D. Smiley, *Constitutional Adaptation and Canadian Federalism Since 1945* (1970) at 40.

26 *Canada Health Act*, S.C. 1984, c. 6.

matters in the past decade. In the 1960s, only one out of every 30 cases decided by the Supreme Court raised a federalism issue. This ratio remained relatively stable throughout the 1970s, despite the change in the leave to appeal procedures instituted in 1974. By the early 1980s, one out of every nine opinions written by the Court was decided on federalism grounds. It is important to remember that these figures do not take into account the impact of the *Charter of Rights* on the Court's workload. With *Charter* cases just beginning to reach the Court in the 1984–85 term, the Court's workload will likely become even more dominated by constitutional issues in the future.

TABLE 1
Federalism Cases Decided by the Supreme Court 1950–1984*

	Federalism Cases	Total Cases	Ratio
1950–59	30	651	4.6%
1960–69	36	1161	3.1%
1970–79	54	1464	3.7%
1980–84	57	524	10.9%

*includes cases reported to December 31, 1984
Source: reported cases, S.C.R.s 1950–85 — includes cases in which constitutional arguments raised, even if case decided on non-constitutional grounds

Not only is the Court deciding more constitutional cases than in the past, it also appears to be assuming a more "activist" stance. As table 2 indicates, the Court today is more likely to strike down a statute on federalism grounds than at any time in the past 20 years. What is equally significant is the changing attitude of the Court towards federal statutes. In the 1950s and 1960s, the Court appears to have regarded federal laws as virtually immune constitutionality; of 20 challenges to federal laws, only two were successful.[27] In the 1980–84 period there were 28 challenges to federal law that reached the Supreme Court and in 12 instances the challenge was successful. This indicates that more challenges to federal laws are reaching the Supreme Court, and with greater success. The extent of the change is indicated by the fact that over the 30-year period ending in 1980, the Court's constitutional docket was dominated by challenges to provincial laws; approximately two-thirds of all federalism cases involved such challenges. In the past five years, this historic relationship

---

27 In one case, the Court ruled the statute to be *ultra vires*, while in the other, the Court ruled that the statute could not be applied to the activity in question.

has been altered, with federalism challenges now being directed equally towards federal and provincial legislation and with virtually identical success.

TABLE 2
Statutes Held to be Ultra Vires*
(On Federalism Grounds)

	Federal Statutes	Provincial Statutes	Total	Percentage of Decisions
1950-59	2/11	11/19	13/30	43%
1960-69	0/9	7/27	7/36	20%
1970-79	4/20	17/34	21/54	39%
1980-84	12/28**	12/30	24/57	42%

*includes statutes held to be inapplicable to private activity on constitutional grounds
***McEvoy v. A.G. N.B.* is attributed to both federal and provincial totals: *ultra vires* in both instances

Of course, this heightened judicial activism does not necessarily imply a more aggressive attitude on the part of the Supreme Court. It is possible that judicial attitudes have remained constant but that other variables have fluctuated, with the effect of multiplying the number of statutes declared *ultra vires*. We can examine at least two such variables; the nature of the statutes being considered by the Court, as well as the attitudes of government towards judicial review itself.

Over the past decade, many of the received understandings surrounding federal-provincial relations were challenged or abandoned. The federal government in particular rejected the norms of negotiation and compromise in favour of greater competition and scope for unilateral action. The national energy programme and the constitutional initiative exemplified the national government's new concern with building more direct ties with Canadian citizens rather than with simply financing the provision of goods and services by the provinces. Moreover, the federal government disputed the claim that provincial cooperation should be secured before acting within areas which were nominally within federal jurisdiction. This more aggressive stance on the part of the national government, rather than judicial activism, may well account for the increase in the numbers of federal laws being ruled *ultra vires*. As the federal government pursues policies which intrude onto areas of established provincial turf, the Court will function as a conservative, checking mechanism, seeking to maintain the existing equilibrium. The predictable result would be that federal statutes would be challenged with greater frequency and success. In effect, the mere act of preserving the constitutional *status quo* would make the Court falsely appear to be adopting a more hostile stance towards federal laws.

The difficulty is that the available evidence fails to support this hypothesis. The cases in which the Court has ruled against the federal government cannot be characterized as responses to aggressive federal initiatives such as the national energy programme or the constitutional reform package. With one or two notable exceptions, the Court has been striking down provisions that have either been in place for many years or are similar to provisions which previously have been upheld in an almost perfunctory manner.[28] For instance, in *McEvoy*,[29] the Court ruled against a joint federal-provincial attempt to restructure the criminal courts, applying the strictures of s. 96 to the federal government for the first time; in *Boggs*,[30] the Court struck down a provision in the *Criminal Code* which made it an offence to drive while one's licence was suspended under provincial law; in *Labatt Breweries*,[31] the Court declared that federal standards for "lite" beer could not be applied to the beer industry, since this would constitute regulation of a "local trade". These federal laws, as well as others which met a similar fate, were hardly symbolic of constitutional hubris on the part of the federal government. Clearly, there is nothing in the character of the laws themselves which adequately explains the about-face performed by the Court with respect to federal legislation.

The other possibility is that the Court has been responding to changing attitudes on the part of government towards constitutional adjudication. In the 1960s, governments consciously attempted to avoid judicial resolution of federal-provincial disputes. Rather than play the zero-sum game of court challenges, governments practiced the politics of positive sum, bargaining to a result which advanced their collective and individual interests.

To a significant degree, this aversion towards constitutional litigation has now disappeared. Governments have increasingly

---

28 According to my calculations, of the twelve cases in which the Court ruled a federal law to be invalid since 1980, only two of these can be attributed to attempts by the federal government to intrude onto established provincial turf: these two instances are the *Ref. re Exported Natural Gas* (1982), 42 N.R. 361 (S.C.C.); and *A.G. Can. v. L.S.U.C.; A.G. Can. v. Jabour*, [1982] 2 S.C.R. 307 (S.C.C.). Of course, the federal constitutional reform package was ruled to be legally valid in the Court's decision in the *Patriation Appeals*, [1981] 1 S.C.R. 753 (S.C.C.).

29 *Re Ct. of Unified Criminal Jurisdiction; McEvoy v. A.G. N.B.*, [1983] 1 S.C.R. 704 (S.C.C.).

30 *R. v. Boggs; Boggs v. R.*, [1981] 1 S.C.R. 49 (S.C.C.).

31 *Labatt Breweries of Can. Ltd. v. A.G. Can.*, [1980] 1 S.C.R. 914 (S.C.C.).

assumed the role of catalysts of constitutional litigation, both in terms of referring cases to the courts and intervening in private litigation. While the vast bulk of constitutional cases still originate through private litigation, there were as many reference cases reaching the Supreme Court in the 1980–84 period as in the previous 20 years. More telling of increased governmental litigiousness is the degree to which governments now intervene in private litigation. As table 3 indicates, during the 1950s and 1960s, most governments devoted only minimal resources towards constitutional litigation. Indeed, the federal government and the provinces of Ontario and Quebec accounted for more than half of the interventions during the 1950–1970 period. This pattern reversed itself in the 1970s, with virtually all governments participating vigorously in constitutional litigation. This was particularly so of the western provinces. By the 1980s, the province of Alberta was the most frequent intervener in federalism cases, surpassing even the federal government.

TABLE 3
Interventions by Government 1950–1984

Government	1950-59	1960-69	1970-79	1980-84	Total
Canada	14	18	29	23	84
Ontario	8	14	22	17	61
Quebec	8	12	21	21	62
Newfoundland	2	1	4	8	15
Nova Scotia	1	1	5	11	18
New Brunswick	3	2	8	18	31
P.E.I.	2	1	2	4	9
Manitoba	2	2	6	11	21
Saskatchewan	2	5	13	17	37
Alberta	4	8	29	26	67
British Columbia	2	2	18	18	40
Total	48	66	157	174	
No. of cases	30	36	54	57	
Interventions per case	1.6	1.8	3.0	3.0	

There does appear to be some link between reference cases and rulings of *ultra vires*. Of the fifteen references that have reached the Supreme Court since 1970, the Court has made a ruling of *ultra vires* in ten of them; contrast this with the fact that of the 96 private challenges reaching the Court over the same period, the Court made a finding of *ultra vires* only 35 times. In effect, the Court was twice as likely to make a declaration of invalidity in a reference case as in a case initiated by a private litigant. Nor can this result be explained by the fact that the reference cases were being initiated by governments hostile to the legislation in question. In the four instances in which a government referred legislation enacted by the other level of government, the Court declared the legislation to be invalid only once. It was precisely in those cases in which a government was referring its own legislation to the Court that rulings of *ultra vires* were most common. The startling thing about this result is that it appears to contradict the common claim that private interests use federalism arguments to escape regulation.[32] The Court appears most receptive to federalism arguments when government, rather than private interest, has instituted the litigation.

There are a variety of reasons why this might be so. The first is that governments tend to refer legislation which is politically highly contentious; this means that there will be well-organized and financed interests willing to mount a concerted lobby against the legislation when it reaches the Court. Secondly, the very act of referring a statute to the Court may act as an implicit signal to the judiciary that the legislation is constitutionally suspect. Whatever the reasons, the increasing willingness on the part of government to refer legislation to the courts cannot itself account for the increased judicial activism of recent years. Both the absolute and the relative number of reference cases is small and the Supreme Court's constitutional docket remains overwhelmingly dominated by private litigation.

This brings us to a consideration of the impact of the dramatic increase in interventions by governments in private constitutional challenges. It might be assumed that when a government intervenes in a private challenge to legislation, the challenge is more likely to succeed; the intervention changes the complexion of the case, transforming a purely private attempt to escape regulation into a choice between competing conceptions of the public good. In fact, a particular provincial complaint during the 1970s was the frequency of hostile federal interventions in constitutional cases. For instance, following the Supreme Court's decisions in *Canadian Industrial Gas & Oil*

---

32 For instances of this line of argument, see P. Weiler, *In the Last Resort* (1974) at 155-185. I argue only that the results "appear" to contradict the claim regarding private interests and federalism litigation. Of course, even in reference cases there are often private interests opposing the legislation and thus, a ruling of *ultra vires* may be indirectly of benefit to these interests. But, at the very least, the data suggests that the Court is not pursuing any conscious policy of assisting private interests in its federalism jurisprudence.

(*CIGOL*)[33] and *Central Canada Potash*[34] in 1978, the province of Saskatchewan was "disturbed" by the fact that the Government of Canada had supported the private litigants in the cases.[35] The participation of the federal government had given legitimacy to the challenge; it was no longer purely private interests opposing the province, but the "national" interest as represented by the government of Canada. Premier Blakeney regarded the federal action as a "betrayal" of previous understandings between the two governments on the energy issue.

Yet when one examines a broader range of outcomes, there is little evidence to support the hypothesis that intervention by government makes private challenges to legislation more likely to succeed. In the 1950s and 1960s, the outcomes in cases in which there were no interventions are virtually indistinguishable from those in which governments did intervene.[36] In the 1970s and 1980s, the cases in which there were interventions by government did have a slightly larger proportion of holdings of *ultra vires*.[37] Yet even here it is difficult to draw a causal link between the government's decision to intervene and a judicial holding of *ultra vires*. In many cases, governments intervened in support of legislation rather than against it. Moreover, even when governments intervened to support private challenges, it may well be that they did so when the issue was particularly contentious and thus, there was an antecedent likelihood that the Court would find in favour of the challenge.

In any event, this focus on the increase in total interventions tends to exaggerate the impact of the change in government behaviour.

---

33 *Cdn. Industrial Gas & Oil (CIGOL) v. Saskatchewan*, [1977] 2 S.C.R. 545 (S.C.C.).

34 *Central Can. Potash Co. v. Saskatchewan*, [1979] 1 S.C.R. 42 (S.C.C.).

35 See Letter from the Premier of Saskatchewan, Allan Blakeney, to the Prime Minister of Canada, Pierre E. Trudeau, 10 October 1978. Saskatchewan was particularly upset by the fact that the government of Canada had become a co-plaintiff in the *Central Can. Potash* case.

36 In the 1950s, there were a total of eighteen private challenges to legislation on federalism grounds. The twelve cases in which there were intervenors split evenly, private litigants winning six; the six cases in which there were no intervenors also split evenly, the private litigants winning three. In the 1960s, there were a total of 31 private challenges. Of the 22 in which there were interventions, the private litigants won only four, while in the nine in which there were no interventions, the private litigants won four.

37 In the 1970s, there were 49 private challenges. Of the 38 cases in which there were interventions, the challenges succeeded fourteen times; in the eleven cases in which there were no interventions, the challenges succeeded three times. In the 1980s, there were 47 private challenges. Of the 36 cases in which there were interventions, the challenges succeeded fifteen times; in the eleven cases in which there were no interventions, the challenges succeeded three times.

While it is true that governments have demonstrated an increasing interest in constitutional litigation, the proportion of cases in which governments intervene has remained fairly constant. Since the 1950s, there has been an intervention by at least one government in roughly four out of every five federalism cases reaching the Supreme Court.[38] The only change is that, whereas in the 1950s there would be only one or two intervenors in a given case, now there may be four or five. It is difficult to see how a change of this order could have a significant impact on the outcomes of federalism cases.

Thus, while these various factors may well be linked in some marginal way with the increasing judicial activism of recent years, they offer, at best, a partial explanation. One is ultimately led to the conclusion that the increasing activism in federalism cases is primarily a consequence of changed judicial attitudes. These evolving attitudes, which can be detected throughout the recent pronouncements of the Court, at bottom depend upon a particular conception of the judicial role. At the heart of the Court's vision is the belief that judges and lawyers constitute a central pillar in the defence of constitutional government in Canada. The paradigm is premised on private decision-making, constrained at the margins by traditional models of adjudication, rather than through managerial or administrative approaches to the economy.

There are numerous illustrations of the paradigm. Perhaps the most obvious exemplar is the judgment of the Court in the *Patriation Appeals*. The Court revealed a willingness to accept primary responsibility for preserving the federal political tradition. The conventions of the constitution, matters which had always been left to the vagaries of the political process, were now regarded as too important to be left in such a fluid state. It was time to usher these amorphous understandings under the protective robes of legal supervision. The claim that conventions remained legally unenforceable was the height of legal formalism, disguising the transformation in their juridical character. The same general themes can be detected in the s. 96 cases, in which the Court ensures that decision-making on "jurisdictional" grounds will be reviewable. This serves to protect traditional models

---

38 Cases in which governments have intervened, by decade:

1950s:	23/30 cases
1960s:	27/36 cases
1970s:	43/54 cases
1980s:	45/57 cases

of adjudication against what the Court regards as the excesses of the regulatory state. The decision of the Court in *Jabour*, while ostensibly aimed at preserving provincial autonomy, simultaneously emphasizes the autonomy and importance of the legal profession.

The point of citing these developments is not to suggest that the Court has suddenly embarked on a policy-making frolic and that it should return to an apolitical, neutral role. The argument is more systemic. My claim is that these recent cases are simply a more overt and measurable manifestation of the policy-making which pervades legal decision-making. The judiciary cannot return to some neutral or objective state of nature, since such objectivity never existed.

These observations have important implications for the continuing debate over the "objectivity" of legal reasoning. Drawing on analogies to literary theory, Ronald Dworkin has argued that judges have a duty to "interpret" legal texts and materials, rather than to "change" them.[39] Judges are like writers who are each asked to write a chapter in a "chain" novel; the novelists are expected to create a single, unified novel rather than a series of independent short stories whose characters happen to have the same names. Each must interpret the work of the earlier members of the chain. They must assess what the characters are "really" like, identify "the" theme of the novel, and establish what the novel amounts to. Dworkin claims that judges stand in a similar position; "he *must* interpret what has gone before because he has a responsibility to advance the enterprise in hand rather than strike out in some new direction of his own."[40]

Yet the recent evolution of judicial review in Canada belies the claim that a sharp distinction can be drawn between "interpreting" legal materials and "changing" them. The recent federalism decisions of the Supreme Court were simultaneously an interpretation as well as a change of what had gone before. They represented an "interpretation" in the sense that the arguments were framed within the parameters established by the existing constitutional jurisprudence. They were simultaneously a "change" in the sense that the outcomes of the cases were significantly different from those in the 1950s and 1960s. This exemplifies Stanley Fish's observation that "[p]aradoxically, one can be faithful to legal history only by revising it, by redescribing it in such a way as to accommodate and render manageable the issues

---

39 R. Dworkin, "How Law is Like Literature" in *A Matter of Principle* (1985) at 146.
40 *Ibid.* at 159.

raised by the present".[41]

The more general point that emerges is that the very dichotomy between objectivity and subjectivity which has fueled debates over judicial review is itself suspect.[42] Building on the "hermeneutic insight" — the view that "a sharp distinction cannot be drawn between understanding the text in its own terms and reading the interpreter's concerns into it"[43] — it becomes unnecessary to discover some independent, apolitical ground for legal reasoning. In this view, the only meaningful use of the term "objectivity" is "the view which would be agreed upon as a result of argument undeflected by irrelevant considerations."[44] Legal reasoning, along with other forms of political argument, is accordingly best understood as contingent yet constrained. It is constrained in the sense that legal argument must interpret and advance the aspirations and ideals which exemplify the political tradition. Yet it is contingent in the sense that the very act of interpreting those ideals changes them; the past is redescribed in order to accommodate the issues raised by the present.[45]

4. THE IMPACT OF ACTIVISM

Acknowledging the political character of constitutional adjudication does little to address the critical, if elusive, issue of the impact of this heightened judicial activism. It is tempting to conclude that the more federalism cases decided by the Court, the greater the impact of the Court's work on federal-provincial relations. But even a cursory analysis of recent federal-provincial disputes suggests that the empirical significance of many of these decisions has been minor. In the energy

---

41 S. Fish, "Working on the Chain Gang: Interpretation in Law and Literature", 60 Tex. L. Rev. 551, 559 (1982).

42 An attack on the objective-subjective dichotomy, as well as other "liberal antinomies", has been a prime element in the "total critique" of the so-called "critical legal studies movement" in America. See generally, R. Unger, *Knowledge and Politics* (1975); Surprisingly, mainstream legal theories have recently shown an impatience with the continuing search for objective legal standards. See L. Tribe, *Constitutional Choices* (1985) at 1-10.

43 D. Hoy, "Interpreting the Law: Hermeneutical and Post Structural Perspectives", 58 S. Cal. L. Rev. 136, 137 (1985).

44 R. Rorty, *Philosophy and the Mirror of Nature* (1979) at 383. "What we need . . . is the ability to think about science in such a way that its being a 'value-based enterprise' occasions no surprise. All that hinders us from doing so is the ingrained notion that 'values' are 'inner', whereas 'facts' are 'outer' and that it is as much a mystery how, beginning with values, we could produce bombs as how, beginning with private inner episodes, we could avoid bumping into things." *Ibid.* at 341-342.

45 For an account of interpretation along these lines, see Fish, *supra*, note 41.

field, for example, the province of Alberta turned to the courts in an attempt to block the federal government's proposed tax on exported natural gas. But before the Supreme Court could rule on the matter, the federal government signed an agreement with the province of Alberta in which it renounced its plans for the tax. In the constitutional reform process, to take a second example, the Supreme Court decision in September 1981 essentially threw the initiative back into the political arena; the accord of November 1981 was acceptable to all parties except Quebec, whose subsequent legal challenge was dismissed by the Supreme Court. This particularistic analysis, in itself, proves little. But it does suggest that merely citing figures about numbers of federalism cases will not support claims about the impact and significance of constitutional adjudication.

One of the central contributions of Ronald Coase was his insight that individuals will seek to bargain around legal rules in order to achieve more efficient results.[46] Of course, there are a whole series of obstacles militating against such bargaining in the federalism context. Chief amongst these is the sheer complexity and cost of any bargaining that might occur. Before we can even contemplate bargaining *between* government, there must be bargaining *within* government, as the respective polities try to make up their "minds" about the best bargaining strategy to pursue. Despite these obstacles, we can expect that governmental elites will continually attempt to limit the effect of judicial rulings which run contrary to what they perceive to be their best interests.

The point can be illustrated by considering the response of federal and provincial governments to the decision of the Supreme Court of Canada in the *Nova Scotia Inter-delegation* case.[47] In this case, the Court ruled that an attempt by one level of government to delegate its power to the other was prohibited by the constitution. It was clearly in the interests of both levels of government to limit the effect of this rule. Translated into market terms, the effect of the ruling was to prevent the various governments from trading their "assets". All governments stood to gain from removing such restraints on alienation; an asset that can be traded is worth more than an asset that must remain in the hands of its legal owner. It is thus hardly surprising to observe that governments subsequently were able largely to nullify the effect of this legal rule. The nullification received Court sanction two years

46 R. Coase, "The Problem of Social Cost", 3 Journ. of Law and Econ. 1 (1961).
47 *A.G. N.S. v. A.G. Can.*, [1951] S.C.R. 31 (S.C.C.).

later in *P.E.I. Potato Marketing Board v. H.B. Willis Inc.*[48] Here, the Court declared that the constitution did not prevent one level of government from delegating power to an administrative body created by the other. This device, combined with the technique of "incorporation by reference",[49] meant that it was now possible to trade legislative powers.

This produces the central law of the federalism equation: it is *always* possible to do indirectly what you cannot do directly. The *Nova Scotia Inter-delegation* case neatly illustrates in a single instance the two primary ways in which such indirection can be accomplished. First, the case illustrates the potential to utilize intergovernmental agreement in order to evade judicially-imposed limitations. Second, the case simultaneously provides an example of governments using an alternative regulatory instrument in place of an instrument or technique that has been ruled invalid. Having discovered that the courts would not countenance direct transfers of jurisdiction, the various governments devised an alternative mechanism which achieved the same result, albeit indirectly.

Given that in virtually any case it is possible to achieve indirectly what you cannot do directly, the interesting question is the extent to which governments actually resort to these various devices. One hypothesis would be that such substitution will occur whenever this would produce the "efficient" result. Yet we can immediately see why this hypothesis will turn out to be false. The most obvious reason is the one suggested by Coase himself; parties will bargain to the most efficient result only when transaction costs are zero. In the real world, and certainly in the context of federalism, transaction costs are never zero. In fact, the transaction costs appear virtually insurmountable, since the "parties" to the agreement are not merely the governments themselves but the millions of constituents who must indirectly feature in the calculations of the governments. Even the rigid party discipline of parliamentary government cannot eliminate the difficulty of achieving the required consensus.

There is a second difficulty. This is with the underlying assumption that, even in the absence of transaction costs, the parties will bargain towards "efficient" results. The difficulty stems from the fact that

---

48 *P.E.I. Potato Marketing Board v. H.B. Willis Inc.*, [1952] 2 S.C.R. 392 (S.C.C.).

49 Here, one jurisdiction simply incorporates the rules or laws in force in another jurisdiction, without repeating those rules. This can be done in an "anticipatory" manner. Not only are the current rules adopted, but any amendment to those rules in the future by the original enacting jurisdiction are automatically deemed to be included in the laws of the incorporating jurisdiction. See *Coughlin v. Ont. Highway Transport Bd.*, [1968] S.C.R. 569 (S.C.C.).

the parties to any such agreement are governments rather than private economic actors. Governments certainly have some interest in the goal of technical efficiency. But there are numerous other factors which influence the shape of government regulation. Governments have a desire to select policies that will result in their re-election.[50] Their policies may thus be directed towards certain powerful interest groups or to an identifiable group of marginal voters. They may opt for policies that provide benefits in concentrated form, so that their visibility is enhanced, and impose costs in dispersed form, so that their visibility is disguised. They may select policies that have a heavy bureaucratic orientation over decentralized forms of resource allocation.[51] This does not mean that considerations of technical efficiency will be irrelevant to the policy process. The more limited point is that technical efficiency is merely one out of a number of competing goals influencing public choice.

Thus, we would expect to observe governments bargaining around the effects of judicial decisions only when these various "political" factors pointed in that direction. It is likely that many of the results would be "inefficient" from the standpoint of technical efficiency. But this is more a product of the political system than any failing on the part of the judiciary. Even if, by some fantastic coincidence, the courts were able to select the result that was efficient from a technical point of view, we would expect to see governments bargaining around the result when there were significant political gains available. There would be little point, therefore, in instructing courts to choose the "efficient" result, even if such an instruction were capable of being executed."[52]

It is possible to advance a hypothesis regarding the extent to which judicial review constrains the ability of government to regulate the economy. Stated simply, this hypothesis is that judicial review con- stitutes a minimal and marginal constraint on the behaviour of government. Moreover, we would expect that constitutional limita- tions will be significant only when they are reinforced by the various

---

50 This theory of "political rationality" governing instrument choice is developed in M.J. Trebilcock *et al.*, *The Choice of Governing Instrument* (Economic Council of Canada, 1982) at 27.

51 For a discussion of the various reasons for such choices, see Trebilcock *et al.*, *ibid.* at 33.

52 See Posner, *Economic Analysis of Law* (1977), whose claim is that courts should choose the efficient result, the result which the parties themselves would have selected in the absence of transaction costs. In effect, Posner's instruction to courts is to try to mimic the market. Posner's argument appears largely irrelevant in the context of federalism.

political factors outlined above. Constitutional limitations standing on their own can be avoided by governments in virtually all cases.

One basis for such a hypothesis is the fact that certain forms of governing instruments play almost no role in constitutional adjudication. Consider that of the 177 federalism cases decided since 1949, there were no challenges to the spending power, one case dealing with state enterprise and four cases challenging a government's proprietary interest. The vast majority of cases have dealt with what might be termed command and control regulation.[53] Thus, it would be very surprising indeed if judicial review constituted a major obstacle to government regulation of economic activity. While certain forms of regulation may be impermissible, others will always be available. Moreover, many of the most important forms of economic regulation appear to be virtually immune from constitutional scrutiny. On the federal level, for example, the instruments of fiscal and monetary policy are largely free of constitutional constraint. The federal government can set macroeconomic policy without having to cast an eye backward on the Supreme Court.

While there seems to be a sound basis for supposing that such a hypothesis regarding the role of judicial review would turn out to be valid, it can only be tested through a detailed consideration of actual government behaviour in response to judicial decisions. Accordingly, this will be a primary concern in the chapters which follow, in which I undertake case studies of particular federalism decisions of the Supreme Court. It is to such detailed analysis that I now turn.

---

53 For a discussion of the various types of governing instruments, see *supra*, note 50, and also chapter 1, note 11.

8

The Court and Constitutional Amendment:
The Battle Over Constitutional Reform
1979–1982

1. INTRODUCTION

In the early 1980s, federal-provincial relations continued to be dominated by disputes over natural resource development and energy rents. But the energy issue was joined at the top of the political agenda by the constitutional question. By the end of the 1970s, the federal government had become determined to "patriate" the Canadian constitution and to entrench a *Charter of Rights* binding on both levels of government. It would seek provincial agreement for its plans but, if such agreement was not forthcoming, Ottawa would break the deadlock by unilaterally requesting a constitutional amendment from Great Britain.

The first federal initiative, Bill C-60 introduced in June 1978, ended in stalemate. However, the second federal initiative in 1980–82 eventually resulted in a compromise plan accepted by nine of the ten provinces and enacted into Canadian law by the British Parliament. The Supreme Court played an important role in both of these episodes, particularly in the events leading up to the federal-provincial constitutional accord of November 1981 and the enactment of a new Canadian constitution. This chapter attempts to identify the constitutional vision which informed the Court's judgments on constitutional amendment in the 1979 to 1982 period. It also seeks to assess what impact, if any, the Court's intervention had on the outcomes of the process.

Four judgments of the Court over the 1979 to 1982 period are scrutinized: the unanimous opinion in the *Senate Reference* of late 1979;[1] the two majority judgments in the *Patriation Appeals* in 1981;[2] and the unanimous judgment in the *Quebec Veto* case of 1982.[3] These cases raised fundamental questions about the nature of Canadian federalism and the Canadian political community. It was therefore quite natural that the Court's response to these issues would be controversial and contested. What was less understandable was the complete failure on the part of the Court to articulate any consistent vision of the Canadian polity. In fact, this chapter argues that the Court played the role of a chameleon in its judgments on constitutional amendment. The Court continually shifted its ground, seeking to embrace in turn a series of quite contradictory images of Canadian federalism. The Court never acknowledged the contradictions or the shifts in its analysis, much less how the sum total of its constitutional prescriptions might be explained or justified.

Turning from the legal reasoning in the cases to the results, I argue that the decisions of the Court had a significant impact on the larger political resolution of the squabbles over constitutional amendment. While the Court's reasoning was hopelessly contradictory, the actual results in the cases were consistent with a "cooperative" view of federal-provincial relations. According to this view, unilateral action by one level of government should be discouraged and political differences should be resolved through *ad hoc* bargaining between governments. Conflict and competition between governments is supposedly evidence of the fact that "the system is not working". I argue that this vision of cooperative federalism, although dominating contemporary political rhetoric in Canada, acts to reinforce the conservative bias of federal systems. It makes change more difficult to achieve and maximizes the interests of governments as such, as

---

1 *Ref. re Legislative Authority of the Parliament of Can. in relation to the Upper House*, [1980] 1 S.C.R. 54 (S.C.C.).

2 *A.G. Man. v. A.G. Can.; A.G. Can. v. A.G. Nfld.; A.G. Que. v. A.G. Can.; A.G. Can. v. A.G. Que.*, [1981] 1 S.C.R. 753 (S.C.C.).

3 *A.G. Que. v. A.G. Can.*, [1982] 2 S.C.R. 793 (S.C.C.)

opposed to the interests of the citizens who elect those governments. I claim that the Court should be less wary of competition and unilateralism in federal-provincial relations, since the ultimate beneficiaries of such political competition are the ordinary citizens of the nation rather than political and bureaucratic elites.

2. PRELUDE: CONSTITUTIONAL AMENDMENT ASSUMES CENTER STAGE

Prior to 1960, Canadians saw little need for any wholesale remodelling of the nation's constitutional understandings. This constitutional complacency may have been somewhat surprising given the fact that our fundamental constitutional document was a nineteenth century statute of the imperial Parliament, amendable only by Westminster. But political leaders in both French and English Canada appeared to regard this vestige of our colonial heritage as an irritant that was more theoretical than practical. The imperial Parliament did not purport to possess any *de facto* authority over the *British North America Act, 1867*; Westminster's residual *de jure* authority would be exercised only with the advice and consent of the Canadian authorities. Moreover, there was apparently little need or desire to update the anachronistic legislative categories in ss. 91 and 92 of the Act. The formal division of powers may well have been hopelessly antiquated but it was also becoming increasingly irrelevant. Governments in the post-war years had discovered a wealth of legislative instruments allowing them to circumvent or to soften the force of constitutional constraints.[4] The *de facto* division of powers and responsibilities between the federal and provincial governments had come to bear little relationship to the formal categories set out in the 1867 Act. To the extent that any explicit constitutional reform was necessary, this could be accomplished in a pragmatic and piecemeal fashion, exemplified by the narrowly focused amendments of 1940 and 1951.

Within two decades, this complacency regarding our constitutional arrangements had evaporated and been replaced by a mood of urgency and crisis. Constitutional reform had emerged from the political shadows to become the central political issue of the early 1980s. The federal government in particular had concluded that the constitutional *status quo* was intolerable and that it would accord the highest priority to achieving sweeping constitutional reform. How can

---

4 See generally, Chapter 1, *supra*.

we account for this constitutional about-face in the 20-year period between 1960 and 1980?

There were two sets of forces which combined to produce this dramatic turn of events.[5] The first challenge to the legitimacy of the *status quo* came from the rise of nationalist sentiment in the province of Quebec. Beginning with the Lesage administration in the early 1960s, successive Quebec governments began calling for a fundamental shift in federal-provincial relations in order to take account of a revitalized yet endangered French-Canadian nation. For the new Quebec, the provincial state was to be both the protector and the expression of the national identity: "The state was nothing in Quebec; now it must be everything".[6] Thus, Quebec's political elites began to call for a variety of constitutional reforms, ranging from a mere strengthening of the province's powers within the existing constitutional system to outright sovereignty from the rest of Canada.[7]

The process of constitutional reform begun by the Confederation for Tomorrow Conference in 1967 and culminating in the Victoria Conference of 1971 was a direct response to these emerging nationalist sentiments in Quebec. Yet during this period, there was no overwhelming sense amongst English Canadians that constitutional reform was imperative. English Canadians appeared to be largely satisfied with the existing constitutional structure. Political elites in English Canada were prepared to debate and accept constitutional reform on the basis that such reform was necessary to maintain harmonious relations with Quebec. The trigger for the constitutional debate was the need to come to terms with Quebec rather than any pervasive sense that the constitution had become unworkable.

Following the collapse of the Victoria agreement in 1971, there was a hiatus in the constitutional reform process. The constitutional question did not resurface until the late 1970s; by this time, the need to seek a new accommodation with Quebec was no longer the sole or even the primary catalyst for the process. The issue of "regionalism" — the conflict between the central heartland of Ontario/Quebec and

---

5 The account which follows is largely uncontroversial and unoriginal. See, e.g., D. Smiley and R.L. Watts, *The Reform of Federal Institutions: Intrastate Federalism in Canada* (Royal Commission on the Economic Union and Development Prospects for Canada, Research Study 39, 1985).

6 P.E. Trudeau, *Federalism and the French Canadians* (1968) at 18. Trudeau, however, was critical of what he saw as the "absolute subordination of economic forces to political forces" in the Quebec of the early 1960s.

7 See generally, E. McWhinney, *Quebec and the Constitution: 1960–1978* (1979).

the hinterlands to the east and west — was now seen as an equally dangerous threat to the survival of the nation. The sense that Canadian federalism faced a "compounded crisis" was captured by the Pepin-Robarts Report of 1979: "We believe that the heart of the present crisis is to be discovered in the intersecting conflicts created by two kinds of cleavages in Canadian society and by the political agencies which express and mediate them. The first and most pressing cleavage is that old Canadian division between 'the French' and 'the English' . . . The second cleavage is that which divides the various regions of Canada and their populations from one another."[8]

Regional conflict is by no means a novel feature of Canadian politics. Western Canada was from the first an economic colony of the country's central heartland, and there have been numerous western revolts against this subordinate position dating back to the 1880s.[9] But historically, western protest had been more concerned with the way in which Ottawa carried out its constitutional responsibilities than with the scope of those responsibilities.[10] It was only in the late 1970s that western political elites began to suspect that the very institutions of the central government itself had to be reformed before their interests would be adequately protected.

The focus of western criticism was on the highly centralized and majoritarian character of national political institutions. Because national power was highly concentrated in the hands of the Prime Minister and his cabinet, it was argued that the federal government had become insensitive to regional interests and concerns. Those institutions which were originally designed to safeguard regional interests, such as the Senate, had never performed this function. The centralized nature of parliamentary government had combined with a "first past the post" electoral system to render the west a permanent minority in the operations of the central government in the decades following the defeat of the Diefenbaker government in 1963. The constitutional agenda of the west was aimed at reforming federal institutions so as to facilitate the representation of regional interests and concerns.

The critique of the institutions of the central government was by no means limited to western politicians and electorates. An

---

8 Task Force on Canadian Unity, *A Future Together.* (1979) at 21.

9 D. Smiley, *Canada in Question: Federalism in the Eighties* (1980) at 261, 269.

10 See R. Gibbins, "Constitutional Politics and the West" in Banting and Simeon, *And No-one Cheered: Federalism, Democracy and the Constitution Act* (1983) at 120–122.

impressive body of academic literature emerged documenting the extent to which the electoral and parliamentary system had suppressed the expression of regional interests.[11] This literature sought to reconceptualize our most basic notions of federalism and federal government. The reformulation was based on an important distinction between "interstate" and "intrastate" models of federalism.[12] "Interstate" federalism refers to the division of powers between the central and provincial governments. "Intrastate" federalism refers to the devices or processes *within* the central government which are designed to safeguard or promote regional interests.

Previous writing on federalism had tended to focus either on the formal division of powers between governments or on the relationships between those governments. K.C. Wheare's classic definition of the federal principle was "the method of dividing powers so that the general and regional governments are each, within a sphere, coordinate and independent".[13] Subsequent writers had criticized the Wheare formulation for its undue emphasis on the mutual independence of governments in a federal system; these critics emphasized the interdependence of governments and the complex pattern of intergovernmental relations which characterized all federal systems.[14] But even these revisionists continued to restrict their analysis to the relationship between the various levels of government in a federal system rather than to the degree to which regional particularisms could be accommodated within the central government itself.

The writing on "intrastate" federalism has illustrated the unduly restrictive nature of these traditional concerns. According to the intrastate model, federalism can be defined in a much broader and unbounded way than has previously been supposed. Federalism is simply a response to the need to protect regional units in the structures and operations of government.[15] But there is no necessary or inevitable

---

11 See, e.g., D. Smiley, "Territorialism and Canadian Public Institutions" in *Canadian Public Policy*, III (1977); W.P. Irvine, *Does Canada Need a New Electoral System?* (1979); A.C. Cairns, *From Interstate to Intrastate Federalism* (1979); R. Gibbins, *Regionalism: Territorial Politics in Canada* (1982).

12 The terms "interstate" and "intrastate" federalism originated with K. Lowenstein, *Political Power and the Governmental Process* (1946) at 405. However, the use of these terms in the recent Canadian literature has diverged somewhat from Lowenstein's formulation. See generally, Smiley and Watts, *supra*, note 5.

13 K.C. Wheare, *Federal government*, 4th ed. (1963) at 10.

14 See, e.g., W.S. Livingston, *Federalism and Constitutional Change* (1956); W.H. Riker, *Federalism: Origin, Operation, Significance* (1964).

15 See Smiley and Watts, *supra*, note 5; P. King, *Federalism and Federation* (1982).

form that this federalist response will take. Thus, one recent definition of federalism was "an institutional arrangement, taking the form of a sovereign state, and distinguished from other such states solely by the fact that its central government incorporates regional units into its decision procedure on some constitutionally entrenched basis."[16] The central point is that protection for regional units or communities can be achieved in at least two quite distinct ways. The first is to assign responsibility for matters in which territorial interests are particularly sensitive to state or provincial governments. The second is to design mechanisms within the national government which will channel and protect regional interests. Either solution should be seen as an acceptance of the "federal principle".

There is no necessary contradiction between these two strategies. Indeed, the *British North America Act* incorporated both interstate and intrastate elements in its attempt to devise a workable scheme of government for the British colonies. This point is easily forgotten, given our long-standing preoccupation with the "interstate" elements of the scheme — the division of powers between the federal and provincial governments. Yet it would appear that the drafters of the Act expected that the primary protection for regional interests would come, not from the provinces, but from within the federal government itself. For instance, the most contentious issue in the drafting of the 1867 Act was not the constitutional distribution of powers between Ottawa and the provinces, but rather the composition and powers of the Senate; six of the fourteen days of the Quebec Conference of 1864 were given over to this issue.[17] The attention given to the role of the Senate is a reflection of the important role which this body was expected to play in protecting regional interests. Unlike its British counterpart, the House of Lords, the Canadian Senate was assigned the task of represented territorial rather than aristocratic interests.[18] The Senate was by no means the sole mechanism for protecting territorial interests in the central government; regional representation in the federal cabinet, as well as the national party system, were regarded as important institutional recognition of regional diversity.[19] As historian P.B. Waite has argued, the drafters of the confederation settlement did not think of the "federal principle" as being embodied

---

16 King, *ibid.* at 77.

17 Smiley and Watts, *supra*, note 5.

18 See C. Campbell, *The Canadian Senate: A Lobby from Within* (1978) at 3; R. Gibbins, *Territorial Politics in Canada and the United States* (1982) at 59-60.

19 Smiley and Watts, *supra*, note 5 at introduction.

in the division of powers between the federal and provincial governments, but rather in the structure of the central legislature and, in particular, "in the balance between the House of Commons on the one hand and the Senate on the other."[20]

The institutional crisis facing the federal government in the late 1970s was attributed to the fact that these regional mechanisms had failed to function effectively. Since senators were appointed by the federal cabinet, they were deprived of effective links with provincial and regional communities. Mackay's study of the Senate concludes that the institution "has rarely been appealed to as the champion of provincial or sectional rights and, even when appealed to, has not consistently supported claims to such rights."[21] The cabinet is no longer a "chamber of political compensation" in which the Prime Minister strikes deals with provincial spokesmen in return for concessions to their regions.[22] Prime Ministers have come increasingly to dominate both cabinet and caucus. The electoral system functions so as to deny particular provinces or regions effective and continuing representations on the government side of the House of Commons.[23]

By the late 1970s, political commentators began writing of a "crisis of representation" in Canada's central institutions.[24] Because regional interests had been so systematically suppressed within the institutions at the centre, the federal government had lost the legitimacy required to reconcile competing regional interests. Ineffectual territorial representation within the national government had weakened political power at the centre of the political system. It had also led to a strengthening of provincial governments and politicians, who increasingly claimed to be the sole credible advocates for regional interests, not only for matters under provincial jurisdiction, but for matters of federal responsibility as well. The federal government was no longer seen as being capable of defining and promoting a national interest which was more than the sum of regional and provincial interests. Persistent regional imbalances in federal institutions had strained the very fabric of confederation, promoted regional polarization and

---

20 P.B. Waite, *The Life and Times of Confederation 1864–1867* (1962) at 110.

21 R.A. Mackay, *The Unreformed Senate of Canada* (1963) at 113.

22 See J. Hamelin, *The First Years of Confederation* (1967), quoted in Smiley, *supra*, note 9 at 276.

23 See A.C. Cairns, "The Electoral System and the Party System in Canada: 1921–1965" (1968), 1 Can. J. Pol. Sc. 55.

24 See Irvine, *supra*, note 11.

intensified territorial conflict and cleavages.[25]

This emerging concern with "intrastate" federalism led to a number of proposals for reform of national institutions along territorial lines. There were two competing reform strategies.[26] The first was a "provincialist" version of intrastate federalism. According to this first view, reform efforts should be concentrated on securing protection for provincial governments *as such* in the operation of the central government. This would extend and institutionalize recent claims by provincial governments that they have a role to play in matters which fall almost exclusively within Ottawa's constitutional jurisdiction.[27] Predictably, this first version of intrastate federalism has proven most popular in the various constitutional reform packages proposed by the provincial governments in the late 1970s and early 1980s.[28] A second strategy, a "centralist" version of intrastate federalism, rejects the proposition that provincial governments as such should be granted representation in central institutions. Reform proposals should be aimed at protecting regional or territorial interests directly rather than the interests of regional governments. Thus, rather than a Senate appointed by the provinces, advocates of this second intrastate model typically propose that senators be directly elected.[29]

These competing reform strategies reflect very profound disagreements about the nature of Canadian federalism and community.[30] The provincialist reform strategy accords primacy to provincial communities and the governments elected by those communities. Provincial governments are accordingly the only legitimate spokespersons for regional interests in all matters, regardless of the fact that, by "constitutional accident", some issues happen to fall under exclusive federal jurisdiction. In contrast, the centralist reform strategy does not deny that provincial governments have a responsibility for representing the interests of their residents within areas of provincial

---

25 For general accounts along these lines, see Gibbins, *supra*, note 11 at 45-78; Royal Commission on the Economic Union and Development prospects for Canada, *Final Report*, Chapter XXI, Vol. III, (1985); P. McCormick, E. Manning, and G. Gibson, *Regional Representation: The Canadian Partnership* (1981).

26 See Cairns, *supra*, note 11 at 11-13.

27 See G. Robertson, "The Role of Interministerial Conferences in the Decision-Making Process" in R. Simeon, ed., *Confrontation and Collaboration: Intergovernmental Relations in Canada Today* (1979) at 81.

28 See, e.g., Government of Alberta, *A Provincially Appointed Senate: A New Federalism for Canada* (1982).

29 See Gibbins, *supra*, note 11; Macdonald Commission, *supra*, note 25 at 88.

30 See the competing visions of the Canadian community outlined in Chapter 1, *supra*.

responsibility. But it claims that there is a larger national interest which transcends regional or local interest. Federal institutions alone are the legitimate forum for the articulation and promotion of such national purposes. Federal senators and members of Parliament are the representatives of regional or provincial interests in matters of national concern.

These two sets of forces — the rise of the new Quebec and regionalism — had combined to produce pervasive dissatisfaction with Canada's constitutional arrangements by the late 1970s. The complacency and conservatism of the early 1960s had given way to a sense that, absent significant constitutional reform, the very future of the nation was in question. It was against this backdrop that the federal government launched two major constitutional reform initiatives.

3. THE FIRST INITIATIVE:
BILL C-60 AND THE SENATE REFERENCE

In June 1978, the federal government introduced a comprehensive set of proposals for constitutional reform, known as the Constitutional Amendment Bill.[31] The Bill purported to divide the constitution into those aspects which might be amended by the action of Parliament alone and those where change would require the involvement of the U.K. authorities and the provinces. The proposed amendments were far-reaching, including a Charter of Rights and Freedoms, a delineation of the respective powers of the Monarch and the Governor-General and a constitutional statement of the relationship between the cabinet and the House of Commons.

The Bill also provided for certain "intrastate" reforms to national political institutions. The most significant of such reforms was the replacement of the Senate by a House of the Federation, whose members would be appointed by the federal and provincial governments. The members of the new second chamber were to be chosen by the party leaders in the House of Commons and legislatures of the provinces in proportion to the respective parties' share of the popular vote in the last federal or provincial election.[32] The powers of the Upper House were to be reduced. The House of the Federation would have only a 2-month suspensive veto over bills enacted by the House of Commons.

---

31 Bill C-60, introduced into the House of Commons by Prime Minister Trudeau on 20 June 1978.

32 See Bill C-60, ss. 62-70. For an overview of the proposed legislation, see P. Hogg, "Comment" (1980), 58 Can. Bar Rev. 631.

However, with respect to matters of "special linguistic significance", it would be necessary to secure the agreement of majorities of the French- and English-speaking members of the Upper House.

The federal government believed that the proposed reform of the Senate could be effected by Parliament acting alone, pursuant to its power under s. 91(1) of the *British North America Act, 1867* to amend the "constitution of Canada".[33] But this claim proved to be controversial[34] and eventually the federal government submitted a reference to the Supreme Court of Canada asking whether Parliament alone might abolish the Senate or change its powers.[35] The Court, in a unanimous opinion published in late 1979, held that Parliament could not abolish the Senate unilaterally.[36] Moreover, Parliament acting alone could not alter the powers of the Senate so as to "seriously impair the position of the Senate in the legislative process;"[37] nor could Parliament alter any of the other features of the Senate which affected the "fundamental character of the Senate as part of the Canadian federal scheme".[38]

(a) The Opinion of the Court

The Court's analysis weaves together two quite distinct lines of argument in order to justify its conclusion that the amendments exceed the powers of Parliament. The primary line of argument is highly formalistic, based on a mechanical parsing of the opening words of s. 91 of the *British North America Act, 1867*. Such formalistic rhetoric remains standard fare in the constitutional opinions of our highest Court.[39] But the Court combines this formalist analysis with a second argument which is much more purposive and contextual. This second line of argument appeals to the actual "intentions" of the fathers of confederation regarding the expected role of the Senate in protecting provincial interests. The combined weight of these two complementary

---

33 Section 91(1) was repealed by the *Constitution Act, 1982* [en. by the Canada Act, 1982 (U.K.), c. 11, s. 1].

34 See Hogg, *supra*, note 32 at 632 (note 7).

35 Order-in-Council P.C. 1978-3581, 23 November 1978, reproduced in the judgment of the Supreme Court of Canada at [1980] 1 S.C.R. 54 at 57-58.

36 See *supra*, note 1.

37 *Ibid.* at 75.

38 *Ibid.* at 76.

39 See the recent analysis of the Court's use of rhetoric by Professor Gold; M. Gold, "The Mask of Objectivity: Politics and Rhetoric in the Supreme Court of Canada" (1985), 7 Sup. Ct. L. Rev. 455.

sets of arguments led the Court to the conclusion that fundamental changes to the Senate could not be accomplished through unilateral action of the Canadian Parliament.

(i) *The formalist argument*

The federal government argued that Parliament's power to alter the powers of the Senate flowed from s. 91(1) of the *British North America Act, 1867*. This section, added to the list of federal powers by the United Kingdom Parliament in 1949, gave Parliament power to amend the "constitution of Canada", subject to a number of exceptions.[40] It was common ground that the powers and composition of the Senate did not fall into any of the named exceptions in s. 91(1); therefore it was argued, the Senate was part of the "constitution of Canada" and its powers could be altered by an ordinary federal statute.

The Court's first response to this broad reading of the phrase "constitution of Canada" in s. 91(1) was that it failed to take account of the opening words of s. 91. The opening words of s. 91 confer federal legislative power upon "the Queen, by and with the Advice and Consent of the Senate and the House of Commons". This reinforces s. 17 of the Act, which defines "Parliament" as consisting of the Queen, the Senate and the House of Commons. Section 91(1) is merely a particularization of the general legislative power possessed by "Parliament". Therefore, argued the Court, this particularized power could not be used to alter the nature of the very institution upon whom the power was conferred; "[i]t [s. 91(1)] cannot be construed as permitting the transfer of the legislative powers enumerated in s. 91 to some body or bodies other than those specifically designated in

---

40 Section 91(1) provided as follows:

1. The amendment from time to time of the Constitution of Canada, except as regards matters coming within the classes of subjects by this Act assigned exclusively to the Legislatures of the provinces, or as regards rights or privileges by this or any other Constitutional Act granted or secured to the Legislature or the Government of a province, or to any class of persons with respect to schools or as regards the use of the English or the French language or as regards the requirement that there shall be a session of the Parliament of Canada at least once each year, and that no House of Commons shall continue for more than five years from the day of the return of the Writs for choosing the House: Provided, however, that a House of Commons may in time of real or apprehended war, invasion or insurrection be continued by the Parliament of Canada if such continuation is not opposed by the votes of more than one-third of the members of such House.

Section 91(1) was repealed by the *Constitution Act, 1982*.

it."[41] This would be the effect of a federal statute abolishing the Senate or altering its powers. Such a change would "involve a transfer by Parliament of all its legislative powers to a new legislative body of which the Senate would not be a member."[42] In effect, the Parliament of Canada was claiming the power to reconstitute itself. Such expansive power was never contemplated by the phrase "the constitution of Canada" in s. 91(1).

The Court sought to reinforce its analysis of s. 91(1) by pointing to the interpretation of an analogous provision in s. 92 of the Act. Section 92(1) empowers the legislatures of the provinces to amend the "Constitution of the Province, except as regards the Office of the Lieutenant Governor". In the case of *Re the Initiative and Referendum Act*,[43] the issue arose as to whether this permitted the Manitoba legislature to provide that laws of the province could be made and repealed by direct vote of the electors instead of only by the legislature. The Manitoba Court of Appeal held that such a provision fell outside of the phrase "constitution of the province" in s. 92(1). The Court reasoned that s. 92 of the Act vested power to make or repeal laws exclusively in the legislature and that it did not contemplate the creation of new legislative bodies; "no matter what changes are made in the constitution, the Provincial Legislature and no other body can legislate on the subjects set forth in the remainder of the sub-sections". This limitation was not affected by the fact that the power of amendment in s. 92(1) operated "notwithstanding anything in this Act". When the matter reached the Privy Council, the board left this point open (the appeal being decided on other grounds). However, Viscount Haldane pointed out that while the legislature might "seek the assistance of subordinate agencies . . . it does not follow that it can create and endow with its own capacity a new legislative power not created by the Act to which it owes its own existence."[44]

According to the Supreme Court, there was an identical objection to any attempt to abolish the Senate. The *British North America Act, 1867* had conferred power on "Parliament", including the Senate, and any change in the composition of the legislative body would have to come from Westminster rather than Ottawa.

There was one overwhelming difficulty with the Court's analysis.

---

41 *Supra*, note 1 at 72.
42 *Ibid.*
43 *Re Initiative and Referendum Act* (1916), 27 Man. R. 1.
44 *Re Initiative and Referendum Act*, [1919] A.C. 935 at 945.

This difficulty arose from the fact that four provinces had abolished their respective legislative councils, relying on the power in s. 92(1) to amend the "constitution of the province". It had always been assumed that these provincial actions were lawful. It was thought that the *Initiative and Referendum* reasoning was distinguishable since the legislatures in these instances were not purporting to confer legislative power on a separate or different body. The legislatures were merely reconstituting or redefining themselves, a power which was contemplated by the amendment provision in s. 92(1).

The Supreme Court in the *Senate Reference* agreed that the previous provincial abolitions of legislative councils had been lawful, but maintained that this did not assist Parliament's claim for a similar power regarding the federal Senate. The Court drew a distinction between the opening words in ss. 91 and 92 of the Act. Section 91 particularizes the participants in the federal law-making process and specifically mentions the Senate. Section 92, on the other hand, merely confers authority to legislate upon the "legislature", without particularizing the elements of that body.

This is surely a distinction without a difference. Although s. 92 itself does not particularize the participants in the provincial law-making process, there are other provisions in the Act which are more specific. Section 71, for example, provides that the legislature of Quebec shall be comprised of "the Lieutenant Governor and of Two Houses, styled the Legislative Council of Quebec and the Legislative Assembly of Quebec." The existence of this particularization did not block the province of Quebec from abolishing its legislative council in 1968.

This produces the following incongruous result. If the drafters of the B.N.A. Act had happened to specify the composition of the "legislature" in s. 92 rather than elsewhere in the Act, this would have rendered the provinces incompetent to abolish their legislative councils. Conversely, if the drafters had simply used the word "Parliament" in s. 91, rather than making specific reference to the Queen, Senate and House of Commons, then Parliament would have been free to abolish the Senate. But such choices in legislative drafting are matters of convenience and form rather than substance. When constitutional choices are made to depend on such historical accidents, constitutional adjudication becomes little more than the "barren exercise in statutory interpretation", which the Court itself is so fond of denouncing.[45]

---

45 See judgment of Dickson J. in *Re Residential Tenancies Act of Ontario*, [1981] 1 S.C.R. 714

There was nothing absurd or mysterious about reading the phrase "constitution of Canada" in s. 91(1) as including the Senate. As Professor Hogg has argued convincingly, whether one adopts a wide or a narrow reading of this phraseology, it is difficult to escape the conclusion that it must include power over the Senate.[46] Thus, even accepting the Court's contention that the "constitution of Canada" referred only to the "constitution of the federal government, as distinct from the provincial governments",[47] this supports rather than undermines the federal position in the reference. No amount of formalistic posturing over the wording of the B.N.A. Act can add up to a plausible rebuttal of that position.

(ii) *The historical argument*

In interpreting the provisions of the *British North America Act*, the Privy Council and the Supreme Court have always purported to be giving effect to the "intentions" of the fathers of confederation. However, their concern has never been with the *actual* beliefs of the fathers of confederation as to the substantive meaning of particular provisions of the Act. Rather, the courts have discovered or inferred the intentions of the drafters through an analysis of the "plain meaning" of the words used in the statute. In the *Senate Reference*, the Court departs from this settled interpretive tradition in order to examine the actual intentions of the fathers of confederation regarding the function and role of the Senate. The Court finds that the Senate was intended to be an important institutional protection for provincial and sectional interests. This supports its conclusion that the Parliament of Canada lacks unilateral power to abolish the Senate.

The historical material relied upon by the Court is the Confederation Debates in the assembly of Canada in 1865. The Court quotes a speech of Sir John A. Macdonald in which he describes the Senate

---

at 722 (S.C.C.). The Supreme Court also attempted to distinguish s. 92(1) from s. 92 by the fact that s. 92(1) includes the phrase "notwithstanding anything in this Act". See *supra*, note 1 at 74. But this argument also appears unsatisfactory. As was pointed out previously, the legislatures had been denied the power to delegate legislative power to other bodies, despite the "notwithstanding" in s. 92(1). It hardly seems plausible to invoke the "notwithstanding" clause in order to justify an abolition of a legislative council but not to justify delegation to a separate body.

46 See Hogg, *supra*, note 32 at 637-639.

47 *Supra*, note 1 at 70.

as a protector of "sectional interests" against "the combinations of majorities in the Assembly".[48] The Honourable George Brown explained to the Assembly that protection for the "diversity of interests" was to be guaranteed in two ways: first, by handing over control of local matters to local legislatures, and second, by providing for equal representation in the Senate for the three "sections" of Ontario, Quebec and the Maritimes.[49] In short, the Senate was explicitly regarded as a body charged with protecting sectional or provincial interests. It was an essential part of the "Canadian federal scheme".[50] Any changes to the essential features of the scheme cannot be made at the whim of one of the parties acting alone:

> The character of the Senate was determined by the British Parliament in response to the proposals submitted by the three provinces in order to meet the requirement of the proposed federal system. It was that Senate, created by the Act, to which a legislative role was given by s. 91. In our opinion, its fundamental character cannot be altered by unilateral action by the Parliament of Canada and s. 91(1) does not give that power.[51]

Essentially, the Court's argument can be reduced to the following three propositions. First, the confederation settlement was a "compact" between the various provinces which was later ratified by the British Parliament. Second, an essential element of the bargain was an Upper Chamber designed to protect sectional or provincial interests from majorities in the House of Commons. Therefore, it is beyond the power of the Canadian Parliament to alter the character of the Senate, regardless of the wording of s. 91(1). In effect, this restrictive reading of s. 91(1) is entailed by the federal character of Canada's constitution.

The "compact theory" has a long and chequered history in Canadian political discourse.[52] The essential feature of the theory is the view that confederation was a contractual arrangement among provincial governments which can only be revised with their unanimous consent. Ironically, the origins of the theory can be traced to statements made by Sir John A. Macdonald in the Confederation Debates describing the federation plan as "in the nature of a treaty

---

48 See *ibid.* at 66-67.
49 *Ibid.* at 67.
50 *Ibid.* at 76.
51 *Ibid.* at 78.
52 See E.R. Black, *Divided Loyalties, Canadian Concepts of Federalism* (1975); D. Creighton, "The Use and Abuse of History" in *Towards the Discovery of Canada* (1972) at 65.

settled between the different colonies".[53] Macdonald claimed that this precluded the possibility of any amendments to the scheme; the proposals would either have to be accepted in their entirety or else interprovincial negotiations would have to be reopened.[54]

The compact theory gained widespread popularity and acceptance in the first 60 or 70 years following confederation. The Judicial Committee of the Privy Council, writers and politicians all assumed, implicitly or explicitly, that confederation was a "treaty" or "pact" which Canadians, as well as the Parliament of the United Kingdom, were bound to respect.[55] But by the 1930s, the assumptions underlying the theory came under attack and were effectively discredited.

The best-known and most cogent legal critique was that advanced by Professor Norman McL. Rogers in 1931.[56] Professor Rogers raised a number of obvious, but thoroughly devastating, objections to the compact theory. He pointed first to the fact that the delegates to the founding conferences in 1864 and 1865 had lacked authorization from either their own legislatures or the Imperial Crown to conclude any binding agreements. Only the Canadian legislature approved the Quebec resolutions. New Brunswick rejected them, and Nova Scotia's legislature was so hostile to the scheme that it was never submitted for consideration. As for the other provinces, British Columbia and Prince Edward Island entered the union after negotiations with the federal government, rather than with the original provinces; the provinces of Alberta and Saskatchewan were created through an ordinary federal statute and denied ownership of their natural resources.

The history of amendment to the *B.N.A. Act* fails to support the assumptions of the compact theory. The constitution has been amended many times since confederation without any provincial consent, much less the unanimous consent supposedly required by the compact theory.[57]Contemporary writing on the compact theory emphasizes that "[c]onstitutional lawyers have effectively refuted the existence of the

---

53 Confederation Debates (1865) at 15, quoted in Black, *ibid.* at 150.

54 *Ibid.*

55 See P. Gerin-Lajoie, *Constitutional Amendment in Canada* (1950) at 206.

56 "The Compact Theory of Confederation", Canadian Political Science Assn. (1931), 2 Proceedings of the Annual Meeting 205.

57 The history of amendments to the *B.N.A. Act* was set out in the judgment of the Court, along with a statement of "four general principles" regarding amendment enunciated in a federal government White Paper in 1965. The fourth general principle in the White Paper stated that "the Canadian Parliament will not request an amendment directly affecting federal-provincial relationships without prior consultation and agreement with the prov-

compact as a legal notion . . .".[58] Thus, the Supreme Court's interpretation of the confederation agreement as a bargain between the various provinces is puzzling and remarkable. Without acknowledging the overwhelming objections to the theory, the Court relies on a conception of confederation that has been effectively discredited for close to 50 years.[59]

Thus, the first proposition in the Court's argument, the reliance on the compact theory of confederation, is constitutionally groundless. What of the second proposition, the claim that the Senate was originally intended to protect sectional interests?

The Supreme Court is quite correct to point out that the Upper House was an embodiment of the "federal principle" and was designed to protect regional interests.[60] But this does not necessarily justify the conclusion that the consent of the provincial *governments* must be obtained for constitutional amendments affecting the Senate. This conclusion follows only if "the provinces" are equated with provincial governments, and if these governments are designated as the only legitimate advocates for regional interest and concern. But there is another possibility. This competing conception would characterize the provincial governments as legitimate advocates for provincial concerns only with respect to those matters falling under provincial jurisdiction. With respect to matters falling under federal jurisdiction, the prov-

---

inces." However, the White Paper also suggested that this principle had only emerged after 1907 and that "the nature and degree of provincial participation in the amending process, however, have not lent themselves to easy definition." See *supra*, note 1 at 64. This fourth principle contradicts, rather than confirms, the compact theory. First, it states that the requirement of provincial consent emerged only after 1907, rather than from the original agreement of the provinces; second, it is deliberately equivocal on the issue of the requirement of unanimity.

58 Black, *supra*, note 52 at 171. See also R. Romanow, J. Whyte and H. Leeson, *Canada . . . Notwithstanding: The Making of the Constitution 1976–1982.* (1984) at 168-170.

59 Some authors have argued that, although the compact theory has no legal foundation, it nevertheless provides an appealing account of the "moral foundations" of Canadian federalism. See, e.g., G.F. Stanley, "Act or Pact? Another Look at Confederation" (1956), Can. Hist. Assoc. Report 1. But even this modified claim is doubtful, for the reasons outlined by Romanow *et al.*:

> Since it [the compact theory] views the basic unit of federalism as provinces rather than people, it denies that the general will of the Canadian people can override the objections of one or a few dissenting provincial governments . . . Supporters of the compact theory failed to acknowledge the existence of the new national community, whose development should not be frustrated by the objections of a small number of participant units.

See Romanow *et al.*, *supra*, note 58 at 169.

60 See discussion in the opening section of this chapter.

ince's federal representatives in Ottawa would be the appropriate voice of provincial interests. On this view, the powers and composition of the Senate would clearly be matters falling outside of the constitutional jurisdiction of the provinces. Therefore, although the Senate is a body designed to guarantee "sectional interests", it does not implicate the interests of provincial governments as such.

Because the Supreme Court failed to make this crucial distinction between "provincial interests" and the interests of provincial governments, it seriously misconstrued the historical evidence regarding the function of the Senate. There is strong historical evidence suggesting that the drafters of the confederation scheme did not regard provincial governments as the sole legitimate advocate for provincial interests. Nor was the Senate expected to protect the interests of provincial governments as such, as opposed to the interests of the citizens and communities in the various regions.

An illuminating illustration is provided by Sir John A. Macdonald, whose views were supposedly the foundation for the Court's opinion in the *Reference*. Macdonald strongly believed that territorial interests must be represented *within* the institutions of the national government rather than *to those institutions* by the provincial governments.[61] For Macdonald, the task of representing provincial or local interests was shared by both levels of government, according to the constitutional allocation of jurisdiction. An illustration of Macdonald's thinking on the issue is the following letter to the Lieutenant-Governor of Nova Scotia in 1886, in which Macdonald argues that the province's representatives in Ottawa were the proper persons to interpret its interests in matters under federal jurisdiction:

> The representatives of Nova Scotia as to all questions respecting the relations between the Dominion and the Province sit in the Dominion Parlt. and are the constitutional exponents of the wishes of the people with regard to such relations. The Provincial members have their powers restricted to the subjects mentioned in the B.N.A. Act and can go no further.[62]

There is nothing in Macdonald's statements regarding the Senate during the Confederation Debates which is inconsistent with these views. In the speech quoted by the Supreme Court, Macdonald merely argues that the Senate is designed to protect sectional "interests" as opposed to the interests of provincial governments. This point seems

---

61 See G. Stevenson, *Unfulfilled Union* (1979) at 68; R. Gibbins, *supra*, note 11 at 78.

62 Macdonald, letter to the Lieutenant-Governor of Nova Scotia in 1886, in Pope, *Correspondence of Sir John Macdonald* (n.d.) at 379, quoted in Stevenson, *supra*, note 61 at 59.

obvious given the fact that representation in the Senate was not according to province but equally divided amongst three "sections"; the delegates to the confederation conferences had explicitly rejected a proposal which would have granted each province equal representation in the Upper House.[63] In sum, Macdonald's view of federalism rejected any facile equation of provincial interests with the interests of provincial governments. He believed that provincial governments were the instruments of their populations for provincial purposes, while federal members of Parliament and senators were provincial representatives for national purposes.

The Supreme Court, in the *Senate Reference*, although purporting to give effect to the "intentions of the drafters", in fact advanced a view which radically contradicted Macdonald's conception. Beginning with the premise that the Senate was designed to protect "sectional interests", the Court jumped to the conclusion that this required the participation of the provincial governments before any changes could be made to the Senate. This ignored the possibility that a province's representatives in Ottawa were the appropriate voice for provincial interests with respect to matters falling within federal jurisdiction.

This confusion between provincial interests and the interests of provincial governments also helps to explain the Court's restrictive and somewhat puzzling reading of the phrase "constitution of Canada" in s. 91(1) of the *B.N.A. Act*. The Court held that the power of amendment in s. 91(1) "relates to the constitution of the federal government in matters of interest only to that government".[64] If an amendment implicates "provincial interests", then it cannot be accomplished through unilateral federal action. Once again, the reason for this rule must be that the provincial governments as such are the only credible defenders of the provincial interest. This explains why amendments to the institutions of the national government require the consent of the provincial governments, even though they clearly fall outside of the jurisdiction allocated to the provinces under s. 92.

At bottom, this reasoning can be characterized as a gloss on the compact theory of confederation. The essence of the compact theory is to regard the national government as the creation of the provinces. There is no national interest which transcends the sum of individual provincial interests. Carried to its logical extreme, it would grant provincial governments the right to control *all* public policy affecting

---

63 See Gibbins, *supra*, note 11 at 59.
64 See *supra*, note 1 at 71.

their citizens, even on matters falling exclusively within Ottawa's jurisdiction.

This "provincialist" view of federalism is one possible conception of the nature of the Canadian community. But it is certainly not the only possible view; nor can it be said that this decentralist vision dominates contemporary political discourse in this country. To offer one prominent counter-example, the *Final Report* of the Macdonald Commission, published in the fall of 1985, explicitly rejected a provincialist view of federalism, arguing that the federal government must be able to define and promote a national interest which is more than the sum of regional parts:

> Commissioners do not, however, accept a model which sees the provincial governments as the sole representatives of regional or provincial interest, and the federal government as the sole articulator for all matters of national interest. Rather, the logic of federalism assigns to provincial governments responsibility for representing the interests of their residents within areas of provincial jurisdiction; and to the national government it assigns the responsibility for articulating the interests of Canadians in areas of federal jurisdiction.[65]

Not only does the Court's analysis take for granted a view of Canadian federalism which is highly controversial, it fails to take account of any of the recent writing on "intrastate federalism". The essential thrust of this literature, as we saw earlier in this chapter, is to loosen and to expand our unduly restrictive conception of the "federal principle". Federalism is not simply the study of the relationships between governments. The federal principle is also embodied in the devices whereby regional interests are protected through the institutions of the central government.

This literature demonstrates that there is no necessary or inevitable connection between the interests of provinces or regions and the governments of those regions. The interests of territorial governments include such things as the re-election of incumbents, bureaucratic expansion and the protection of the constitutional powers of the provincial state.[66] Such bureaucratic or state interests are not necessarily shared by the citizens of those regions. In any event, a major theme of the writing on intrastate federalism has been the need to strengthen the powers of the federal government in relation to the provinces. The assumption is that the absence of effective regional representation in the institutions of the central government has

---

65 Macdonald Commission, *supra*, note 25 at 70-71.
66 See discussion in Gibbins, *supra*, note 11 at 45-46.

weakened national political institutions. This suggests that the remedy is to strengthen the representation of regions within federal institutions, rather than the representation of provincial governments.[67]

Had the Court considered and analyzed this literature, it might well have remained unpersuaded of the distinction between provincial interests and the interests of provincial governments. But the Court appeared oblivious to these sophisticated and continuing debates over the nature of Canadian federalism. What is perhaps most troubling is that the Court purported to ground its analysis in the historical intentions of the fathers of confederation. But the Court's historical analysis was simplistic and sloppy, misconstruing the views of the drafters regarding the Senate. Ironically, the Court's foray into historical inquiry in this case tends to confirm the wisdom of the traditional rule which excluded such material from the judicial record.

Ultimately, neither of the arguments advanced by the Court provides a satisfactory basis for its opinion. The formalistic argument based on the opening words of s. 91 depends upon an implausible distinction between the phrase "constitution of Canada" in s. 91 and "constitution of the Province" in s. 92. The historical argument combines a series of historical misconceptions with the view that provincial interests are to be equated with the interests of provincial governments. Extending the logic of the "compact theory", the Court's analysis appears to assume that there is no "national interest" which transcends the sum of individual provincial interests. The remaining issue is the impact of this judicial analysis on the politics of Canadian federalism.

(b) The Impact of the Opinion

It is tempting to suggest that the Supreme Court's opinion in this case had a rather minimal impact on the constitutional amendment process. The argument for minimal impact would point to political factors as being far more important in blocking attempted reform of the Senate. First, the proposal for a House of the Federation, as set out in Bill C-60, received little political support and one leading commentator predicted in late 1979 that the proposal "is likely to be soon forgotten."[69] Second, the proposal was overtaken by onrushing

---

67 See Smiley and Watts, *supra*, note 5, "The Assumptions of Intrastate Federalism"; Macdonald Commission, *supra*, note 25 at 88.

68 No footnote 68.

69 Smiley, *supra*, note 9 at 85.

political events. Bill C-60 died on the order paper when Parliament was dissolved in May 1979 and the Trudeau government was defeated in the subsequent election. When the Liberals were re-elected in February 1980, the constitutional agenda of the Prime Minister no longer included comprehensive reform of the Senate.

Yet this account appears to seriously underestimate the actual impact of the Court's decision. This is not to suggest that the constitutional decision represents the sole or even the primary impediment to Senate reform. Nor does the opinion in the *Senate Reference* make future reform efforts futile. But the Court's decision has inserted an important new political obstacle into the process. Whereas previously it was thought that the consent of Parliament alone was sufficient, it is now necessary to obtain the consent of the provincial authorities before Senate reform can proceed. The requirement of provincial consent has since been constitutionally codified in s. 42(1)(*b*) of the *Constitution Act, 1982*; this provision states that the "powers of the Senate and the methods of selecting Senators" can only be changed with the consent of the legislatures of two-thirds of the provinces which comprise together at least half of the population of all the provinces.

This requirement does leave some scope for Senate amendments without provincial consent. Moreover, one should not necessarily assume provincial intransigence on this issue. Nevertheless, it will be rather difficult to secure provincial consent for a number of the current proposals for Senate reform. Most of the current reform proposals envisage an elected Senate.[70] They propose to strengthen the representation of provincial or regional interests in the central government, as distinct from the interests of provincial governments as such. There is little reason to expect provincial political elites to regard these "centralist" variants of intrastate federalism with much favour. Indeed, an important justification of such reforms is that they will strengthen the legitimacy of the federal government at the expense of the provinces. The incentives for provincial political elites lie in the opposite direction, in favour of institutionalizing some role for provincial governments directly in the operations of the federal government.

Thus, while the Court's decision in the *Senate Reference* may not have precluded Senate reform, it has unquestionably restricted the

---

70 See, e.g., Macdonald Commission, *supra*, note 25 at Chapter 21; Smiley and Watts, *supra*, note 5 at Chapter VII; Gibbins, *supra*, note 11.

directions which reform might take. By explicitly recognizing a constitutional role for the provincial governments in the process, it has made it more likely that a reconstituted Upper House will be a representative of provincial governments rather than of provincial interests more broadly defined. These constitutional constraints can be overcome only through the expenditure of considerable political will and resources.

4. THE SECOND INITIATIVE: UNILATERAL FEDERAL ACTION AND THE PATRIATION APPEALS

The federal government was unable to secure provincial agreement for the comprehensive constitutional changes proposed in Bill C-60.[71] With the defeat of the Trudeau government in May 1979, the issue of constitutional reform lost its sense of urgency and priority. Then, following the surprising defeat of the conservative government of Mr. Clark and the return to power of the Liberals in February 1980, constitutional reform was once again placed at the top of the political agenda. Buoyed by its success in the Quebec referendum in May 1980, the federal government convened a constitutional conference in early September. However, the September conference was a complete failure, ending in an atmosphere of confrontation and recrimination between the federal and provincial governments.[72] It was widely expected that the federal government would take some form of unilateral action in an attempt to break the logjam over constitutional reform.[73]

The federal government announced its response on 2 October 1980. The Federal Minister of Justice tabled a "Proposed Resolution" which requested the Queen to "cause to be laid before the Parliament of the United Kingdom" an act to be known as the *Canada Act*. The *Canada Act* would abolish the power of the United Kingdom Parliament to legislate for Canada and provide a domestic procedure for amending the Canadian constitution. The statute would also entrench a "Charter of Rights and Freedoms" which would be binding on both the federal and provincial governments.

---

71 For a summary of the discussions over Bill C-60, see Smiley, *supra*, note 9 at 81-83.

72 For a detailed account of the events leading up to the conference, as well as the conference itself, see Romanow *et al.*, *supra*, note 58 at 60-105.

73 This had been the strategy proposed in the leaked "Kirby memorandum": see Federal-Provincial Relations Office, *Report to Cabinet on Constitutional Discussions, Summer 1980 and the Outlook for the First Ministers Conference and Beyond* (30 August 1980).

Only Ontario and New Brunswick supported the federal initiative. The eight dissenting provinces sought to block the resolution by referring the matter to various provincial Courts of Appeal. The references, to the Courts of Appeal of Manitoba, Quebec and Newfoundland, raised three issues. First, did the proposed constitutional amendments affect the "powers, rights or privileges" of the provinces; second, was there a "constitutional convention" requiring provincial consent before such a resolution could be submitted to Great Britain; third, was there some legal rule or principle requiring provincial consent in these circumstances?[74]

The provinces lost in both the Quebec and Manitoba courts, but a unanimous Newfoundland Court of Appeal held that provincial consent was legally required before the amendments could become part of Canadian law.[75] Following the Newfoundland decision, the federal government announced that it would not submit the resolution to Britain before the Supreme Court of Canada was given an opportunity to rule on its constitutional validity. The case was argued before the Supreme Court in May 1981.

(a) The Positions of the Parties

The argument offered by the federal government in favour of its proposed action was deceptively simple. The federal government did not claim any *legal* authority to amend the *B.N.A. Act* or even to "cause" it to be amended. Rather, Ottawa claimed that full legal authority to amend the constitution continued to reside in the United Kingdom Parliament.[76] There was a constitutional convention that British authority would only be exercised upon the request and with

---

74 Although the wording of the three references varied, each raised these three issues in one form or another. When the cases reached the Supreme Court, only the second and third issues remained contentious, as the federal government conceded that the proposed amendments affected provincial powers.

75 *A.G. Can. v. A.G. Nfld.* (1981), 82 A.P.R. 503.

76 See factum of the Attorney-General of Canada, p. 63. The argument was based on the wording of the *Statute of Westminster, 1931*, (22 & 23 Geo. V), c. 4. It was argued that the general effect of this statute was to terminate the power of Great Britain to legislate for Canada without Canadian consent, and to permit Canada to repeal prior British laws which applied here. However, this legal recognition of Canadian independence did not apply to the amendment of the *B.N.A. Act*, due to s. 7(1) of the *Statute of Westminster, 1931*, which states:

> Nothing in this Act shall be deemed to apply to the repeal, amendment or alteration of the British North America Acts, 1867 to 1930, or any order, rule or regulation made thereunder.

the consent of the Senate and House of Commons, but conventions were said to raise questions of political exigency rather than legal obligation. Thus, the argument of the Attorney-General of Canada was that Westminster could legally amend the *B.N.A. Act* at its sole discretion and any resulting amendment would be valid and enforceable in Canadian law. No Canadian consent of any kind (and *a fortiori* no provincial consent) was "constitutionally required".

With respect to the issue of whether there was a "convention" or political norm requiring provincial consent, the federal strategy was to point to the diverse and conflicting procedures which had been employed in previous amendments to the *B.N.A. Act*. The federal lawyers argued that, while a number of these amendments had received provincial consent, many of them had been enacted without provincial consultation or else over provincial objections. The federal position was that there was no moral or political obligation of obtaining provincial consent before requesting an amendment to the *B.N.A. Act*.

There was no single or common provincial position in the reference. Some provinces, for example, argued that unanimous provincial consent was required before the resolution could proceed, while Saskatchewan maintained that some lesser but unspecified measure of provincial consent would have been sufficient. The diverse and sometimes conflicting nature of the provincial arguments makes it impossible to ascribe a position to "the provinces". However, of all the arguments raised by the provinces, there was one in particular which was extremely powerful and compelling and which constituted the most serious obstacle to the federal position on the "legal" question.[77]

This provincial argument can be stated in the form of two propositions. The first proposition is a claim about Canadian independence. It rejects the federal government's assertion that the United Kingdom Parliament retained absolute, unfettered legal authority over the amendment of the *B.N.A. Act*. On this view, the sovereignty of Canada is inconsistent with the power in any other state, including Great Britain, to enact law for Canada. Thus, the role of the United Kingdom Parliament in the amendment process must be merely formal. Amendments passed by Great Britain to the Act will take effect as

---

77 My reference to the "legal" question parallels the distinction between "law" and "convention" utilized by the Court in its judgment in the case. Conventions can be distinguished from laws on the basis they are norms which are recognized as morally or politically binding, but which cannot be enforced in a court of law.

part of Canadian law only if they have received the consent of the proper Canadian authorities. If Britain were to attempt to amend the constitution without a proper request from Canada, the Canadian courts would be entitled to ignore the amendment. In short, the first proposition in the argument is a simple claim that *some form* of Canadian consent is legally required for amendments to the Canadian constitution.

The second proposition in the argument in a claim about the nature of the Canadian consent which is legally required. Canada is not just a sovereign state; it is also a federal state. Federalism implies that there are two levels of government, neither of which has the unilateral power to alter or reduce the powers of the other. This suggests that the consent of the federal government alone is insufficient to ground an amendment which would affect provincial legislative powers. The federal government is competent to speak only on s. 91 matters; the logic of federalism is that any changes to the powers of the provinces under s. 92 must receive some measure of provincial consent. This does not mean that the provinces have the power to directly request an amendment from Britain. It simply requires that no amendment which affects provincial powers should be recognized by Canadian courts as part of Canadian law without some measure of provincial consent.[78]

These submissions on the "legal issue" were coupled with an equally cogent argument with respect to the issue of whether there was a "convention", or political norm, requiring provincial consent. On this question, the provinces sought to counter federal suggestions that the history of constitutional amendment was too diverse to support a constitutional convention. The provincial strategy was to attempt to distinguish those amendments which had altered provincial legislative powers from other amendments to the *B.N.A. Act.* The provinces argued that in each of the five instances in which provincial legislative powers had been affected, provincial consent had been obtained. Conversely, there were a number of other such amendments which had not been forwarded to Great Britain for action because of provincial opposition. In this way, the provinces were able to explain the fact that, on a number of occasions, their consent had not been obtained for constitutional amendments by Britain. The provinces were able to demonstrate that in all those instances when provincial consent

---

78 For elaboration of the arguments summarized here, see B. Schwartz, "General National Agreement: The Legal Sanction for Constitutional Reform in Canada" (1981), 6 Queen's L.J. 513a; Romanow *et al., supra,* note 58 at 164-168.

had not been obtained, the amendment had not affected provincial legislative powers. This confirmed rather than contradicted the existence of a constitutional convention with respect to the class of amendments which affected provincial legislative powers. Since the proposed amendment fell into this class, the convention would be breached if the federal government forwarded the resolution to Britain without obtaining provincial agreement.

The arguments raised on the reference were extraordinarily subtle and complex. They implicated fundamental issues about the nature of Canadian federalism and independence. But given the Supreme Court's judgment just two years earlier in the *Senate Reference*, the provinces had good reason to be hopeful of success. In the *Senate Reference*, the Court had adopted a radically provincialist view of Canadian federalism. It had cabined and cribbed the federal power of constitutional amendment under s. 91(1) to those few matters which were "of interest" only to the federal government. Of course, the issue in the 1981 appeals was different; now, the Court was dealing with an amendment to be enacted by Westminster rather than by the federal Parliament under s. 91(1). But six of the eight justices who had decided the *Senate Reference* were also sitting on the *Patriation Appeals*. If those justices adopted the same premises about Canadian federalism which had informed their analysis in the *Senate Reference*, it was difficult to imagine how the federal arguments in this case could succeed.

(b) The Opinion of the Court

The decision of the Supreme Court, handed down on 28 September 1981 before a battery of television cameras, denied clear victory to either side in the dispute. The Court ruled that there was no legal rule blocking the proposed patriation plan; however, a majority of the Court held that there was a constitutional convention requiring provincial consent in these circumstances. The decision may well have reflected shrewd political judgment on the part of the Court; as is well known, the effect of the judgment was to force the parties back to the bargaining table for one final effort to reach a compromise solution.[79] Yet, whatever its political merits, the Court's legal analysis was confusing, internally inconsistent and a total contradiction of its opinion in the *Senate Reference* just two years earlier.

---

79 For an argument along these lines, see P. Russell, "Bold Statecraft Based on Questionable Jurisprudence".

The internal inconsistency in the Court's analysis is most evident in the majority opinion on the "legal issue". Here, the Court had to deal with the contention that the United Kingdom Parliament possessed unlimited legal power to amend Canada's constitution. At a number of points in the judgment, the Court appears to explicitly accept the view that Westminster's authority remains absolute and that no Canadian consent of any kind is required as a matter of law.

The first instance of this occurs when the Court analyzes the impact of the *Statute of Westminster, 1931*. The Court holds that the effect of s. 7(1) of the Statute[80] was to preserve the unlimited authority of Britain in terms of constitutional amendment:

> What s. 7(1), reinforced by s. 7(3), appeared to do was to maintain the *status quo ante*; that is, to leave any changes in the *British North America Act, 1867* (that is, such changes which, under its terms, could not be carried out by legislation of the Provinces or of the Dominion) to the prevailing situation, namely, with the legislative authority of the United Kingdom Parliament being left untouched.[81]

Later, in response to the provincial argument that the federal government lacked power to do indirectly which it could not do directly, the Supreme Court repeated this view of Westminster's authority:

> . . . it is to confuse the issue of process, which is the basic question here, with the legal competence of the British Parliament when resort is had to the direct-indirect argument. The legal competence of that Parliament, for the reasons already given, remains unimpaired, and it is for it alone to determine if and how it will act.[82]

The view that it is for Britain "alone" to determine "if and how it will act" is a particularly explicit acknowledgment of Canada's legal subordination to British authority. On this view, there is no legal requirement of Canadian consent, either from the federal or provincial governments. If Britain were to decide unilaterally or "alone" to amend the *B.N.A. Act*, such action would apparently be recognized and enforced by the Canadian courts. There would no doubt be a breach of a convention requiring Canadian consent but, as the Court emphasizes, conventions are not legally enforceable.

---

80 *Ref. re Amendment of the Constitution of Can. (Nos. 1, 2, 3)* (1981), 125 D.L.R. (3d) 1 at 37.

81 *Ibid.* at 41. The point is reinforced later in the judgment: "There is here, however, an unprecedented situation in which the one constant since the enactment of the *British North America Act* in 1867 has been the legal authority of the United Kingdom Parliament to amend it." *Ibid.* at 47.

82 *Ibid.* at 41.

The Court's acceptance of Canada's colonial status seems curiously formalistic and remote from political reality. However, given the fact that it was the federal government itself which had argued this view before the Court, the judicial acceptance of it is perhaps understandable. The more puzzling aspect of the Court's judgment is that numerous other passages in the same opinion explicitly reject the suggestion that Canada lacks independence from Great Britain. This competing and contradictory line of argument claims that Canada achieved independence from Britain many decades ago. The reason why provincial consent is not required is said to be because the resolution deals with a matter of "foreign affairs".

This line of argument appears early in the opinion, when the Court emphasizes that Canada has international recognition as an "independent, autonomous and self-governing state". It suffers from an "internal deficiency" in the sense of lacking the power to amend its constitution, but there is no suggestion that any other state has unilateral power to effect constitutional amendments for Canada.[83] The recognition of Canadian independence is unequivocally reiterated later in the judgment:

> . . . the Statute of Westminster, 1931 . . . put internal independence from Great Britain on a legal foundation. The remaining badge of subservience, the need to resort to the British Parliament to amend the British North America Act, 1867, although preserved by the Statute of Westminster, 1931, did not carry any diminution of Canada's legal right in international law, and as a matter of Canadian constitutional law, to assert its independence in external relations, be they with Great Britain or other countries. The matter is emphasized by the judgment of this Court in *Reference re Ownership of Off-shore Mineral Rights* (1967), 65 D.L.R. (2d) 353 at p. 375, [1967] S.C.R. 792 at p. 816, 62 W.W.R. 21. This is a relevant consideration in the appeals which are before this Court.[84]

Here, there is no hint of a continuing colonial relationship with Great Britain. The need to resort to Westminster for constitutional amendments does not diminish Canada's independence as a matter of "Canadian constitutional law". The implication seems to be that Britain retains a formal power of amendment only. Any unilateral attempt by Great Britain to amend the *British North America Act* would

---

83 *Ibid.* at 21.
84 *Ibid.* at 44. The passage in the *Off-shore Minerals* case referred to reads as follows: "There can be no doubt now that Canada has become a sovereign State. Its sovereignty was acquired in the period between its separate signature of the Treaty of Versailles in 1919 and the *Statute of Westminster, 1931*. . . ."

be void as a matter of Canadian constitutional law, since it would fail to take account of Canada's legal independence.

Thus, the reason why provincial consent is not required cannot depend on the "unimpaired" authority of Westminster. Rather, the proposed resolution does not require provincial consent because it involves a matter of "external relations": "[t]his Court is being asked . . . to say that the internal distribution of legislative power must be projected externally, as a matter of law, although there is no legal warrant for this assertion."[85] The provinces have no role to play in the foreign relations between the sovereign states of Canada and Great Britain. There is no legal rule preventing the federal government, in its "foreign relations" with Great Britain, from requesting a constitutional amendment which would limit provincial powers. The Court rejects the suggestion that this is in any way inconsistent with "federalism". In the Court's view, there is no such thing as a "standardized federal system". The Court points out that there are many "unitary" features of Canadian federalism, such as the federal declaratory power and the power of disallowance. In any event, the "essential federal character of the country is preserved under the enactments proposed by the Resolution."[86]

What all of this amounts to is unclear, other than that the federal proposal is legally valid. Some commentators read the Court as holding that provincial consent is not required because Westminster retains absolute authority over the *B.N.A. Act*.[87] Others argue that the Court recognized Canada's independence and dispensed with provincial consent because of the foreign relations aspect of the proposal.[88] These are equally plausible readings of the opinion of the majority on the legal issue. In blunt terms, the opinion is an incoherent and internally contradictory jumble of assertions rather than a reasoned argument. The Court asserts the unlimited authority of Great Britain over the *B.N.A. Act* while simultaneously claiming that Canada is a sovereign, independent state.

This sense of internal contradiction is deepened when we compare the majority opinion on the legal issue with the majority opinion on the issue of convention. The Court accepts the provincial claim that there is a convention requiring a "substantial measure of provincial

---

85 *Ibid.* at 47.

86 *Ibid.*

87 See P. Hogg, "Constitutional Law — Amendment of the British North America Act — Role of the Provinces" (1982), 60 Can. Bar Rev. 307 at 325.

88 See B. Slattery, "The Independence of Canada" (1983), 5 Sup. Ct. L. Rev. 369 at 396-397.

consent" for amendments which affect provincial legislative powers. The reason for this rule, according to the Court, is the "federal principle"; "[t]he federal principle cannot be reconciled with a state of affairs where the modification of provincial legislative powers could be obtained by the unilateral action of the federal authorities."[89] The Court also rejects the federal government's contention that the proposal does not offend the "federal principle" since it does not alter the federal character of the country. The Court's curt and devastating reply to this federal submission is that, while Canada would remain a federation, it would be a different federation, made different at the instance of the federal authorities alone. According to the Court, "[i]t is this process itself which offends the federal principle."[90]

There is a very deep tension between the Court's view of federalism in these two majority opinions. In dealing with the legal issue, the Court maintained that there was no standardized "federal system", and thus, federalism was not offended by a unilateral federal power to amend the constitution. Moreover, the Court pointed out that the essential federal character of the country would be preserved under the proposed amendments. The opinion on the conventional issue amounts to a cogent rejection and rebuttal of the Court's own analysis on the legal issue. The argument on convention asserts that the federal principle would indeed be offended by unilateral federal power to secure constitutional amendments. It illuminates the fallacy in the view that federalism is not offended here because the federal character of the country is preserved.

The Court's contrasting views of federalism can be better understood through reference to the typology of federal concepts developed by political scientist Edwin Black, in his book *Divided Loyalties*.[91] The majority opinion on the legal issue exemplifies what Black terms the "centralist" concept. This view is associated with the political ideas of Sir John A. Macdonald, who believed in a unitary state and wished to subordinate the provincial governments to national authority. The Court's opinion on the conventional issue, on the other hand, assumes what Black terms a "coordinate" view of federalism. This is a so-called "classical" conception of federalism, in which each

---

89 *Supra*, note 81 at 104.

90 *Ibid.* at 106.

91 See Black, *supra*, note 52. The five concepts or images of Canadian federalism identified by Black are: centralist, administrative, coordinate, dualist and compact.

level of government is independent and supreme within a clearly defined area of jurisdiction.

Black's typology also illustrates that both of these majority opinions essentially reject the underlying view of federalism advanced in the *Senate Reference*. The contrast between the *Senate Reference* and the majority legal opinion in the *Patriation Appeals* is fairly obvious. The Court in the *Senate Reference* gave a particularly constricted interpretation of federal powers of amendment under s. 91(1), while the majority in the *Patriation* case saw federal power as essentially unlimited. But there is also a wide divergence between the Court's approach in the *Senate Reference* and its opinion on the conventional issue in the *Patriation* case.

Recall the Court's unwillingness in the *Senate Reference* to entertain any distinction between "provincial interests" as such and the interests of provincial governments. This view, consistent with what Black terms the "compact theory" of confederation, would require the consent of the provincial governments whenever an amendment was "of interest" to a province. The analysis of constitutional conventions in the *Patriation Appeals* proceeds on quite a different footing. This latter analysis distinguishes constitutional amendments which directly affect provincial legislative powers from other types of amendments. The Court takes the view that only amendments affecting legislative powers of the provinces require provincial consent. The other side of the coin is that, even though an amendment might be "of interest" to a province, this does not entail any requirement, in either law or convention, that a province consent to it. It is on this basis that the Court explains the many amendments to the *B.N.A. Act* which have been "of interest" to the provinces but which were enacted without any provincial consent. For example, the amendment of 1915, which re-defined the senatorial divisions of Canada, was enacted with the consent of the Senate and House of Commons alone. No provincial consent was obtained.

This analysis reflects a commitment to a classical conception of federalism. The provinces' jurisdiction is limited to the subjects enumerated in s. 92. Unless an amendment touches on those exclusive powers, there is no need for the provincial governments to be consulted. This is why the amendment of 1915, although "of interest" to the provinces, did not require provincial consent. This approach can be contrasted with the analysis of the Court in the *Senate Reference*. In the *Senate Reference* there is no distinction made between amendments which affect provincial powers under s. 92 and those which are merely "of interest" to the provinces. *Any* amendment which has an impact on a province requires provincial participation, regardless of whether it involves a matter under ss. 91 or 92.

The shifts in the Court's conceptions of federalism are depicted in Table 1. The *Senate Reference* embraces a compact theory of federalism while rejecting both the centralist and classical images. There is no indication in the judgment of the Court's view of the "two nations" theory.[92] In the "legal" opinion in the *Patriation Appeals*, the Court rejects the compact theory and embraces a centralist view of Canadian federalism. The judgment on the conventional issue in the same case shifts once again, this time to a classical concept of federalism.

TABLE 1
Images of Federalism in the Supreme Court 1979–1982

Case	Compact Theory	Two Nations	Classical Federalism	Centralist Federalism
Senate Ref.	yes	?	no	no
Patriation (Law)	no	no	no	yes
Patriation (Convention)	no	?	yes	no
Quebec Veto	no	no	?	?

The table includes a reference to the subsequent judgment in the *Quebec Veto* case[93] to illustrate further shifts in the Court's view of federalism. This reference was initiated by the province of Quebec to determine whether its consent was necessary to the "substantial measure" of provincial consent that the Court had said was required by Canadian convention. The irresistible implication of the Court's reasoning in the first reference was that Quebec's consent was required. In the first reference, the Court had relied upon the constitutional precedents of 1964 and 1971 as evidence of the existence of a convention. These "negative" precedents were instances in which proposed amendments had been blocked due to the opposition of Quebec alone. Yet, in the *Quebec Veto* opinion, the Court rejected the argument that Quebec's consent was constitutionally required on the grounds that there had never been an explicit recognition of such a right. As commentators on the opinion have emphasized, this amounts to an

---

92 A variant of the compact theory, this view characterizes confederation as a compact between two founding races or cultures. See Black, *supra*, note 52 at 199-201.

93 See *supra*, note 3.

implicit rejection of the Court's own analysis of constitutional convention in the *Patriation Appeals*.[94]

5. THE COURT AND CONSTITUTIONAL AMENDMENT: AN OVERVIEW

There are two larger issues which remain unanswered. The first is whether there is any possibility of making sense out of this series of contradictory judgments on constitutional amendment. The second is an assessment of the impact of the Court's role on the eventual political resolution of the issues.

It should be evident by this point that it is futile to attempt to "reconcile" the reasoning of the Court in these cases. In one sense, the contradictions between the opinions should come as no surprise. The Court is divided in these cases over the nature of Canadian federalism and the Canadian political community. There is no consensus on these fundamental issues in the larger political arena; our political discourse combines and includes elements of a whole range of ideological images of federalism.[95] The "legal" analysis of the Supreme Court is essentially an elaboration and application of one or another of these various ideological images. The contradictions and divisions in the Court's opinions are simply a reflection of the heterogeneity of the political debates on federalism. The contradictions in the Court's analysis are a direct consequence of the fact that there are a whole range of contradictory "federal images" which have credibility in the political arena.

While there is little consistency in the legal reasoning of the Court, it may be possible to discern a pattern to the *results* in the cases. In general terms, the results seem consistent with a view of federalism which seeks to maximize countervailing power and cooperation between governments. At the same time, the cases reflect a hostility to unilateralism, independent action by any one government in the federation.

This pattern emerges most clearly in the *Patriation Appeals*. What is striking about the result in that reference is the careful balance between federal and provincial power struck by the Court. While the Court had declared that the federal plan was "legal", the justices had

---

94 For devastating critiques of the *Quebec Veto* case, see A. Petter, "Maître chez who? The Quebec veto reference", Comment on *A.G. Que. v. A.G. Can.*, [1982] 2 S.C.R. 793 (S.C.C.), in (1984), 6 Supreme Court L.R. 387; see Gold, *supra*, note 39.

95 See Black, *supra*, note 52 at 10.

coupled this with a finding that the proposal violated constitutional convention. This lent credibility to the opponents of the resolution in the federal conservative party and the eight dissenting provinces. Even if the resolution cleared the House of Commons, it was now questionable whether Westminster would grant final approval.[96]

If the Court had weakened the hand of Ottawa, it had also dealt a setback to the provinces. The Court had rejected provincial claims that unanimous provincial consent was a prerequisite to constitutional amendment. The effect of the Court's judgment was to simultaneously whittle down the claims of both sides, thereby precluding the possibility of unilateral action by either of them. If constitutional amendment was to be achieved at all, it would have to come through a process of further negotiation and compromise between the various governments.

This hostility to unilateral action and a preference for cooperative, joint solutions is reflected in the *Senate Reference* as well. Essentially, the Court determined that the federal government had no real unilateral right of constitutional amendment; any amendment which was "of interest" to a province would require some form of provincial participation. Aside from minor "housekeeping" matters, it is difficult to imagine a constitutional amendment which would *not* be "of interest" to one or more of the provinces. In substance, if not in form, the Court had read the power of amendment in s. 91(1) right out of the *B.N.A. Act*. It had essentially precluded unilateral action and mandated the involvement of both levels of government in all significant constitutional change.

This interpretation also fits with the result in the *Quebec Veto* case. In this case, the Court was no longer confronted with unilateral action on the part of the federal government. Ottawa had been able to secure the consent of nine of the ten provincial governments for a significantly revised constitutional proposal. It was now the government of Quebec rather than the federal government which seemed to be invoking unilateral rights; Quebec asserted a right to "veto" constitutional amendments agreed to by ten other governments. Within the Court's constitutional vision, provincial unilateralism is no more legitimate than federal unilateralism. The fact that the final constitutional amendment had been the product of joint federal-provincial agreement seemed to satisfy the Court. It refused to weigh the quality

---

96 See Romanow *et al.*, *supra*, note 58 at 188.

of the provincial consent or the significance of Quebec's exclusion from the deal.

The Court's vision in these cases might be termed one of "cooperative federalism". According to this vision, federalism is functioning properly when there is a minimum of discord and division between the various levels of government. Disputes are resolved through a process of bureaucratic bargaining and negotiation rather than political confrontation. Conversely, federalism is malfunctioning when these processes of "elite accommodation" malfunction, resulting in political competition and unilateral action on the part of governments.

In embracing this vision of "cooperative federalism", the Supreme Court is merely giving effect to a vision of Canadian federalism which has become a kind of new orthodoxy in both popular and elite circles. The popular political rhetoric of the 1980s has been pervaded by the values of cooperation. The Mulroney conservatives waged their 1984 campaign on a platform of reconciliation with the provinces. The conservative claim was that an aggressive and insensitive federal government under Pierre Trudeau's liberals had alienated provincial leaders and scuttled the proper functioning of the federal system. Following their victory, the conservatives devoted significant political resources to rebuilding a spirit of cooperation, reaching important agreements on energy resource development with the West and with Newfoundland. The academic literature on federalism has likewise reflected a preoccupation with promoting cooperation between governments through "executive federalism".[97]

There are important political costs associated with an attempt to promote cooperation at the expense of competition. As Albert Breton points out in his brilliant essay published as part of the MacDonald Commission's *Final Report*, federalism is to a large extent premised on the values of competition.[98] Competition is not necessarily to be avoided or condemned. Many social and political institutions are deliberately organized along competitive lines; one obvious example is the body of rules which mandates competition in the market and makes certain forms of cooperative behaviour a criminal offence.

In terms of federal politics, the most important consequence associated with the promotion of cooperation is the condemnation of

---

97 See Smiley, *supra*, note 9.
98 See A. Breton, "Supplementary Statement", in Macdonald Commission, *supra*, note 25 at 486.

unilateral action by one level of government. As Breton argues, this has far greater practical effect on the federal government than on the provinces, for the simple reason that the federal government is more likely to be in a position to act unilaterally.[99] It also means that the political system will have a built-in conservative tendency, making change more difficult to achieve. This tendency was manifested in the reaction of the political actors to the Court decisions in both the *Senate Reference* and the *Patriation Appeals*. The effect of the *Senate Reference* was to make constitutional amendments to the Senate extremely difficult to achieve.[100] The *patriation* case had an identical impact. Had the Court ruled in favour of the federal government on the convention issue or simply refused to answer the question, the political opposition to the federal plan would have been muted. This, in turn, would have assured the resolution's safe passage through the Parliament at Westminster. The Court's ruling in favour of the provinces on this issue effectively scuttled the unilateral federal proposal and made further constitutional negotiations necessary.

The effect of the Court's intervention can be measured through a comparison of the original federal proposals with the revised resolution which was eventually forwarded to Westminster. The chief beneficiaries of the modifications appear to have been the provincial governments. The amending formula in Part V of the statute was modified so as to permit provincial governments to "opt out" of future constitutional changes limiting their rights. An override provision was inserted into the constitution, permitting either level of government to provide that a law would have legal force notwithstanding certain rights protected by the *Charter*. One of the primary democratic features of the original federal proposal, a plan to permit constitutional change through public referendum, was dropped due to provincial opposition. As Reginald Whitaker has put it:

> It is most striking that it was the democratic elements of the federal proposal which were bargained away.[101]

The fact that the parties were able to reach agreement at all demonstrates that cooperative federalism is not necessarily a recipe for political paralysis. The effect of proscribing unilateral action is simply to increase the costs associated with achieving significant

---

99 See *ibid.* at 98.

100 See discussion *supra* at note 69 and accompanying text.

101 "Democracy and the Canadian Constitution" in K. Banting and R. Simeon (eds.) *And No One Cheered: Federalism, Democracy and the Constitution Act* (1983) at 257.

change. In this instance, the strong public sentiment in favour of change was sufficient to induce governments to devote the necessary resources to the process and to make the necessary compromises. But this will not always be the case, as the continuing inaction over Senate reform illustrates. Moreover, a system of cooperative federalism operates primarily as a protection for the interests of political elites rather than those of citizens. Political conflict is automatically translated into the idiom of "intergovernmental affairs", a dialect which gives primacy to the prerogatives and privileges of provincial and federal states. This suggests that, ultimately, it is citizens who benefit the most from political competition between governments and who suffer the greatest from its absence.

9

Federalism and the Economy

The constitutional question was one of the two great issues dominating the federal-provincial agenda in the late 1970s and early 1980s; the other was the economy. Confronted by economic downturns and limited tax revenues, governments in Canada became embroiled in a series of disputes over energy, the development of natural resources and the control of the natural environment.

Predictably, the Supreme Court of Canada was often a high-profile player in such federal-provincial economic disputes. In the next two chapters, I present an overview of the nature and significance of the Court's role in such disputes. My focus is a series of important Court decisions which delineated the scope of federal and provincial regulatory powers over the economy. In this chapter, I examine the decisions from an "internal" perspective. My analysis centers on the reasoning and the arguments of the cases in order to ascertain the general themes and mood of the Court's work in the area.[1]

In Chapter 10, I shift to an "external" perspective. I attempt to determine the extent to which governments have been constrained

---

1 The material in Chapter 9 is drawn largely from P. Monahan, "The Supreme Court and the Economy" in *The Supreme Court of Canada as an Instrument of Political Change* (Royal Commission on the Economic Union and Development Prospects for Canada, Vol. 47, 1985).

in their public policy choices by this series of Supreme Court judgments. The focus here is on the reaction of governments to the decisions and, specifically, on the extent to which governments have been able to substitute alternative regulatory instruments in place of instruments struck down by the Court. From this perspective, it becomes apparent that the decisions of the Court had a rather marginal impact on the eventual public policy outcomes. In each of the instances examined, governments were able to achieve the identical policy goal by deploying a substitute policy instrument. Thus, while the Court often assumed a high profile in such disputes, the actual significance of its role is, at the very least, rather difficult to measure.

1. THE CONTEMPORARY DOCTRINE

Two distinct generalizations may be advanced about the trade and commerce cases of the past ten years. First, the Supreme Court has modified its previous attitude of deference to federal laws. This does not mean that the Court has become hostile to or suspicious of federal attempts to regulate the economy. The point is that the Court is no longer as reluctant to strike down federal economic legislation as it was in the past. The second generalization flows from those instances in which the Court has ruled against the federal government. The Court did not decide these cases through a sensitive balancing of the values at stake in the litigation. Instead, it simply reverted to categories and assumptions that had been dominant in the Privy Council era. The Court's reasoning attempted to draw bright lines between federal and provincial areas of jurisdiction.

This story begins with the decision of the Court in *Re Agricultural Products Marketing Act*.[2] In the aftermath of the Supreme Court's decision in the *Manitoba Egg* case,[3] it had become clear that some form of interprovincial cooperation would be necessary if the market for eggs were to be effectively regulated. The federal government and the provinces eventually agreed on an intricate scheme requiring dovetailing legislation from both levels of government. The scheme was designed to regulate comprehensively all dealings in eggs, whether for local, interprovincial or export trade. Overall quotas for each province were fixed by the federally established Canadian Egg Marketing Agency (CEMA). The agency was also responsible for

---

2 *Re Agricultural Products Marketing Act*, [1978] 2 S.C.R. 1198 (S.C.C.).
3 *A.G. Man. v. Man. Egg & Poultry Assn.*, [1971] S.C.R. 689 (S.C.C.).

purchasing and disposing of any surplus eggs that were within the allotted provincial quota. This guaranteed a fixed price for all eggs within the quota, regardless of whether they were actually required for the table market. The provincial agency would set individual quotas based on the province's overall quota. There were extensive cross-delegations of authority from one level of government to the agency established by the other level. Both federal and provincial agencies financed their operations and redistributed receipts through levies on producers.

A host of constitutional issues was raised by this legislative framework. The judgments contain intricate discussions of the delegation doctrine and the constitutional characterization of producer levies, issues that are not germane to the present discussion. The interest of this chapter extends only to the analysis of the trade and commerce power in the judgment of Mr. Justice Pigeon. The discussion arose in the context of certain quotas that had been imposed on egg producers by the Ontario Farm Products Marketing Board. Not only did these quotas limit the number of eggs that could be marketed by provincial producers, they also directly regulated their production of eggs and their possession of fowl. The production quotas did not distinguish those producers who sold their product locally from those who exported their eggs. All producers were subject to these controls, regardless of the destination of the product. Those challenging the validity of the legislation claimed that the province had overreached its authority. Provincial production quotas were valid only to the extent that they applied to goods that would eventually be sold locally. Goods that would enter the stream of interprovincial trade had to be regulated by Parliament.

It would not have been difficult to construct some functional counterargument in favour of the provincial quotas. For instance, it could have been suggested that it was impossible to identify, at the point of production, whether the goods were eventually to be sold locally or interprovincially.[4] Any requirement that separate regimes be established for local as opposed to interprovincial producers would have been unworkable. But Pigeon J. did not rely on any such limited, functional argument. Instead, he advanced the sweeping generalization that a province had control over all "production" of eggs. The

---

4 Corry, *Difficulties of Divided Jurisdiction*. Study for the Rowell-Sirois Royal Commission on Dominion-Provincial Relations (1939), cited by Laskin C.J. at [1978] 2 S.C.R. 1198 at 1263 (S.C.C.).

destination of the eggs was irrelevant. One did not have to inquire whether most or even all of a producer's eggs would eventually leave the province. The only relevant issue was that the province had enacted "production" quotas rather than "marketing" quotas; "marketing does not include production and, therefore, provincial control of production is *prima facie* valid."[5]

This distinction between "marketing" and "production is reminiscent of U.S. cases in the early twentieth century interpreting Congress' power over interstate commerce. These cases relied on a distinction between "commerce" on the one hand and "manufacture" or "production" on the other. Congress was said to lack power to interfere with production or manufacture, regardless of their importance or interconnection with interstate trade. For instance, in *U.S. v. E.C. Knight Co.*,[6] the U.S. Supreme Court held that the *Sherman Antitrust Act* did not prohibit a near monopoly in the manufacture of refined sugar. This was because "commerce succeeds to manufacture and is not part of it." This distinction relieved the Court of the responsibility of determining the impact of this manufacturing monopoly on interstate commerce itself. The attempt to regulate manufacture was absolutely void regardless of how socially desirable or necessary it might have been. If the polity was not satisfied with this result, it might amend the constitution. The judiciary was merely charged with interpreting the constitution, not with rewriting it.

The difficulty with this line of argument was its extreme artificiality. Economic reality simply does not conform to any rigid distinction between manufacture and commerce. Choices made at the production stage have a direct impact on the marketing of any product. A market constitutes a unified whole rather than isolated fragments or subdivisions. It was precisely because of these underlying economic factors that the U.S. Supreme Court subsequently abandoned its early categorical approach. The later jurisprudence emphasized the effect of an activity on commerce as opposed to "rubrics concerning its boundaries."[7]

> The artificial and mechanical separation of 'production' and 'manufacturing' from 'commerce', without regard to their economic continuity, the effects of the former two upon the latter, and the varying methods by which the several processes are organized, related and carried on in different industries or indeed

---

5 *Supra*, note 2 at 1296.

6 *U.S. v. E.C. Knight Co.*, 156 U.S. 1 (1895).

7 *Mandeville Island Farms Inc. v. American Crystal Sugar Co.*, 334 U.S. 219 at 233 (1948).

within a single industry, no longer suffices to put either production or manufacturing and refining processes beyond reach of Congress' authority.[8]

The Canadian Supreme Court has not been oblivious to these considerations. Indeed, it is possible to identify other recent cases in which the distinction between "production" and "trade" was simply ignored. In these instances, the Court displayed an awareness of the economic continuity between these various forms of activity.

A good illustration is the *Potash* case,[9] decided less than a year after *Re Agricultural Products Marketing Act*. This litigation arose out of attempts by the government of Saskatchewan to stabilize the North American market for potash. Saskatchewan is one of the largest potash producers in the world, exporting the bulk of its production to the United States. In the late 1960s, there was a serious excess of supply and a drop in the world price. The Saskatchewan government, in concert with the largest U.S. potash supplier, devised a plan to limit production and increase market prices. The scheme fixed production quotas for potash producers and established a floor price for potash free on board the mine as a condition for obtaining a licence. The legislation was challenged by Central Canada Potash, a Saskatchewan producer that had an assured market for production in excess of its production allocation.

It would have been possible to uphold this legislation on the basis of the categorical distinction between production and trade. The argument would have focused on the fact that the scheme established production quotas rather than marketing quotas. But merely to state such an argument is to reveal its inadequacy. The whole purpose of the legislation was to stabilize the market for potash in the United States. The regulatory framework operated at the point of production, but its purpose was to ensure that Saskatchewan producers received a fair return on the sale of their resources outside the province. These facts illustrate the artificiality of a rigid distinction between production and trade. Indeed, Chief Justice Laskin simply glossed over the distinction and concluded that the legislation was *ultra vires* the province. In Laskin C.J.C.'s view, the Court had to determine the "true nature and character" of the legislation. This issue could be resolved only by considering "the circumstances under which the *Potash Conservation Regulations, 1960* came into being, [and] the market to which they were

---

8 *Ibid.* at 229.

9 *Central Can. Potash Co. v. Saskatchewan*, [1979] 1 S.C.R. 42 (S.C.C.). The discussion that follows has benefited greatly from a series of conversations with P. Hogg.

applied and in which they had their substantial operation."[10] Looking to those broader factors, the Chief Justice had little difficulty in concluding that they amounted to an attempt to regulate the export market in potash. The fact that the legislation took the form of quotas on production was irrelevant.

Laskin C.J.C. did make a half-hearted attempt to distinguish *Potash* from the *Agricultural Products Reference*. According to Laskin C.J.C., the crucial difference between the cases was that price fixing was a "central feature" of the Saskatchewan legislation. The reply to this argument is that price fixing was an equally central feature of the legislation considered in the *Agricultural Products* case. The prices paid to producers of eggs were fixed each week by the local boards and CEMA on a "cost of production formula."[11] The suggested distinction between the cases is not merely flimsy, but nonexistent.

The Court's analysis in these cases is instructive in jurisprudential terms. In one instance, the Court purports to decide a case on the basis of an artificial distinction between production and trade. Subsequently, the distinction is simply ignored, in substance if not in form. But because the initial distinction is never authoritatively repudiated, it retains doctrinal legitimacy. There are thus two lines of cases, espousing contradictory methodologies, both of which are logically available for use in subsequent litigation. Nor is there any theory to indicate the instances in which the principle is to be preferred over the counterprinciple. The notion of consistency in such a body of materials is little more than rhetorical posturing.

Consider the case of *Labatt v. Attorney-General of Canada*.[12] At issue was the validity of s. 6 of the federal *Food and Drugs Act*,[13] which prohibited anyone from marketing certain food unless it complied with the prescribed standards for such food. Labatt's marketed a beer called "Special Lite Beer" without complying with the standard for "light beer" prescribed in the regulations. Mr. Justice Estey delivered the judgment of the majority of the court on the constitutional issue. He purported to synthesize the jurisprudence that had developed surrounding the trade and commerce power. Relying on such cases as *Eastern Terminal*,[14] he concluded that Parliament had no authority under the first branch of *Parsons* to regulate "individual trades or sections of

---

10 *Ibid.* at 75.
11 *Supra*, note 2 at 1217.
12 *Labatt Breweries of Can. Ltd. v. A.G. Can.*, [1980] 1 S.C.R. 914 (S.C.C.).
13 *Food and Drugs Act*, R.S.C. 1970, c. F-27.
14 *R. v. Eastern Terminal Elevator Co.*, [1925] S.C.R. 434 (S.C.C.).

industry.''[15] Estey J. suggested that the second branch of *Parsons* could only support legislation that dealt with trade in a ''sweeping, general sense,''[16] such as the incorporation statute upheld in *Wharton*.[17] Turning to the facts of the particular case, Estey J. concluded that the legislation could not be supported on the basis of the trade and commerce power. The section fell outside the first branch of *Parsons* since it was not concerned with trade but with production. The act regulated the brewing process itself by means of a ''legal recipe,'' and was not aimed at the movement of products through the channels of trade.[18] Neither could the second branch of *Parsons* be used here, since the regulations related to a single industry rather than to trade in general.

This analysis is essentially a reassertion of a categorical mode of reasoning. The discussion of the first branch of *Parsons* is premised on the artificial distinction between trade and production. Estey J. emphasizes that the distinction between the flow of commerce and production and local sale was ''pointedly made'' by Mr. Justice Pigeon in the *Agricultural Products Marketing Act* case. There is no discussion of the fact that this same distinction was simply glossed over in the *Potash* case. Nor is there any awareness of the makeshift quality of the distinction. The analysis of the second branch of *Parsons* assumes a similar tack. The second branch is said to support laws that regulate trade in general, as opposed to particular trades. This analysis is also categorical in nature. It emphasizes the purely formal aspects of a given statute. If the law fails to satisfy those purely formal requirements, it is void, regardless of its social utility.

The difficulty with these various distinctions and arguments is simply that they ignore the fundamental issue raised in the case, whether this type of law should be enacted on the federal or the provincial level. The purpose of the *Food and Drugs Act* was to reduce confusion and ignorance in the market by specifying uniform standards for food.[19] The expectation was that improving the quality of the information possessed by the consumer would enable individuals to spend their money more rationally. The issue is whether such a policy goal should be a national or a local responsibility. In his judgment, Estey J. failed to address the question of the provinces' ability to remove

---

15 *Supra*, note 12 at 937.

16 *Ibid.* at 940.

17 *John Deere Plow Co. v. Wharton*, [1915] A.C. 330.

18 *Supra*, note 12 at 939, 943.

19 See McQueen, ''Commentary'' (1980-81), 5 Can. Bus. L.J. 225 at 227. See further discussion, *infra*, Chapter 10.

the "noise and static"[20] from the Canadian marketplace, or to consider whether central control over product standards might compromise values of local autonomy in some important way. The only "evidence" before the Court on these issues was the labels from the beer, which indicated that Labatt's operated manufacturing establishments in a number of provinces. Estey J. relied on these labels in concluding that the beer industry was local in nature. But the beer industry in Canada, as in other western countries, is dominated by a relatively small number of huge corporations.[21] The location of the manufacturing establishments does not alter the national character of the industry. By focusing exclusively on the location of the brewing plants, Estey J. was distorting the basic structure and operation of the industry. Instead of examining the economic reality of the beer industry, he was preoccupied with the arbitrary and artificial distinction between the production of beer and trade in beer.

In *R. v. Dominion Stores Ltd.*,[22] the Court had another opportunity to clarify the reach of the trade and commerce power. Given the factual circumstances of the case, the indefatigable distinction between production and trade did not feature in the reasoning of the Court. But the reasons and the result were no less unsatisfactory than they had been in *Labatt*. In *Dominion Stores*, the federal government had created certain national grade names for agricultural products and set standards to be met by sellers who utilized the grade names.[23] Traders engaged in interprovincial and export trade were required to use the applicable names, while traders engaged in purely intraprovincial trade could use the grade names if they desired, provided that they complied with the accompanying standard. A charge was laid under the federal act against Dominion Stores, a wholly intraprovincial trader[24] that had allegedly been selling apples under the grade name "Canada Extra Fancy" without complying with the standards prescribed for that grade name. Dominion Stores challenged the ability of the federal government to prosecute a local trader.

Arguably, the case was indistinguishable from an earlier Privy

---

20 *Ibid.* at 227.
21 For a discussion of the historical evolution of the industry in Ontario, see the judgment of Chief Justice McRuer in *R. v. Cdn. Breweries Ltd.*, [1960] O.R. 601 (Ont. H.C.).
22 *R. v. Dom. Stores Ltd.*, [1980] 1 S.C.R. 844 (S.C.C.).
23 *Canada Agricultural Products Standards Act*, R.S.C. 1970, c. A-8, Pt. I.
24 It was assumed for the purposes of the appeal that the prosecution related to a wholly intraprovincial transaction.

Council decision, the *Canada Standard* case.[25] The federal government had enacted that the words "Canada Standard" should be a national trade mark, and that the application of that mark to any commodity warranted it to conform to a certain standard. Although the Supreme Court of Canada had ruled the legislation invalid, the Privy Council overturned this decision, invoking Dominion authority over "general" trade and commerce. It was obvious, thought Lord Atkin, that the Dominion had authority to create a uniform law of trade marks,[26] and it was impossible to distinguish between trade mark rights for individual traders and the establishment of a national mark. The trial court in the *Dominion Stores* case relied on *Canada Standard* in upholding the application of the act.[27] Mr. Justice Grange pointed out that the meaning of the term "general" regulation of trade and commerce was uncertain. One knew from the authorities that it did *not* include the regulation of particular trades within a province, "nor does it appear to include the regulation of many trades . . . nor even of all trades . . . if that trade is or can be intraprovincial."[28] Beyond these negative limitations, there was little guidance in the cases. It did appear, however, that the power included the authority to create national marks of quality, since this very point had been decided in the *Canada Standard* case. In Grange J.'s opinion, the purpose of the *Canada Agricultural Products Standards Act* was precisely to create a national standard to be signified by a national grade name, and thus the case was indistinguishable from *Canada Standard*. He dismissed the argument that the federal act amounted to the regulation of local trade. "The answer to that contention," his Lordship opined, "can only be that in law it is not."[29]

This disposition was affirmed by the Ontario Court of Appeal, but the Supreme Court reversed it by a 5–4 majority. The majority opinion was written by Mr. Justice Estey, who argued that there was no inconsistency between his conclusions and the result in the *Canada Standard* case. The main point emphasized by Estey J. was that the statute was mandatory, in substance if not in form, in its application

---

25 *A.G. Ont. v. A.G. Can.*, [1937] A.C. 405.

26 "There could hardly be a more appropriate form of the exercise of [the trade and commerce] power than the creation and regulation of a uniform law of trade marks." (*Ibid.* at 417). There was at the time a well-established national code for trade marks, the *Trade Marks and Design Act*, R.S.C. 1927, c. 201.

27 *R. v. Dom. Stores Ltd.* (1978), 79 D.L.R. (3d) 627 (Ont. H.C.).

28 *Ibid.* at 630.

29 *Ibid.* at 632.

to local traders. This result was produced by the interaction between the federal statute and a sister provincial act, the *Farm Products Grades and Sales Act*.[30] This made it compulsory for local traders to use certain provincial grade names, and the prescribed names were identical to the ones contained in the federal scheme. Thus "stripping off the complexities of the constitutional argument and reducing the transaction to its real proportions,"[31] the local traders were obliged to adopt the federal grade names and to comply with the applicable federal standard. This meant that the federal statute was in reality a "marketing scheme" as opposed to a "trade marks scheme," and the *Canada Standard* case did not apply. It went without saying, of course, that a marketing scheme directed at intraprovincial trade was beyond federal power.[32]

One might contest Estey J.'s conclusion that the statute was mandatory in relation to local traders.[33] But there is a deeper issue: why this should matter? Justice Estey's assumption was that a voluntary system of grade names was valid, while a mandatory system was not. But this is not necessarily so. If the federal government has authority to establish national grade names, the reason must be that this is a matter of general concern throughout the Dominion. This was apparently the conclusion of the Privy Council in the *Canada Standard* case. If this is accepted, then whether the grade names are mandatory or voluntary should be constitutionally irrelevant. It is for Parliament and not the courts to determine whether a mandatory programme is warranted. The problem was that if Estey had approached the matter on this relatively straightforward footing, he would have had to abandon the "settled" principle that Parliament could not regulate local trade. If the Supreme Court had upheld a system of mandatory grade names for local traders, it would have been impossible to deny federal authority over all aspects of "local" trade. The dominant body of doctrine in the area would have been turned on its head.

To avoid this result, Estey J. seized on the fact that the legislation in the *Canada Standard* case happened to impose only voluntary

---

30 *Farm Products Grades and Sales Act*, R.S.O. 1970, c. 161.

31 *Supra*, note 21 at 859.

32 Estey J. cited the familiar litany of cases such as *A.G. B.C. v. A.G. Can.*, [1937] A.C. 377; *Ref. re Farm Products Marketing Act*, [1957] S.C.R. 198 (S.C.C.).

33 Professor J.C. Macpherson criticizes the judgment on these grounds. In his view, "the provincial law was a red herring which should not have influenced the characterization of the federal law." See "Developments in Constitutional Law: The 1979-80 Term" (1981), 2 Sup. Ct. L. Rev. 60-61. The difficulty with this objection is that it is not clear that the provincial law was a red herring; this would depend on the legislative history of the enactments.

standards. But the use of the voluntary/mandatory distinction brings another problem to mind. If mandatory national standards for local traders are invalid because they regulate intraprovincial trade, the basis for even voluntary federal standards in this area is questionable. It becomes more than a little strained to argue that voluntary standards are more "general" than mandatory standards and are for this reason supportable under the second branch of *Parsons*. Thus, the result in *Dominion Stores* leads to the conclusion that the federal government has no authority to enact product standards for wholly local traders — in short, that *Canada Standard* was "wrongly decided". Such conundrums arise only because of the irrelevance of the voluntary/mandatory distinction itself. Like the distinction between production and trade, the voluntary/mandatory dichotomy simply fails to address the underlying policy issues raised by the case. In fact, the whole purpose of invoking these sorts of distinctions is to permit the courts to avoid having to confront these political choices.

The Court's most recent pronouncements on the trade and commerce power came in two companion cases, *Canadian National Transportation Limited et al. v. Attorney General of Canada*[34] and *R. v. Wetmore et al. (Kripps Pharmacy)*.[35] The primary issue in the cases was the authority of the Attorney General of Canada to conduct criminal prosecutions.[36] However, the judgments do contain some discussion of the scope of federal authority over trade and commerce. In *Kripps Pharmacy*, the accused were charged under the *Food and Drugs Act* with selling drugs manufactured or stored under unsanitary conditions and with promoting drugs in a misleading manner. The majority judgment of Chief Justice Laskin concluded that the relevant sections of the Act were supportable under Parliament's authority in relation to criminal law. But Laskin C.J.C. went on to suggest that certain provisions might also be valid under the trade and commerce power:

> This Court was concerned in *Labatt Breweries of Can. Ltd. v. A.G. Can.*, [1980] 1 S.C.R. 914, 9 B.L.R. 181, 30 N.R. 496, with a proceeding relating to sections 6 and 25 and the regulations thereunder, of this Act. While these sections and the provisions herein involved are both found in Part II of the Act, very different issues arise in this appeal.
>
> An examination of the various provisions of the *Food and Drugs Act* shows

---

34 *C.N. Transportation Ltd. v. A.G. Can.*, [1983] 2 S.C.R. 206 (S.C.C.).

35 *R. v. Wetmore*, [1983] 2 S.C.R. 284 (S.C.C.). For a discussion of the cases and their implications for competition policy, see N. Finkelstein, Comment (1984), 62 Can. Bar Rev. 182.

36 For a discussion of the implications of the primary holding in the cases, see A. Petter, Comment (1985), 63 Can. Bar Rev. 162.

that it goes beyond mere prohibition to bring it solely within s. 91(27) but that it also involves a prescription of standards, including labelling and packaging as well as control of manufacture. The ramifications of the legislation, encompassing food, drugs, cosmetics and devices and the emphasis on marketing standards seem to me to subjoin a trade and commerce aspect beyond mere criminal law alone. There appear to be three categories of provisions in the *Food and Drugs Act*. Those that are in s. 8 are aimed at protecting the physical health and safety of the public. Those that are in s. 9 are aimed at marketing and those dealing with controlled drugs in Part III of the Act are aimed at protecting the moral health of the public. One may properly characterize the first and third categories as falling under the criminal law power but the second category certainly invites the application of the trade and commerce power.[37]

The section Laskin C.J.C. regards as "inviting" the application of the trade and commerce power is s. 9 of the *Food and Drugs Act*, which prohibits the labelling, packaging, treating, processing, selling or advertising of drugs in a manner that is "false, misleading or deceptive or is likely to create an erroneous impression. . . ." The difficulty is how this observation can be squared with Estey J.'s opinion in *Labatt*. *Labatt* decided that s. 6 of the *Food and Drugs Act* was *ultra vires*. It is not clear what the relevant distinction between the two sections might be. Like s. 6, s. 9 of the Act reaches back into the production of drugs in the province. *Labatt* emphasized that the regulation of production was a local matter falling under provincial jurisdiction, outside the scope of the "first branch" of the *Parsons* test. Nor could the second branch of *Parsons* apply, since the section does not deal with trade "in general." As the dissenting judgment of Mr. Justice Dickson points out, s. 9 amounts to the "detailed regulation of the pharmaceutical industry."[38] There is no discussion of any of these matters in the majority judgment, other than the meaningless observation that the issues arising in *Kripps* were "very different" from those considered in *Labatt*. The reader is left to ponder why the differences between the two cases are relevant or significant.

If *Labatt* was the sequel to the *Agricultural Products Reference*, *Kripps* is the sequel to *Potash*. The *Agricultural Products Reference* relied on the distinction between production and marketing, while *Potash* ignored it. Although *Labatt* revived the distinction, it was ignored once again in *Kripps*. The astounding feature of these cases is the judicial oblivion to the inconsistencies between them. *Labatt* applies a categorical mode of reasoning to federalism problems. Each level of government

---

37 *Supra*, note 35 at 288.
38 *Ibid.* at 294.

possesses exclusive authority over a zone of absolute entitlement. These premises are rejected by the majority in *Kripps*. The federal government's authority over trade and commerce is framed in much more flexible and pragmatic terms. In a future case, one could plausibly justify a variety of different results, depending on the line of cases designated as "controlling".

The dissenting judgments of Mr. Justice Dickson (as he then was) in both *Kripps* and *Canadian National Transportation* undertake to reconcile these cases. The task is one of herculean proportions. If Dickson J. ultimately falls short, this is due only to the illogical and contradictory state of the materials with which he is forced to work. Dickson J. is sensitive to the fundamental value choices the judiciary is called upon to make in constitutional cases. In his view, the scope of the trade and commerce power is not dictated by doctrine or defined by logic. It will depend on the degree to which federal economic regulation "encroaches on the degree of local autonomy contemplated by the constitution."[39] The difficulty is in reconciling this flexible, balancing attitude with the contradictions implicit in the doctrine. Dickson J. holds that the "second branch" of *Parsons* authorizes legislation aimed at the economy "as a single integrated economic unit rather than as a collection of separate local enterprises." There is a clear demarcation between "measures validly directed at a general regulation of the national economy and those merely aimed at centralized control over a large number of local economic entities."[40]

The question is how to interpret this form of words. On the one hand, Dickson J. may be advocating a pragmatic case-by-case balancing of the various federal and provincial interests implicated in a given case. On this interpretation, there is no categorical demarcation between federal and provincial jurisdiction. Dickson J. lends support to this view later in the judgment when he identifies a number of functional criteria as "indicia" supporting federal authority.[41] At the same time, Justice Dickson refuses to acknowledge the tension between such an approach and the judgment of Estey J. in the *Labatt* case. Indeed, he explicitly adopts Estey J.'s statement that "what is clearly not of

---

39 *Supra*, note 34 at 260.

40 *Ibid.* at 267.

41 Included in such criteria are the presence of a regulatory scheme, the fact that the provinces would be incapable of passing the enactment, and evidence that failure to include one or more provinces would jeopardize successful operation in other parts of the country. *Ibid.* at 267.

national concern is the regulation of a single trade or industry".[42] This implies that the real test is not a functional one at all; instead, it is a purely formal question of whether the legislation singles out a particular industry. On this view, any federal attempt to regulate a particular industry is void, regardless of the functional utility of such regulation. Only where the law deals with trade in general is there scope for federal economic regulation.

This ambiguity is played out in Dickson J.'s substantive discussion of the two statutes in *C.N.* and *Kripps*. In *C.N.* he upholds the conspiracy section of the *Combines Investigation Act* on the basis of the second branch of *Parsons*. The analysis is wholly functional. The statutory provision is part of a regulatory scheme. It applies to a wide range of unfair competitive practices across the economy. The conduct being prohibited is of national significance, and could not be effectively regulated by the provinces. Then, in *Kripps*, he holds that the relevant provisions of the *Food and Drugs Act* cannot be supported under the trade and commerce power. Indeed, Dickson J. contends that he cannot see "any justification" for classifying s. 9(1) as falling under s. 91(2) of the *Constitution Act, 1867*. This is because the section regulates a "single trade or business." The nationwide scope of the industry is irrelevant, as are all the other functional indicia articulated in *C.N.* All that matters is that the regulations "amount simply to the detailed regulation of the pharmaceutical industry and consequently fall within the portion of economic regulation allocated to the provinces by virtue of s. 92(13)."[43]

The dissenting opinions of Dickson J. in *C.N.* and *Kripps* exemplify the current state of doctrine on the trade and commerce power. The dominant paradigm recognizes the inevitable necessity of balancing competing values in a pragmatic, utilitarian fashion. There can be no bright lines between provincial and federal jurisdiction. This dominant paradigm is associated with a clear tendency to uphold the validity of federal economic regulation. The dominance of this way of thinking does not go unchallenged, however. The doctrine is riddled with anomalies, fragments that have survived the collapse of the Privy Council era. These anomalies are premised on the antique notion of power absolute within a sphere and a rejection of the idea that it is necessary to balance competing values; the jurist simply decides the case by identifying the proper "matter" at issue. The anomalies

---

42 *Ibid.* at 265-266 (citing Estey J. from *Labatt*).

43 *Supra*, note 38.

are associated with a tendency to invalidate federal laws. But because these cases fail to analyze the values at stake in any meaningful way, the doctrine as a whole assumes a makeshift and haphazard form.

The larger question which remains to be answered is whether these doctrinal disputes have any larger significance. It may be, for example, that governments are able to resort to alternative regulatory devices in order to substitute around adverse Supreme Court rulings. In such cases, the legislature would be able to pursue the identical policy goal, notwithstanding the fact that it might have "lost" the constitutional litigation. I turn to this important empirical question in the next chapter.

10

Does Federalism Review Matter?

Legal scholars have long regarded judicial review as a central feature of Canadian federalism. Like the American constitution, the *British North America Act* did not make any explicit reference to the institution of judicial review. Yet legal scholars very soon came to the view that the very idea of federalism seemed to imply some form of judicial supervision of legislation. Federalism was premised on the notion of the limitation and categorization of state power. Limitations on power only become meaningful if there is some means of enforcing the limits. Hence the rationale for judicial review; the courts serve as a kind of constitutional police, ensuring fidelity to the intentions of the fathers of confederation. This does not mean to suggest that the judiciary was regarded as playing any creative or original role in the politics of federalism. In the years immediately following confederation, legal scholars tended to subscribe to a "plain meaning" theory of legal interpretation. Thus, judicial review was regarded as a neutral and objective process, in which courts elaborated the "plain meaning" of the *B.N.A. Act* in order to ensure that governments did not stray outside the zones of jurisdiction allocated to them under the Act. The point is that without the central role played by the judiciary in enforcing the confederation bargain, federalism itself seemed a logical and legal impossibility.

Beginning in the 1930s, legal scholars began to question whether judicial review was as neutral and uncreative as had previously been believed. Led by young iconoclasts such as Bora Laskin, Canadian legal writers began to realize that the interpretations handed down by the Privy Council were by no means neutral or objective. Looking back on the work of the Privy Council as a whole, the generation of the 1930s and 1940s became convinced that judicial interpretation had failed to keep faith with the intentions of the fathers of confederation. According to the picture painted by scholars at the time, the Privy Council had emasculated federal authority through a peculiar and perverse reading of the plain meaning of the *B.N.A. Act*.[1] Instead of the centralized federal power envisaged by the framers and embodied in the language of the Act, the Privy Council had substituted their own idiosyncratic and romantic brand of classical, decentralized federalism. The result was that the provinces had been saddled with responsibilities which they were plainly incompetent to discharge. The members of the Privy Council were commonly characterized as "bungling intruders" whose misreading of the *B.N.A. Act* had crippled the ability of the federal government to respond to the "complications of modern industry and of modern business".[2]

In later years, the decentralizing tendencies of judicial interpretations came to be seen as evidence of a conservative bias against state intervention. Writing in the 1950s, Professor Mallory argued that the engine of constitutional doctrine was the reaction of a free economy against regulation. Business raised claims of *ultra vires*, not because of any inherent concern with the integrity of the federal system, but simply out of a self-interested desire to escape state regulation. Mallory criticized the constitutional decisions of the Privy Council as evidence of an anti-statist, laissez-faire mentality on the part of the judiciary.[3] Professor Weiler refined and developed Mallory's insights in his important writing on Canadian federalism in the 1970s. Weiler observed that the primary beneficiaries of judicial review in federalism cases appeared to be business interests, who used the courts in order to impeach the validity of laws enacted by representative legislatures. Business had no particular preference for federal as opposed to provincial interests; there was no necessary connection between

---

1 See, e.g., V.C. MacDonald, "Judicial Interpretations of the Canadian Constitution" (1935), 1 U.T.L.J. 260.

2 W.P.M. Kennedy, *Some Aspects of the Theories and Workings of Constitutional Law*, at 92.

3 See J.R. Mallory, *Social Credit and the Federal Power in Canada* (1954); "The Courts and the Sovereignty of the Canadian Parliament" (1944), 10 Can. J. Econ. 166.

"decentralization" and the advancement of business interests. The overriding motive of business was simply to escape regulation by the state. Thus, the constitutional strategy of business was wholly instrumental, framed in terms of defending either federal or provincial jurisdiction as circumstance required. In Weiler's view, the point of a federal system was to allocate governing power to different regions and groups, not to confer immunities from regulation on private citizens. Weiler's response was to propose that private citizens be forced to obtain the consent of the Attorney General before being permitted to bring a constitutional challenge on federalism grounds.[4]

Even this brief survey indicates that there has been a quite radical evolution in Canadian attitudes towards judicial review over the past century. But there has also been one constant throughout this evolution. This constant has been the assumption that judicial review has been and is central to the federal system of government. From the very earliest years of Canadian federalism, commentators have all agreed that judicial review matters. The outcome of constitutional litigation is thought to make a real difference for individuals and for government. This assumption was shared even by the earliest writers on judicial review, who tended to regard the process as neutral and objective. These early writers saw judicial review as being of the utmost importance, since it served to keep the original confederation bargain intact. The presence of judicial review meant that constitutional change had to originate in the majesty of the British Parliament rather than on the whim of Canadian legislators. Later writers, who regarded judicial review as much more creative, continued to subscribe to the belief that legal interpretations had been central to the evolution of Canadian federalism. Indeed, the Privy Council was seen as the chief culprit in a process whereby a highly centralized federal bargain was transformed into a decentralized system of federalism.[5]

As was pointed out in Chapter Seven, there is good reason to question these assumptions about the instrumental effects of judicial interpretations of the *B.N.A. Act*. The primary reason is that the assumption of instrumental impact ignores the central economic phenomenon of substitution. Individuals who are legally barred from achieving their goals in a particular way may not abandon the goal;

---

4 P. Weiler, *In the Last Resort* (1974) at 181. Weiler's claims about the conservative bias of federalism have been widely accepted.

5 For a contrasting view, which argues that the Privy Council played a much a less significant role in the evolution of Canadian federalism, see A.C. Cairns, "The Judicial Committee and its Critics" (1971), 4 Can J. Pol. Sc. 301.

rather, they may employ an alternate legal device to achieve the identical goal or they may make a side payment to a third party in return for removal of the legal impediment. The possibility of this type of substitution applies no less to governments than it does to private individuals. Thus, it may be totally incorrect to assume that governments are significantly constrained by the outcomes of constitutional cases. They may be able to substitute around those decisions and achieve their original goals through alternative means.

As was discussed in Chapter 7, there appear to be a variety of ways in which governments or individuals can avoid or modify the effect of constraints associated with federalism. Federalism is premised on a theory of the exhaustion of powers; if one government is denied jurisdiction over a particular matter, then the other level of government must necessarily possess such jurisdiction. Accordingly, if the Supreme Court finds that legislation enacted by one level of government is *ultra vires* on federalism grounds, there are a variety of regulatory alternatives still available. First, the other level of government may choose to enact the legislation in substantially the same form. Alternatively, the results of the litigation may be reversed by intergovernmental agreement, in which the "winning" level of government delegates to the "loser" part or all of the disputed jurisdiction. Finally, the "losing" level of government may simply reassert regulation over the activity in question through substituting an alternative policy instrument in place of the one struck down by the Court.

This leads to the following fundamental maxim of Canadian federalism; contrary to repeated judicial pronouncements to the contrary,[6] it is *always* possible to do indirectly what you cannot do directly. The only relevant question is whether the costs of indirection are so high that they outweigh the benefits.

Yet this "fundamental maxim" is less of a final conclusion than an invitation to further inquiry. Specifically, having noted the theoretical availability of regulatory substitutes, to what extent do governments actually employ such substitutes in order to avoid the constraining effects of judicial interpretations? The remainder of this chapter is an attempt to offer a general and tentative answer to that important question. I begin by setting out a series of principles which must underpin analysis of this issue. I then apply and test these principles through two case studies of the interaction of government and the

---

6 See, e.g., the dissenting judgment of Martland and Ritchie JJ. in the *Patriation Appeals*, in which the various authorities on the issue are referred to.

judiciary. The focus of these case studies is the series of trade and commerce cases decided by the Supreme Court in the late 1970s and analyzed in Chapter 9. As we observed in Chapter 9, the reasoning in many of these decisions was weak; the Court seemed to have a rather poor understanding of the actual purpose and effect of the legislation being considered. Yet, what we will discover in this chapter is that these decisions appear to have had a very modest impact on the formulation of public policy. Governments have been able to overcome the effects of these adverse judicial rulings through inter-governmental agreement or by enacting alternative legislation. Based on the analysis developed in these case studies, I attempt to draw out a series of more general conclusions regarding the instrumental impact of federalism adjudication.

1. GENERAL PRINCIPLES

The suggestion that judicial decisions may have a limited impact on public policy formation is obviously traceable back to the seminal work of Ronald Coase.[7] In his classic "The Problem of Social Cost", Coase demonstrated that, in the absence of transactions costs, parties will bargain to the efficient result regardless of the rule of liability announced by the Court. What was radical about this thesis was the idea that a judicial determination of liability might not conclusively dictate the allocation of resources between parties.

Yet it is important to remember that the originality and novelty of Coase's work can easily be overestimated. First, it is sometimes mistakenly assumed that the "Coase theorem" is an attempt to demonstrate that legal rules are irrelevant. But this was clearly not the point of Coase's argument at all. Coase argued that rules of liability will not affect the allocation of resources only if there are no transactions costs. If bargaining is costly, there is no guarantee that the parties will agree on the efficient allocation of resources. Moreover, since bargaining is almost always costly, the legal rule will often conclusively determine the allocation of resources.

Applying this first principle to the legal rules of federalism, it should be obvious that there are enormous transactions costs associated with bargaining between governments. Rather than the relatively simple situation described by Coase in which a rancher and farmer bargain over crop damage, federalism brings together eleven govern-

---

7 See R. Coase, "The Problem of Social Cost" (1960), 3 J. Law & Econ.

ments, each responsible to a large and heterogeneous electorate. Further, the "parties" must bargain in the constant glare of the media. Observers of Canadian federalism have long recognized that the process is a costly one; in fact, many political scientists claim that it has become even more difficult in recent decades to achieve federal-provincial consensus. This observation is based on the fact that in the era of "executive federalism", politicians have tended to supplant bureaucrats at the negotiating table. This has politicized the negotiating process, making it less likely that the participants will approach the issues on the basis of a common set of assumptions or goals.[8]

There is a second general principle that must be emphasized in any attempt to transpose Coase's insights to the federalism context. As Coase himself pointed out, even if a legal rule has no effect on the allocation of resources, it will still have a distributive impact. In Coasean terms, the liability rule determines which of the parties will be forced to make a side payment in order to achieve the efficient result. In the context of federal-provincial bargaining, this means that even when governments bargain around a legal decision, it would be erroneous to suppose that the legal result was therefore irrelevant. Presumably, one or more of the parties was forced to make concessions in order to secure the bargain. The legal decision was central to this process because it dictated the initial entitlements of the parties and placed one or the other in the position of having to offer concessions.

A good illustration of this point is the political negotiations following the decision of the Supreme Court in the *Patriation Appeals* in the fall of 1981. The negotiations following the Court's decision eventually produced an agreement between the federal government and nine of the ten provinces; this accord was then forwarded to Westminster and enacted into law. But the fact that the governments managed to reach this agreement should not lead one to suppose that the constitutional decision of the Court was therefore irrelevant. The federal government made a number of important concessions in order to obtain provincial consent. It is unlikely that it would have been forced to make these concessions had the Supreme Court ruled that the original federal proposals were "constitutional".[9]

---

8 See generally, D. Smiley, *Canada in Question: Federalism in the Eighties*, (3rd ed., 1980).

9 Of course, I use the term "constitutional" in its "conventional" sense, as defined by the Supreme Court in its judgment. For an analysis of the impact of the Court's judgment in this case on the subsequent negotiations, see R. Romanow, J. Whyte and H. Leeson, *Canada . . . Notwithstanding: The Making of the Constitution 1976-1982* (1984) at 188-212.

These general observations suggest the following, important conclusion: federal-provincial bargaining may indicate the importance as opposed to the marginality of constitutional constraints. If governments are prepared to bear the significant costs of intergovernmental bargaining, this must be because there are even higher costs associated with leaving the court-defined legal regime in place. Moreover, even when governments are successful in reaching agreement, they will have been forced to make concessions which probably would have been unnecessary had the judicial interpretation been different.

The corollary is that constitutional decisions will likely have the least constraining impact in cases where regulatory substitution can occur without recourse to interprovincial bargaining. In these instances, although the Court may have ruled a particular legal instrument to be *ultra vires*, the government is able to put in place an alternative instrument which will achieve the same goals in roughly the same way. Moreover, it can do so without the necessity of bargaining with the other level of government or of offering concessions.

An example of such substitution is the current litigation surrounding the constitutionality of Ontario's film censorship system. In 1983, the Ontario Divisional Court ruled that Ontario's current censorship regime violated the *Charter* since the standards employed by the censor board were not "prescribed by law".[10] The ruling was upheld in the Court of Appeal and the matter is currently under appeal to the Supreme Court of Canada. In the meantime, however, the provincial government has amended the legislation so as to require the censor board to employ criteria set out in regulations. The irony is that the standards in the regulations are just as amorphous as the informal guidelines which the censor board had followed in the past; the only difference is that these standards are now legally binding on the board. If the amendments survive *Charter* scrutiny, the ultimate impact of the litigation on Ontario's censorship regime will have been negligible.

This leads to the following hypothesis: the availability of close regulatory substitutes is the single most-important factor determining the instrumental impact of federalism review. If close substitutes are available, the impact of the judicial interpretation will likely be marginal. Conversely, if there are no close substitutes, the government will be forced either to abandon or to modify its goals, or else to

---

10 *Re Ont. Film & Video Appreciation Soc. and Ont. Bd. of Censors* (1983), 147 D.L.R. (3d) 58 (Ont. Div. Ct.).

enter into negotiations with the competing level of government. Because the transactions costs associated with such negotiations are extraordinarily high, a bargain will result only if the government is prepared to commit significant resources to the process. In any event, even if an agreement is reached, the government which lost the court battle will probably have made significant concessions.

If this hypothesis is correct, then the task becomes one of identifying those instances in which there are likely to be close regulatory substitutes available to government. The difficulty with formulating a universal generalization in this regard is immediately obvious; to a large extent, the availability of regulatory substitutes depends on how broadly or narrowly the Court frames the particular constitutional constraint. If the constraint is framed narrowly, then it will be a relatively simple matter for the state to frame an alternative instrument which will pass constitutional muster. A broadly-framed constraint is much less easy to evade.

Notwithstanding these obstacles, it may still be possible to formulate a number of meaningful generalizations regarding the issue. I turn now to two case studies of the interplay between judicial interpretation and state regulation. The case studies will serve two purposes; they will offer a test of the hypothesis outlined above as well as an opportunity to generate a more precise gauge of the circumstances in which governments are able to make use of regulatory substitutes.

2. FEDERAL PRODUCT REGULATION: THE AFTERMATH OF DOMINION STORES AND LABATT BREWERIES OF CANADA LTD.

In *R. v. Dominion Stores Ltd.*[11] and *Labatt Breweries of Canada Ltd. v. A.G. Can.*[12] the Supreme Court had limited federal power to provide for national product standards. In *Dominion Stores*, the Court had ruled that a scheme prescribing grade names and standards associated with those names could not be applied to intraprovincial traders. In *Labatt*, the Court had struck down s. 6 of the *Food and Drugs Act*, ruling that s. 6 was an impermissible attempt to regulate local trade. Both of these decisions were widely criticized by commentators at the time, who saw the rulings as threatening national product standards and

---

11 *R. v. Dom. Stores Ltd.*, [1980] 1 S.C.R. 844 (S.C.C.).
12 *Labatt Breweries of Can. Ltd. v. A.G. Can.*, [1980] 1 S.C.R. 914 (S.C.C.).

thus as promoting increased consumer ignorance and confusion in the market.

Today, close to a decade after the rulings in these cases, the chaos and confusion which these commentators feared has failed to materialize. This is not to suggest that consumers are now able to obtain accurate and full information on all the products they buy. The point is simply that the feared balkanization of the Canadian market, in which individual provinces would prescribe different standards and specifications for goods sold there, has not developed. There has been little complaint from federal policy-makers about the deterioration of national product standards or calls for urgent legislative or constitutional reform. Neither of the statutes which was the subject of litigation has been amended. In short, the cases appear to have had little or no impact on the manner in which goods are packaged and sold in Canada or on the agenda of public policy-makers. How can we account for the negligible impact of the cases, particularly in light of the predictions of dire consequences which were heard in the months immediately following the release of the decisions?

Consider first the aftermath of the *Dominion Stores* case. The key to understanding the limited impact of this case is the long history of constitutional litigation dealing with the regulation of farm products. Federal-provincial attempts to regulate the marketing of farm products date back to the mid-1930s. The Privy Council had determined that the regulation of intraprovincial trade in natural products was a provincial responsibility, while only Parliament could regulate interprovincial and international trade.[13] The two levels of government had overcome this division of responsibility through interprovincial bargaining and agreement. The relevant standards would be set through federal-provincial agreement; each province would then implement the agreement for products traded locally, while the federal government would enact legislation covering interprovincial and international trade. In this way a common set of product standards would apply across the country, notwithstanding the constitutional division of responsibility.

This system of dovetailing legislation was in place long before the litigation involving *Dominion Stores*. Part II of the *Canada Agricultural Products Standards Act*[14] established a compulsory scheme of grade names

---

13 *A.G. B.C. v. A.G. Can.*, [1937] A.C. 377 (holding federal Natural Products Marketing Act *ultra vires*).
14 *Canada Agricultural Products Standards Act*, R.S.C. 1970, c. A-8.

and standards for products moving in interprovincial and export trade. The same set of grade names and standards applied to local traders in Ontario pursuant to the *Farm Products Grades and Sales Act.*[15] The validity of these provisions was not at issue in the appeal. What was challenged was Part I of the federal legislation, which sought to establish a voluntary system of grade names and standards for products traded locally. It was this voluntary system of grade names which was ruled unconstitutional by the Court.

This legislative background makes it easy to understand why the decision in *Dominion Stores* has had minimal impact on the regulation of natural products. Notwithstanding the Court's ruling, the same set of natural product standards remains validly in force. The only difference is that prosecutions must be brought under Part II of the federal Act or the relevant provincial legislation, depending upon the origin of the product in question. The consequence is that it will be necessary for investigators to obtain information on the origin of the product before laying a charge. But there is no reason in principle why such information could not be obtained.

Perhaps the greatest irony of the case is that there was evidence that the apples which were the subject of the charge in *Dominion Stores* had been traded interprovincially.[16] Thus, although the charge was laid under Part I of the federal Act, the investigators could have proceeded under Part II, which contained compulsory standards for interprovincial traders. Had this latter option been chosen, there would have been no constitutional defence to the charge and the only issue would have been whether the apples complied with the relevant standard. Thus, the constitutional issue was manufactured by a discretionary decision to proceed under Part I of the legislation.

In short, the *Dominion Stores* case was little more than a footnote to the long history of constitutional litigation involving the marketing of farm products. The federal and provincial governments had previously agreed on a package of dovetailing legislation establishing a common set of regulatory standards. The *Dominion Stores* case did not call into question the validity of that federal-provincial arrangement. The only effect of the case was to prevent the federal government from applying a "voluntary" scheme of regulation to products traded

---

15 *Farm Products Grades and Sales Act*, R.S.O. 1970, c. 161.

16 This is reflected in the judgment of Chief Justice Laskin: "There was some intimation that the apples referred to in the charge were produce of British Columbia, but this is not reflected in the charge nor was it a consideration on the argument of the constitutional issue . . .". *Supra*, note 11 at 847.

locally. Given the continued consensus between federal and provincial governments over the relevant standards to be applied in this area, the impact of the decision has been minimal.

There was no similar set of dovetailing federal-provincial legislation in the *Labatt Breweries* case. Section 6 of the federal *Food and Drugs Act* purported to set down national standards for all food products, without distinguishing whether they were traded locally or interprovincially. There was no comparable provincial legislation in place. Thus, one might have expected that the Court's ruling that s. 6 was *ultra vires* to have had a fairly significant impact on food products standards. Yet this impact has yet to materialize. In general, food products sold in Canada continue to meet the standards set down in the federal legislation. Federal officials responsible for compliance with the so-called "food recipe" standards report very few violations in the wake of the *Labatt Breweries* case.[17]

What is the explanation for this continued compliance with standards which are apparently unenforceable? An explanation which appears initially plausible is based on the observation that the food industry has an interest in a common set of food standards. A common set of standards enables the industry to signal to consumers the varying nature and quality of products which may otherwise appear indistinguishable. Consider the sale of "ground beef" as an illustration of this signalling function. The quality of ground beef varies according to the fat content of the meat, yet fat content cannot be determined through visual inspection. The solution is to establish different grades of ground beef according to the fat content of the meat (i.e., "lean", "medium" or "regular") and to package and sell the meat accordingly. The industry has a clear interest in establishing such standards since they can then differentiate between and charge appropriate prices for products which appear indistinguishable through visual inspection. Consumers also have an interest in such standards since they obtain accurate information about the quality of the product they are buying and (in the example above) they are given a choice between three grades of ground beef rather than one.

Given the clear consumer and industry interest in establishing labelling standards, one might expect such standards to arise spon-

---

17 Telephone interviews with G. Reasbeck, Chief of the Retail Food Division, Consumer and Corporate Affairs, Ottawa, and M. Rosenberg, Senior Counsel, Legal Services, Department of Consumer and Corporate Affairs, Ottawa. There are approximately 300 "food recipe" standards established under the *Food and Drugs Act*.

taneously in a market. The reason why this does not occur is because of the difficulty in policing compliance with the standards. Once a product standard is established, there is an immediate incentive to attempt to substitute a lower quality product in place of one of higher quality. To return to the ground beef example, once three grades of ground beef have been established, there is an incentive to market "regular" ground beef as either "medium" or "lean" beef and charge a higher price for the product. This incentive to cheat is all the more powerful because consumers are unable to distinguish the quality of the product through visual inspection. The way out of this dilemma is to establish the product standards through legislation. If the product standards are established and enforced by the state, cheaters can be identified and prosecuted. State intervention makes possible the efficiency gains associated with product standards.[18]

This analysis, far from explaining the continued voluntary compliance with the food standards, makes such compliance all the more curious. Given the inability of the federal government to enforce compliance with the standards, why has there not been a dramatic increase in the numbers of sellers seeking to substitute lower quality products in place of higher quality ones?

There are undoubtedly a number of factors which have contributed to the absence of widespread violations of the Act. First, the product standards were already in place and had become widely accepted by the industry as being in its own best interest. Thus, it is hardly surprising that the bulk of the industry would continue to support the product standards even after the result in *Labatt Breweries*. Second, the federal government still possesses considerable authority to enforce the product standards. Since the *Labatt Breweries* litigation, federal officials have sought to enforce the product standards through prosecutions under s. 5 of the *Food and Drugs Act*, which provides:

> 5.(1) No person shall label, package, treat, process, sell or advertise any food in a manner that is false, misleading or deceptive or is likely to create an erroneous impression regarding its character, value, quantity, composition, merit or safety.[19]

It is arguable that prosecutions under s. 5 are somewhat more difficult than prosecutions under s. 6. Under s. 6, the relevant test was whether an article was "likely to be mistaken" for food for which a standard had been prescribed under the regulations. If it was likely

---

18 Significantly, most of the food recipe standards were established at the request of the industry.
19 *Food and Drugs Act*, R.S.C. 1970, c. F-27.

to be mistaken for such food, then it had to comply with the applicable standard. In contrast, s. 5(1) makes it an offence to package food in a manner that is "false, misleading or deceptive or is likely to create an erroneous impression regarding its character…". It is arguable that the standard under s. 5 is somewhat higher, since there is an obligation to demonstrate that the labelling of the food is "misleading": it may be, for example, that food has not been labelled in accordance with the regulations, but that it cannot be demonstrated that this improper labelling was "false, misleading or deceptive".

Yet, on further examination, it is apparent that there are also certain broad similarities between the standards established under ss. 5 and 6. Section 6 itself did not directly require compliance with the food standards in the regulations. It was also necessary to demonstrate a "misleading" of the public in order to prosecute under s. 6; the offence in s. 6 was one of packaging , selling or advertising food "in such a manner that it is likely to be mistaken" for food subject to the regulations. Nor was this "misleading" element of the offence a mere *pro forma* requirement. It should be recalled that the trial judge in the *Labatt Breweries* case had found that "the plaintiff's Special Lite beverage ("food") has not been labelled, packaged or advertised in such a manner that it is likely to be mistaken for the beverage "light beer" ("Food").[20] Thus, even though Labatt's Special Lite did not comply with the standard for "light beer", the trial judge was prepared to grant a declaration that there had not been a violation of s. 6 of the Act. In short, while s. 5 of the Act does not permit direct enforcement of the standards in the regulations, neither did s. 6. Instead, both sections depend on some demonstration that there has been a misleading of the public.

This leads to the obvious question: is s. 5 of the Act also vulnerable to a constitutional challenge? While the answer is not altogether free from doubt, it would appear that s. 5 of the Act could be defended as an exercise of Parliament's jurisdiction over "criminal law". The criminal law power has always included the authority to proscribe trade practices contrary to the interest of the community such as misleading, false or deceptive advertising. There is a strong argument to the effect that s. 5 is a valid exercise of that power.[21]

---

20 *Labatt Breweries of Can. Ltd. v. A.G. Can.* (1978), 84 D. L. R. (3d) 61 at 67 (S.C.C.).

21 The matter is not altogether free from doubt, as the following passage from the judgment of Estey J. in *Labatt Breweries* makes clear:

   That there is an area of legitimate regulations in respect of trade practices contrary to the interest of the community such as misleading, false or deceptive advertising and

In short, while the federal government can no longer utilize s. 6 in order to enforce the food product standards, it has a relatively close regulatory substitute in s. 5. Moreover, there is an alternative basis for directly and conclusively enforcing the standards set out in the *Food and Drugs Act*. This alternative is to seek the cooperation of the provinces and to establish a framework similar to that already in place for natural products. Under such a scheme, Parliament could enact food product standards for goods moving in interprovincial and export trade. The provinces would enact parallel standards for goods produced and traded locally. In this way, a common set of food product standards would be binding and enforceable throughout Canada. Federal-provincial negotiations aimed at establishing such a scheme are underway and the federal government expects to introduce legislation setting standards for interprovincial and export trade before the next election.[22]

In summary, neither *Dominion Stores* nor *Labatt Breweries* has had any significant impact on the manner in which goods are marketed or on government policy. The impact of the *Dominion Stores* litigation was minimal due to the existence of dovetailing federal and provincial legislation regulating natural products. As for *Labatt Breweries*, the industry has continued to voluntarily comply with the food recipe standards, notwithstanding the outcome of the litigation. Over the longer term, there are a number of alternative regulatory instruments which can be utilized in order to ensure appropriate compliance with the standards. Neither case seems to have made a great deal of difference for the politics of Canadian federalism.

3. NATURAL RESOURCE REGULATION: THE AFTERMATH OF *CIGOL* AND *CENTRAL CANADA*

In the late 1970s, the Supreme Court appeared to have dealt a body blow to provincial attempts to regulate the natural resource

---

misbranding, is not under debate. In the statue now before us, the question of mislabelling arises only after the category of light beer is created and the specifications for its production are assigned. When all this has been ordained, the use of the words "Special Life" (sic) by the appellant may be said to be misleading to the beer buying public. The contest, however, is not in respect of this second stage, but rather the first stage, that is the right in the Federal Parliament and the Federal Government to establish the standards of production and content of this product.

Supra, note 12 at 933-934.

22 Reasbeck, *supra*, note 17.

industry. In *CIGOL*,[23] the Court struck down a provincial tax designed to capture the dramatic increase in oil prices resulting from the 1973 Middle East war. In *Central Canada*,[24] the Court ruled invalid a provincial scheme establishing quotas and minimum prices for the production of potash in Saskatchewan. There were howls of protest from the western provinces following these decisions. The provinces complained that fundamental issues of federal-provincial politics were being resolved by an institution "not in the mainstream of the political process."[25] Various Premiers claimed that the Supreme Court was "biased" in favour of the federal government and that the method of appointment to the Court had to be changed to allow for provincial participation.[26]

A decade after these controversial decisions, constitutional questions no longer seem to feature in discussions of the energy issue. The public policy agenda has become preoccupied with the global oversupply of oil and the resultant drop in world oil prices. The constraints facing contemporary Canadian governments in the energy field are constraints arising from market forces, rather than from the constitutional jurisprudence of the Supreme Court. Indeed, Quebec, rather than the west, has become the principal advocate of Supreme Court reform. Once again, the obvious question: how did provincial governments, particularly those in the west, manage to overcome the constitutional obstacles which seemed so pressing and problematic less than a decade ago?

Consider first the aftermath and provincial response to the *CIGOL* case. The immediate priority of the province of Saskatchewan was to ensure that it would not have to refund the $500 million collected under the invalid production tax. The government achieved this result by levying an income tax on the oil industry, retroactive to 31 December 1973.[27] This alternative form of tax was constitutionally valid, since income taxes are direct taxes and within the provincial taxing power under s. 92(2) of the *B.N.A. Act*. The $500 million previously collected by the government under the invalid production

23 *Cdn. Industrial Gas & Oil (CIGOL) v. Saskatchewan*, [1977] 2 S.C.R. 545 (S.C.C.).

24 *Central Can. Potash Co. v. Saskatchewan*, [1979] 1 S.C.R. 42 (S.C.C.).

25 See "Reform of the Supreme Court of Canada", *British Columbia's Constitutional Proposals* (Paper No. 4, October 1978) at 45.

26 For an academic discussion of whether these claims of bias can be substantiated, see P. Hogg, "Is the Supreme Court of Canada biased in Constitutional Cases?" (1979), 57 Can. Bar Rev. 721 (arguing that there is no basis for the claim that the Court has been biased in favour of the federal government in constitutional litigation).

27 See the *Oil Well Income Tax Act*, R.S.S. 1978 (Supp.), c. 0-31.

tax was to be set off against the liability arising from the income tax. The legislation also imposed limits on the deductability of expenses for the purpose of calculating liability for tax.

This income tax allowed the government to achieve its main goal, which was to ensure that the increase in energy rents resulting from the oil crisis remained in Saskatchewan. But income taxes are more complex and costly to administer than production taxes. In order to levy an income tax there must be a calculation of the "profit" that is subject to tax; a production tax can be levied on the more straight-forward basis of the bare number of units produced or sold. Moreover, an income tax presents opportunities and incentives for tax avoidance behaviour by those subject to the tax. Tax avoidance is a marginal consideration in the administration of a production tax. This means that, although the income tax was an adequate regulatory substitute for the production tax struck down in *CIGOL*, it was not a perfect substitute. The income tax was more costly to the government, in terms of the additional resources which had to be committed to enforcement. The income tax also carried with it a social cost — the cost of the resources invested in socially unproductive tax avoidance behaviour by the industry.

Having imposed an income tax as an interim measure, the province continued to press for some form of constitutional amendment to remedy fully its difficulty. Fortuitously for Saskatchewan, by 1981 the federal government badly needed western support for its constitutional reform package. In an attempt to gather support, the federal government agreed to amend s. 92 of the *B.N.A. Act* so as to broaden provincial powers over the natural resource sector. The new s. 92(a) of the Act, enacted as part of the constitutional reform package by Westminster in 1982, granted provinces power to make "laws in relation to the raising of money by any mode or system of taxation in respect of . . . non-renewable natural resources . . . " This amendment eliminated the requirement that a provincial tax be "direct" rather than "indirect".

The constitutional amendment has enabled the province of Saskatchewan to enact the *Freehold Oil and Gas Production Tax Act*, 1982[28] as well as the *Mineral Taxation Act, 1983.*[29] The first Act provides for a production tax on the freehold oil and gas produced in the province; the second Act levies a production tax on the production of specified

---

28 S.S. 1982-83, c. F-22.1.
29 S.S. 1983-84, c. E-10.2.

minerals. In short, the province has now fully regained the constitutional ground it lost in *CIGOL*.

What assessment can be offered of the instrumental impact of the Court's decision? First, it is clear that the decision was not nearly as crippling to provincial regulatory power as had been suggested initially. The province was able to replace immediately the invalid production tax with an icome tax, thereby avoiding any significant revenue loss. At the same time, there were nontrivial costs associated with the imposition of an income tax in place of a production tax. In short, while the decision was not the disaster which some had feared, neither was it wholly irrelevant to the formulation of provincial energy policy.

Second, the fact that the result in the case was later reversed by constitutional amendment does not mean that the litigation was thereby rendered meaningless. Because the rule announced by the Court had to some extent limited provincial power, the federal government had been provided with an important constitutional bargaining chip. The federal government was able to play that chip when it was faced with widespread opposition to its constitutional proposals. Had the *CIGOL* litigation been decided the other way, the federal government would have had to have offered some other constitutional concession in order to achieve the same result.

There is a final point that needs to be emphasized, relating to the nature of the federal-provincial bargaining surrounding this issue. The energy issue in the late 1970s and early 1980s was framed and understood in explicitly regional terms, with the resource-rich provinces being pitted against consuming provinces. Federal-provincial bargaining on such a regionally-sensitive issue requires the active involvement of the highest political levels of the respective governments. Further, agreement is impossible without each side being seen to offer significant political concessions to the other. In contrast, the issues arising from the *Dominion Stores* and *Labatt Breweries* litigation have not been perceived as explicitly regional issues. Federal-provincial bargaining on food product standards, for example, is understood as an issue which seems to affect all regions of the country in roughly equal fashion. There are a number of consequences which flow from this difference. First, it is possible to achieve federal-provincial consensus on such "technical" issues without the active involvement of the highest political levels. Second, because the negotiations can be framed in technical rather than political terms there is no necessity for each side to be seen to be offering "concessions" to the other.

These distinctions are important in terms of predicting those cases in which federal-provincial bargaining is likely to be successful; I will return to them in the final section of this chapter.

What of the response to the Supreme Court's decision in the *Central Canada* case? As with *CIGOL*, the ultimate impact on provincial regulatory power was much less severe than had been feared initially. In this case, however, the circumstances which produced this result were largely fortuitous. The provincial regulatory scheme had been enacted in the late 1960s, in response to a serious excess of supply and a drop in the world price of potash. By the time the Supreme Court decision in the case was handed down in 1978, the market for potash had changed. Due in part to the success of the provincial scheme limiting production and fixing prices, the market had stabilized. The industry no longer needed production quotas or price-fixing in order to survive. Thus, the Court's ruling that the provincial scheme was unconstitutional had no appreciable impact on the market or the provincial economy.[30]

Potash producers in Saskatchewan during this period had also been contemplating a constitutional challenge to potash "prorationing fees", levied under the *Potash Proration Fees Regulations, 1972*. The potash producers had laid the groundwork for this challenge by successfully arguing that a province had to refund money collected under an unconstitutional law.[31] However, in 1979 the producers abandoned their constitutional challenge against the prorationing fees by entering into the *Potash Resource Payment Agreement, 1979*. Under this agreement, the producers agreed to abandon their constitutional challenges and to render payments to the province in accordance with a fixed schedule. In return, the province agreed not to levy any further proration fees.[32]

It is easy to identify the gains each party obtained from this agreement. The province obtained a guaranteed series of payments from the industry, thus avoiding the uncertainty associated with the pending constitutional challenges. The industry gained the certainty of knowing in advance what rate of tax it would have to pay to the province, avoiding the possibility of sudden, unexpected increases in their tax liability. By entering into this agreement, both parties

---

30 Telephone interview with G. Peacock, Counsel, Constitutional Law Division, Ministry of the Attorney-General for Saskatchewan, December 1986.

31 See *Amax Potash Ltd. v. Saskatchewan*, [1977] 2 S.C.R. 576 (S.C.C.), ruling s. 5(7) of the provincial *Proceedings Against the Crown Act*, R.S.S. 1978, c. P-27 to be unconstitutional.

32 The agreement was to remain in force for five years . It was renewed in 1984 and currently remains in force.

purchased certainty about the intentions and future behaviour of the other.

In short, by the late 1970s, constitutional constraints had faded in significance in the relationship between the province of Saskatchewan and the potash industy. This situation was in part a product of the market conditions prevailing at the time, which made strict provincial regulation unnecessary. It was also due to the fact that the province and the industry had purchased constitutional peace through the *Potash Resource Payment Agreement*. The enactment of s. 92(a) of the *Constitution Act, 1867* served to confirm provincial power to regulate the potash industry. Section 92(a) grants the province power to enact laws in relation to the management and conservation of non-renewable natural resources.[33] This suggests that, should the market for potash collapse in the future, the province will have ample constitutional authority to restore stability to the market.[34]

4. CONCLUSION: THE IMPACT OF CONSTITUTIONAL CONSTRAINT

What general conclusions can be drawn from these case studies of the impact of constitutional adjudication on Canadian government? The first conclusion is obvious: the outcomes of constitutional cases are much less determinative of public policy than is often supposed by lawyers and legal scholars. In each of the cases examined, the constitutional result was initially seen as a significant setback to the losing government. Yet in each instance, the governments concerned have been able to achieve the same regulatory goals through alternative instruments. It must be conceded that in certain instances this conclusion had resulted largely from market forces rather than from the conscious intervention of government. The point remains that there was no instance in which the constitutional rule announced by the Court determined the eventual behaviour of the parties.

This does not mean that constitutional constraints are wholly

---

33 Section 92(a) provides as follows:

92(a).(1) In each province, the legislature may exclusively make laws in relation to . . .

  (b) development, conservation and management of non-renewable natural resources and forestry resources in the province, including laws in relation to the rate of primary production therefrom;

34 This matter is not altogether free from doubt. For a discussion of the effect and ambiguity of s. 92(a), see W. Moull, "Section 92(a) of the Constitution Act, 1867" (1984), 61 Can. Bar Rev. 715.

illusory. As I have emphasized throughout this chapter, often the only means of overcoming a constitutional constraint is through intergovernmental agreement: in such instances, the constitutional decision fixes the initial bargaining position of the parties. In other instances, the alternative regulatory instrument is an imperfect substitute for the device struck down by the Court. The point is simply that constitutional reasons will rarely constitute conclusive reasons against undertaking particular public policies. Federalism does not create regulatory vacuums. There will inevitably be a variety of regulatory instruments or legal arrangements which could be utilized in order to achieve a given policy goal. Constitutional reasons may operate so as to rule out the use of some of those regulatory instruments or legal arrangements. But constitutional constraints will rarely make all of the possible instruments off limits. In this sense, constitutional constraints must be seen in relativistic terms. They operate so as to increase the costs associated with achieving policy goals, forcing government to employ alternative regulatory instruments or else to coordinate efforts with those of other levels of government. Policy-makers are then faced with a choice; either bear the increased costs associated with the alternative instrument or abandon the goal. Constitutional constraints help to shape the legislative demand curve.

Once the relativistic nature of constitutional constraint is understood, the task becomes one of identifying those instances in which the constraints are most significant. A useful way of approaching this task is to classify regulatory instruments in the manner suggested in Chapter 7. There are at least three independent sources of regulatory authority: the power to spend, the power to tax and traditional "command and control" regulation.[35] In very general terms, the constitutional constraints surrounding the first two categories seem somewhat less significant than those surrounding the third. Consider the use of the so-called "spending power" by government. Of the close to 200 federalism decisions of the Supreme Court since 1949, there have been no cases dealing with the state's power to spend public funds. Most commentators on the issue assume that the spending power is not subject to the constraints of federalism.[36] In like fashion, the taxing power of the federal government is largely unencumbered given its mandate in s. 91(2) of the *Constitution Act, 1867* to raise money by "any mode or system of taxation". Provincial taxing powers are limited

---

35 See discussion, *supra*, Chapter 7.
36 For a discussion, see P. Hogg, *Constitutional Law in Canada* (2nd ed., 1985) at 123-126.

to "direct" taxation. Yet the vast bulk of provincial taxing measures has been held to fall within this definition; moreover, those exactions which have been held to be "indirect taxes" can often be reformulated so as to satisfy constitutional requirements. An illustration was provided by our case study of the decision in *Canadian Industrial Gas and Oil v. Government of Saskatchewan.*[37] Following the adverse Court ruling, the government imposed an income tax on the industry. Although this tax was not a perfect substitute for the production tax, it enabled the government to avoid a loss in revenue.

The relatively modest constitutional constraints in these areas can be contrasted with the limitations surrounding direct regulation by the state. So-called "command and control" regulation is easily the most susceptible to challenge on federalism grounds: most federalism cases since 1949 have involved challenges to such regulation. Further, the analysis in the case studies suggested that constitutional constraints in this area could often only be overcome through intergovernmental agreement. In *Dominion Stores*, for example, we saw the key role played by intergovernmental agreement in overcoming constitutional constraints. In the absence of such agreement, effective and coordinated regulation of the national market for natural products would have been impossible. Similarly, in the *Central Canada* case, the provincial scheme fixing quotas and prices could not have been replaced by the government of Saskatchewan acting alone. What was required was a constitutional amendment granting the province broad new powers of regulation over the potash industry.

This analysis produces the following important conclusion. Regulation which takes the form of taxes or transfers is likely to be freer of constitutional constraints than traditional "command and control" regulation. The corollary is that, in those instances when the judiciary does find that a taxing or spending measure is invalid, there is likely to be a close regulatory substitute available to government. This regulatory substitute can be inserted unilaterally, without the necessity to secure agreement from other governments. Conversely, when a "command and control" regulation is ruled invalid, it is more likely that some form of intergovernmental bargaining and agreement will be necessary in order to devise a substitute measure. Of course, such bargaining is extremely costly and may often not produce any agreement.

This analysis has important implications for the state's ability to

---

37 *Supra*, note 23.

pursue the goals of allocative efficiency and income redistribution. The most effective and accepted means of redistributing income is through the system of taxes and transfers. Since these regulatory instruments are relatively immune from constitutional constraint, it is unlikely that constitutional considerations have figured in any prominent way in state policy regarding wealth redistribution. The same cannot be said with respect to attempts by the state to pursue the goal of allocative efficiency. The system of taxes and transfers is often inadequate to correct market failure. In order to effectively pursue the goal of allocative efficiency, government will often have to resort to direct prohibitions or orders — in short, "command and control" regulation. Consider, as an illustration, state attempts to promote and maintain a competitive market. The most obvious and accepted manner of promoting competition is through some form of competition policy, which consists of a series of enforceable prohibitions and commands. Significantly, attempts to promote competitive markets in this way in Canada have always had to grapple with serious constitutional obstacles. The courts have traditionally taken the view that the only constitutional basis for federal competition legislation is the criminal law power. This has forced the federal government to frame the *Combines Investigation Act* as a criminal statute and employ criminal standards of proof. Most commentators believe that the criminal law is an inappropriate mechanism for controlling anti-competitive behaviour and argue that civil sanctions would be much more effective. But the federal government has been prevented from moving to a civil system because of the restrictive conception of competition policy advanced by the Supreme Court.

It is one thing to suggest that these constitutional constraints have resulted in some efficiency loss; it is quite another to suggest the magnitude of that loss or even how the loss might be calculated. But the precise calculation of the efficiency loss in this particular instance is really beside the point. The example is designed to illustrate the following general conclusions: to the extent that federalism doctrine has had an impact on Canadian public policy, the impact has been in terms of allocative efficiency rather than wealth redistribution.

This conclusion directly contradicts the views of those commentators who have claimed that federalism has had a "conservative" bias, limiting the ability of the state to assist the poor or economically disadvantaged.[38] According to these critics, the main shortcoming of

---

38 See, e.g., Mallory, *supra*, note 3 at 53-56.

federal political systems is that they provide multiple veto points for the economically powerful to block government attempts to assist the economically disadvantaged. The classic expositor of this view in Canada has been Professor Mallory and, more recently, Professor Paul Weiler.[39] The analysis in this chapter suggests that both Mallory and Weiler were mistaken in supposing that the alleged "anti-state" bias of the courts has had any significant impact on redistributive public policy. Because of the existence of close regulatory substitutes, judicial review has not constituted a major impediment to federal or provincial attempts to redistribute wealth or income. This is not to suggest that either level of government in Canada has been particularly committed to the goal of wealth redistribution. There have obviously been a whole series of political factors constraining such policies and it appears that inequalities in wealth and income have not been altered significantly in the past 40 years. The point is simply that it is wide of the mark to seek to attribute this political inertia to constitutional considerations.

The other conclusion which emerges from the case studies is that the likelihood of securing interprovincial agreement is much higher on some issues than on others. In particular, it appears easiest to obtain interprovincial agreement on issues that can be framed as "technical" and focused on a specific and limited subject matter. These issues can be dealt with by officials who subscribe to a common set of professional norms. Further, governments are perceived to share a set of common interests on these issues and thus there is no necessity for a set of explicit trade-offs or concessions from each side.[40] The *Dominion Stores* and *Labatt Breweries* cases raised issues which fell into this first category. Conversely, issues which are framed in explicitly regional terms require the involvement of the highest political levels of the government, with the negotiations being conducted under the constant glare of the media. Further, any agreement which is concluded will be subject to intense public debate in order to determine whether each side made "appropriate" concessions. While it is not impossible to secure federal-provincial agreements in such circumstances, it is certainly more difficult than if the issue is framed in technical terms. The conflicts over energy rents in the late 1970s and early 1980s exemplified such a highly politicized and regionalized issue.

In the decades immediately following the second world war, the vast majority of federal-provincial issues tended to fall into the first

---

39 Weiler, *supra*, note 4 at 181.
40 See Smiley, *supra*, note 8 at 96.

category rather than the second. But over the past decade in particular, the politics of Canadian federalism has been increasingly dominated by issues framed in explicitly regional terms.[41] The confused and embattled negotiations over the free trade issue are a striking illustration of the current tensions in the system. This has made federal-provincial bargaining and cooperation more difficult and, ultimately, increased the significance of constitutional constraints in the Canadian federal system.

41 For a discussion, see Smiley, *ibid.* at 92-116.

11

The Court into the 1990s

For most of its 112-year history, the Supreme Court of Canada was the forgotten institution of Canadian politics. Outside of the specialized legal community, there were few Canadians with any awareness or understanding of who comprised the Supreme Court or of what it did. Within the past decade, however, all this appears to have changed quite dramatically. The Court has become a focus of increasing attention and scrutiny, with the personalities and politics of the Court the subject of media commentary and speculation. Whereas a decade ago the Court heard and decided cases almost unnoticed, today's Supreme Court hearings are *bona fide* media "events"; on important cases reporters fill the courtroom, attempting to decipher and interpret the rather baffling arguments presented to the Court and the questions posed by the justices. The Court may not yet have captured the imagination of the Canadian body politic, but at least it appears to have stirred a modicum of genuine interest in the beast.

What accounts for these decades of public indifference, followed by the sudden appetite for information about the Court? The explanation seems rather simple. Until the early 1980s, the constitutional work of the Court was concerned almost exclusively with federalism disputes involving the proper allocation of power. Such arguments over the proper allocation of power appear esoteric and remote from the concerns of the average citizen. Moreover, as the analysis in chapter 10 demonstrated, the Court's work in the federalism area has had a limited impact on policy choices by government. Even in cases where the Court determined that a particular piece of legislation was *ultra vires*, there were usually a range of close regulatory substitutes available to government. Governments have usually been able to manoeuvre around unfavourable Court rulings, either by bargaining with other governments or by fashioning an alternative regulation which would survive judicial scrutiny.

Thus the Supreme Court laboured in obscurity for the simple reason that its work did not appear to have a significant impact on the lives of ordinary Canadians. Even in those rare instances where the Court attracted political criticism, such as in its decisions involving resource rents in the late 1970s, the notoriety was short-lived. Once governments realized that they were able to work around the unfavourable court rulings, public criticism of the Court lost most of its energy.

The single greatest factor altering these public attitudes towards the Court has been the enactment of the *Charter*. Disputes under the *Charter* do not simply involve the competing bureaucratic claims of governments. The *Charter* visibly implicates the interests of citizens by questioning the ability of *any* majority to pursue a given policy. Further, the enactment of the *Charter* has meant that a broad range of controversial issues that had previously been decided in the political arena are now being channelled into the courts. Nor is the *Charter's* impact limited to those issues, such as abortion, Sunday closing or the right to strike, which have actually been litigated. The *Charter* is becoming an important feature of political debate generally, as both governments and individuals claim that "Charter considerations" support their preferred political outcome. In fact, it is becoming increasingly commonplace to observe political debate being preoccupied with the narrow question of whether a proposed course of action does or does not violate the *Charter*. In Ontario, for example, the debate over the merits of extending full funding to Roman Catholic schools was eventually reduced to a matter of determining whether the funding violated the *Charter*. The ground-rules of political argument were turned on their head, with a judicial ruling on the constitutionality of the legislation taken as determinative of the political merits of the issue. The legislation was referred to the courts and promptly disappeared from the political agenda.

Given the centrality of the *Charter* in the politics of the 1980s, it is hardly surprising that the Supreme Court should have attained such sudden and unprecedented prominence. But public attention also inevitably entails public criticism. The Court is now saddled with the responsibility of deciding whether laws on abortion, capital punishment or Sunday closing violate the constitution. On these politically volatile questions the Court will be in for sustained and vocal criticism, no matter what it decides. If the Court upholds legislative power in the face of *Charter* attack, opponents of the legislation will label the Court as insensitive to minority interests. If, on the other hand, the Court rules legislation to be unconstitutional because of the *Charter*, it will provoke the anger of governments and the frustration of those who stood to benefit from the impugned legislation. In short, no matter what the Court decides, it will increasingly serve as a lightning rod for criticism and controversy. There will inevitably be questions raised regarding the legitimacy of the Court's role and the wisdom of entrusting such broad discretion to the judiciary.

In my view, such a debate over the legitimacy of judicial review under the *Charter* is both healthy and necessary. As I have argued in this book, the enactment of the *Charter* did not resolve the issue of the legitimacy of the Court's role; it simply caused that debate to take a different and more limited form. The enactment of the *Charter* resolved what might be termed the "big" question — whether to entrench fundamental rights in the Constitution in the first place. But it left open the more limited question of the nature and scope of the Court's role in interpreting and applying those fundamental rights. In other words, what remains to be resolved is whether there are meaningful limits to the judicial function under the *Charter*. Is the effect of the *Charter* simply to hand over to the courts a whole host of questions previously decided in the political arena? Or is there a more limited and focused way of conceiving of the purpose and function of judicial review under the *Charter*?

In this book, I have argued that the Supreme Court's role under the *Charter* is, indeed, a limited one. The *Charter* was not designed simply to displace politics in favour of the courts. As I argued in Chapter 6, the *Charter* recognizes a positive role for the state of creating and maintaining political freedom. The courts should read the *Charter* as primarily designed to increase the opportunities for political debate and dialogue, rather than as creating artificial boundaries around the political process.

The early *Charter* decisions of the Court rarely address these larger considerations in explicit terms. But, as suggested in Chapter 4, these early decisions implicitly reject the view of the *Charter* that I have put forward. The Supreme Court's early jurisprudence proceeds from the assumption that there is an inevitable contradiction between individual liberty on the one hand, and state power on the other. On this view, individual freedom, which is conceived of as a realm of personal "privacy", is necessarily compromised by the coercive intervention of the state. Of course, state attempts to intervene in and regulate the private realm are not *per se* impermissible; given the conflicting desires of individuals, some form of state regulation is obviously inevitable and desirable. But because state intervention necessarily interferes with individual freedom, it should be subjected to stringent criticism and scrutiny.

The Court's background assumptions are revealed most clearly in the *Oakes* case, in which the Court attempts to develop a general methodology governing the application of section 1. According to the Court, the section 1 inquiry must be premised on the understanding that a protected right is being limited and that limits on rights are "exceptions to their general guarantee". This means that the standard of justification demanded of governments under section 1 must be rigorous; limits on rights can be permitted only in furtherance of collective goals of "fundamental importance". The goals of the law must relate to concerns that are "pressing and substantial" and must impair the protected right as little as possible.[1] In essence, what *Oakes* prescribes is a modified form of "strict scrutiny" as the basis of analysis under section 1.

This "rigorous" approach to section 1 fits comfortably with the widely-held view that there is an inevitable tension between state interests and individual liberty. According to the conventional view, liberty is a private, individual matter, a realm of "privacy" that exists apart from and independent of the state or the community. Freedom is the protection of individual subjectivity against social oppression, "the absence of coercive social restraint against doing, or being, or becoming as one will."[2] The cornerstones of this realm of natural liberty are the institutions of property, contract and the market. Because liberty is conceived in this way, there is an inevitable contradiction between liberty interests and state or community

---

1 See generally chapter 4 for analysis and discussion of *Oakes*.
2 F. Michelman, "The Supreme Court 1985 Term, Foreword: Traces of Self-Government", 100 Harv. L. Rev. 4 at 25 (1986).

interests. State intervention is by definition coercive; it intrudes into the realm of privacy and subjectivity, forbidding certain choices and mandating others. Of course, the conventional view recognizes that state intrusion into the private sphere is often necessary since "freedom is not absolute". But a society dedicated to the preservation of individual liberty would be wise to scrutinize carefully the justifications that are offered for such "coercion". Otherwise, it is said, individual autonomy will be sacrificed and bureaucratic tyranny guaranteed. The Supreme Court in *Oakes*, by reading a form of strict scrutiny into section 1, reflects this vision of liberty as privacy and of state intervention as coercion.

These assumptions about the relationship between the public and private realms are so widely held that they appear almost axiomatic. The trouble is that, far from being axiomatic, such assumptions are in reality highly contestable. Consider first the alleged distinction between the public and private realms. According to the conventional view, liberty is a zone of prepolitical autonomy that inheres naturally in individuals. State regulation represents public "intervention" into this private realm and is therefore to be regarded with suspicion. But it turns out that the central elements of this private realm — property, contract and the market — either depend upon or assume the intervention of the state.

This elementary point can be illustrated through a simple example, designed to illustrate the public character of property rights.[3] Suppose that A has possession of a rare silver water goblet, but that B, through trickery, stealth or superior strength, manages to take it from A. A claims that the water goblet was his property and demands that the state force B to return it to him. One option is for the state to recognize A's property right and to declare that B unlawfully appropriated the goblet and must therefore return it. But this is not the only decision rule open to the state. The state might declare that it is permissible for individuals to obtain goods through trickery, stealth or superior strength. If this second decision rule were selected, the state would refuse to force B to return the goblet to A.

Advocates of a private property regime sometimes invoke "individual liberty" in support of their claims. But the example shows why

---

3 The example in the text is based on the reasoning and analysis of, amongst others, Hohfeld, "Some Fundamental Legal Conceptions as Applied in Legal Reasoning", 23 Yale L.J. 16 (1913); Hale, "Coercion and Distribution in a Supposedly Non-coercive State", 38 Political Science Quarterly 470 (1923).

this attempt to link individual liberty with private property is fallacious. The idea of "liberty" provides no basis for choosing between the two hypothetical decision rules outlined above. The first decision rule protects the liberty of A by limiting the liberty of B, while the second decision rule protects the liberty of B by limiting the liberty of A. Each decision rule protects certain liberties, but not others. Thus the idea of "liberty" is insufficient to dictate a choice in favour of the first rule over the second. Nor can the private property decision rule be defended on the basis that it limits state "intervention". Both rules assume state intervention. The issue is not whether the state will intervene in the dispute between A and B, but rather, on whose behalf and in whose interest will the state intervene.

The larger point which emerges from this discussion is that there is no such thing as a realm of "pure" autonomy.[4] The dichotomy between the supposedly private realms of property and market and the public realm of the state is simply mistaken. The market, private property, and liberty of contract all depend upon and assume the intervention of the state in one form or another. Thus "nonintervention" is a baseless criteria for determining state policy on such questions. The state is already there. The question is not whether to intervene, but how.

This false dichotomy between public and private realms is only the first difficulty with the analysis in *Oakes*. A related problem is the narrow conception of individual liberty which underlies the judgment. Liberty is equated with privacy, as a zone of personal subjectivity into which the individual can retreat. But liberty can be framed in positive as well as negative terms, as the opportunity to realize one's life plans rather than simply as the absence of restraint.[5] Positive liberty reflects the ideal of action and self-direction according to reasons one gives to oneself.[6] Further, this conception of liberty as "self-government"[7] does not entail any necessary association between liberty and privacy; positive liberty does not seek to establish the "protection of private judgment as the summit of political virtue".[8]

---

4 There is, of course, nothing novel in this claim; one of the significant accomplishments of the legal realists was to demonstrate the illusory character of the public/private distinction. For a general discussion, see Kennedy and Michelman, "Are Property and Contract Efficient?" 8 Hofstra L. Rev. 729 (1980).

5 See I. Berlin, "Two Concepts of Liberty", in *Four Essays on Liberty* 118 (1979).

6 For a discussion, see Michelman, *supra*, note 2 at 25-31.

7 This description of positive liberty is Michelman's; see *supra*, note 2 at 26.

8 Lasch, "Why The Left Has No Future", 1 Tikkun 92 at 97 (no. 2, 1986).

Instead, a positive view of liberty is entirely compatible with a view of the individual as socially situated, formulating his or her life plans in a community of equals. The point is made eloquently by Frank Michelman:

> This view of the human condition implies that self-cognition and ensuing self-legislation must, to a like extent, be socially situated; norms must be formed through public dialogue and expressed as public law. Normative reason, it thus seems, cannot be a solitary activity. Its exercise requires knowledge, including self-knowledge, obtainable only by encounter with different outlooks in public argument. Thus its requisite forum is a political community of equals, and its requisite temper is a willingness to submit opinions to public exposure and debate.[9]

What this preceding discussion suggests is that the vision of state and society which underlies the Supreme Court's reasoning in *Oakes* is deeply flawed. *Oakes* is founded on a deep suspicion of the state, assuming that state power is necessarily intrusive into the private realm of individual liberty. Liberty itself is equated with privacy and the absence of social restraint. Given these background assumptions, it is easy to understand how the Court came to the conclusion that limits on rights are permissible only in exceptional circumstances.

Yet, as I have argued, the dichotomy between public and private realms is largely illusory. The supposedly private realms of property and market are themselves part of the public sphere. In like manner, liberty itself can be viewed as the product rather than the enemy of public institutions. Individuals are socially situated; their life plans are not the result of inexplicable private impulses, but are produced through public dialogue and debate with their fellow citizens. On this "republican" view, the task of politics is not to deregulate society, but to ensure that public institutions are accountable and responsive to ordinary citizens.

What relevance does this extended discussion of the nature of freedom and of politics have for interpretation under the *Charter*? The basic point, which I developed in Chapter 6, is that the *Charter* itself rejects the idea that there is any necessary contradiction between state regulation and individual freedom. The *Charter* seeks to give expression to the notion that state intervention can often enhance individual freedom, rather than subvert it. Although framed in the rhetoric of liberal individualism, the *Charter* simultaneously emphasizes communitarian and republican values. This is hardly suprising, given the

---

9 Michelman, *supra*, note 2 at 27 (footnotes omitted).

particular emphasis on communitarian values in the Canadian political tradition.

The fundamental problem with the Supreme Court's opinion in *Oakes* is that it ignores the communitarian values embedded in the *Charter* and in Canadian political life. *Oakes* assumes that the *Charter* represents a decisive break with Canada's communitarian political tradition. The Court reads the *Charter* as though it were a manifesto of liberal individualism, mandating judicial suspicion of state attempts to limit the private liberty of the individual. In Chapter 6, I suggested why I find this reading of the *Charter* unpersuasive. I proposed an alternative interpretation of the larger purposes of the *Charter*, one which regards the document as primarily dedicated to the enhancement of democratic values. On this alternative view, the point of the *Charter* is to enhance the opportunities for democratic debate and dialogue rather than to draw boundaries around the political process.

The theory of judicial review which I propose is one which limits the judicial role under the *Charter*. I argue that courts should direct their energies primarily towards policing the political process, rather than to determining the correct allocation of resources in society. For some, this is precisely the difficulty with my theory. A critic of my argument would claim that it fails to give adequate protection to minorities or to disadvantaged groups in Canadian society. The critic would point out that the interests of minorities or the disadvantaged have historically been ignored in the political process. According to the critic, the purpose of the *Charter* is to redress this historic imbalance by curbing the rights of the majority and protecting the interests of the minority. My theory, because it emphasizes the integrity of the political process rather than the interests of minorities, strips the *Charter* of its purpose and meaning.

There are two responses to this objection. First, I maintain that my analysis of the *Charter* more accurately reflects the larger values embodied in the document, as well as the traditions of Canadian politics. I have already developed this argument at length in Chapter 6 and will not repeat it here.

Second, my argument is by no means unsympathetic to minority interests or the interests of disadvantaged Canadians. But I believe that, in general, those interests can best be protected through the political process itself rather than through assigning this task to the judiciary. The judiciary in Canada has never been particularly sympathetic to the interests of minorities or the disadvantaged. Where the interests of the disadvantaged have been advanced, this has usually been accomplished through political rather than judicial means. Indeed, the judiciary has historically been rather suspicious of state initiatives designed to regulate private power so as to protect the economically or socially disadvantaged. Furthermore, even if the judiciary were to reverse its traditional suspicions and to suddenly become the champion of minorities, the long-term benefits would be questionable. Over the past generation, the political left in the United States has relied on the courts and the federal bureaucracy to advance its goals of affirmative action and racial integration. By relying on these undemocratic means to achieve its goals, the left has ultimately lost public confidence and support for its policies.[10] In short, a political strategy emphasizing undemocratic means to achieve its ends has only exacerbated the very evil it sought to cure.

I have been critical of the early performance of the Supreme Court under the *Charter*. I believe that the Court has thus far failed to come to terms with the significance of the document for Canadian political life. But the *Charter* is still in its infancy and the doctrines developed by the Court remain fluid and malleable. I have put forward an alternative interpretation of the *Charter*, one which squarely faces the issue of the legitimacy of judicial review. I do not pretend to have finally resolved that debate. But I hope, at least, to have demonstrated why the debate can no longer be avoided.

---

10 For a discussion of the difficulties faced by both the American left and right, see C. Lasch, "What's Wrong with the Right", 1 Tikkun 23 (no. 1, 1986).

Index